Leading with Values

Positivity, Virtue, and High Performance

Edited by

EDWARD D. HESS

KIM S. CAMERON

CAMBRIDGE
UNIVERSITY PRESS

CAMBRIDGE UNIVERSITY PRESS
Cambridge, New York, Melbourne, Madrid, Cape Town, Singapore, São Paulo

Cambridge University Press
The Edinburgh Building, Cambridge CB2 2RU, UK

Published in the United States of America by Cambridge University Press, New York

www.cambridge.org
Information on this title: www.cambridge.org/9780521686037

© Cambridge University Press 2006

First published 2006

Printed in the United Kingdom at the University Press, Cambridge

A catalogue record for this publication is available from the British Library

ISBN-13   978-0-521-86686-6 hardback
ISBN-10   0-521-86686-3 hardback

ISBN-13   978-0-521-68603-7 paperback
ISBN-10   0-521-68603-2 paperback

Edward D. Hess dedicates this book to Jimmy Blanchard; Tom Cousins; Sonny Deriso; Gardiner Garrard, III; Bill Turner; and Billy Wren who made all of this possible.

Kim Cameron dedicates this book to the outstanding leaders represented in the chapters of this book. Hopefully, their leadership will inspire many generations of leaders to come.

Contents

Tables

Figures

Notes on contributors

SARAH BOIK is business office manager of the Physician Billing Department of Foote Hospital in Jackson, Michigan. Sarah is a highly skilled manager with over 25 years of experience running physician practices and executing hospital finance. Sarah currently manages an extremely high-performing accounts receivable unit that has grown from 5 to just over 40 employees under her guidance. In this outstanding work unit, she has implemented a highly creative business office reorganization, including establishing formal work teams, implementing collective productivity measures, and generating an exceptional work environment that has dramatically reduced employee turnover and increased morale.

GARY W. BOUCH is Senior Vice President, Operations and Transportation Officer at FedEx Freight. He has spent over seven years with Freight, most recently as Vice President of Operations and Transportation. Prior to joining FedEx Freight, Gary learned the transportation industry at Airborne, P.I.E., Yellow, Rider, Con-Way, and ABF. Gary is also an attorney, and practiced with the law firm of Scholl & Hamlin in New York. He lives with his wife and children in Harrison, Arkansas.

DAVID S. BRIGHT is a visiting assistant professor in the Department of Organizational Behavior, and a research fellow in the Center for Business as an Agent of World Benefit, both at Case Western Reserve University. His research interest centers on forgiveness and virtuousness as related to employee engagement, especially where people develop strengthened commitment to organization success and experience connections with others. He recently completed his doctoral studies at Case Western Reserve University.

KIM S. CAMERON is Professor of Management and Organization at the University of Michigan Business School and Professor of Higher

Education in the School of Education at the University of Michigan. His current research focuses on the virtuousness of, and in, organizations and their relationships to organizational success. This work was recognized as one of the 20 highest impact ideas of 2004 by the *Harvard Business Review*. His past research on organizational downsizing, effectiveness, quality culture, and development of management skills has been published in more than 80 articles and nine books.

ROBERT DRAZIN is Professor of Organization and Management, and faculty director for the Center for Entrepreneurship and Corporate Growth at Goizueta Business School, Emory University. Prior to joining the Goizueta Business School faculty, Robert taught at the Graduate School of Business at Columbia University. His research in the areas of organization theory and the management of innovation and growth in large corporations has been published in, *The Search for Organic Growth*, Hess and Kazanjian (eds.), Cambridge University Press, 2006) as well as numerous other books; and in such journals as the *Academy of Management Journal*, *Organization Science*, *Management Science*, *Administrative Science Quarterly*, and the *Academy of Management Review*.

MARYANN GLYNN is Professor of Organization and Management at Goizueta Business School, Emory University. Prior to joining the Goizueta faculty, MaryAnn served on the faculty of Yale University's School of Organization and Management, and as a Visiting Professor of the Steven M. Ross School of Business, University of Michigan, 2002–2004. Her work has been published in such books as, *The Search for Organic Growth*, Hess and Kazanjian (eds.), Cambridge University Press, 2006), and numerous others, as well as many leading journals, including the Academy of Management Journal, Organization Science and Strategic Management Journal.

EDWARD D. HESS is Adjunct Professor of Organization and Management; Founder and Executive Director of the Center for Entrepreneurship and Corporate Growth; and Founder and Executive Director of the Values-Based Leadership Institute at the Goizueta Business School at Emory. Prior to joining Goizueta, Ed had over 30 years' experience as a lawyer, investment banker, and strategy consultant. He is the author of, *Make It Happen* (EDHLTD, 2000);

The Successful Family Business: Proactively Managing the Family and the Business (Praeger, 2005); *The Search for Organic Growth*, Hess and Kazanjian (eds.) (Cambridge University Press, 2006); *The 6 Keys to Organic Growth: How Great Companies Consistently Grow from Within* (McGraw Hill, 2006), and the author of over 40 articles on Leadership, Strategy, Execution, Growth, and Finance.

HEATHER JAMERSON is a Ph.D. candidate in sociology at Emory University. Her research and teaching interests include global political economy, economic sociology, ethics, and culture. In addition to teaching in the sociology department, Heather has co-taught Ethics at Candler School of Theology, and Principled Leadership at Goizueta Business School. Her current research projects include a co-authored case study on principled leadership in the revitalization of East Lake in Atlanta, and her dissertation on the wine industry in the US.

FARAH MIHOUBI is a graduate of the Wharton School of Business and recently completed her Master's degree in Consumer Economics from the University of Georgia. She spent a number of years researching, and creating innovative teaching materials for undergraduate and MBA students at Emory University's Goizueta Business School. She is currently obtaining her certification for a career in financial literacy/life path coaching.

MICHAEL B. PARKYN is a Lieutenant Colonel and F/A-18 Hornet pilot in the United States Marine Corps. A graduate of the United States Naval Academy and veteran of combat operations in Kuwait, Iraq and Afghanistan, Lieutenant Colonel Parkyn has been a student and practitioner of leadership for over two decades. Lieutenant Colonel Parkyn currently serves as the Director of Leader Development at the Marine Corps University in Quantico, Virginia, where he resides with his wife and five daughters.

EDWARD H. POWLEY, PH.D. is a visiting assistant professor of management in the Marketing and Policy Studies department at the Weatherhead School of Management at Case Western Reserve University. He has consulted and conducted research with the US Environmental Protection Agency, US Navy, Roadway Express, the Society for Organizational Learning's Sustainability Consortium, and Weatherhead's Business as an Agent of World Benefit project. His published articles cover such topics as organizational change, appreciative inquiry, and ritual.

SCOTT N. TAYLOR is a Ph.D. candidate in organizational behavior at the Weatherhead School of Management, Case Western Reserve University. He has been an instructor and facilitator of leadership development, employee training, emotional intelligence, and organizational behavior courses to business executives and graduate students. His current research focuses on leader assessment and development, emotional intelligence, the sustainability of individual change, and 360-degree feedback. He has published articles covering topics such as leadership development, sustainable individual change, 360-degree assessment, management education, and executive coaching.

PAOLO TRIPODI is the Donald Bren Chair of Ethics and Leadership at the Marine Corps University. He served as an Ethics Fellow at the Center for the Study of Professional Military Ethics at the US Naval Academy, and as the 2002 Jerome E. Levy Visiting Fellow at the Naval War College. Dr. Tripodi was a senior lecturer in security studies at the Nottingham Trent University. His publications include: *The Colonial Legacy in Somalia* (Macmillan, 1999); and he has written articles for *Medicine, Conflict and Survival*, the *Journal of Strategic Studies*, and numerous others.

KARL E. WEICK is the Rensis Likert Distinguished University Professor of Organizational Behavior and Psychology, and Professor of Psychology at the University of Michigan. He is a former editor of the journal *Administrative Science Quarterly* (1977–1985) and co-author with Kathleen Sutcliffe on the book *Managing the Unexpected* (2001). Dr. Weick's research interests include collective sensemaking under pressure, medical errors, handoffs and transitions in dynamic events, high reliability performance, improvisation, and continuous change.

MONICA WORLINE is Assistant Professor of Organization and Management at Goizueta Business School, Emory University. Monica's areas of specialization include the expression of courage and compassion in work organizations, positive deviance in organizations, and positive dynamics and processes. Monica earned her Ph.D. in Organizational Psychology from the University of Michigan. She came to the study of organizations by way of Silicon Valley, where she worked as an entrepreneur, co-founded a successful software firm, and co-developed an influential knowledge development and training organization. Her work has been published in such journals as *Organization Science*, as well as numerous other journals and books.

DAN YAROSLASKI is a Major in the United States Marine Corps. A native of California, he enlisted in the Marine Corps Reserve as an infantryman in 1988. Upon graduating from Loyola Marymount University in Los Angeles, California, he received an active duty commission as a 2nd Lieutenant with a specialty of Assault Amphibian Vehicle Officer. He has served in numerous locations both in the United States and abroad, to include a combat tour in Iraq. Major Yaroslaski received his Masters of Military of Science degree in 2004, while attending the Marine Corps Command and Staff Course.

Acknowledgments

From Ed

I would be remiss in not expressing thanks to the many people who made this book possible. First, to Al Hartgraves; Greg Waymire; Robert Drazin; Mary Ann Glynn and L. G. Thomas, III; at Goizueta Business School for giving me the opportunity to teach and to continue my life-long learning. Secondly, to Gardiner Garrard, III; Walter M. Deriso, Jr., Jimmy Blanchard; Tom Cousins; Lillian Giornelli and Billy Wren for helping create and support the Values-Based Leadership Institute. To Professors Diana Robertson and Monica Worline for bringing together a world class faculty for our conference; and to Dr. Katy Plowright at Cambridge University Press who believed in this project and brought it to fruition. To all our authors I say, "Thank You" for giving and sharing. To my support staff at Goizueta Business School, Gail Mooney and Carol Gee, a big job well done – this would not have happened without your help.

To my co-author, Kim Cameron, who made this a better book because of his laser-like intelligence and his strong personal commitment to scholarship. Kim, this book was a joy because of you. Your positive leadership, kindness and uplifting spirit motivated all of us to perform better and more quickly. Thank you – you are a good soul.

From Kim

This book project is a product of the extraordinary efforts of a myriad of people – willing and tenacious authors, a helpful editorial staff, and a supportive publisher, especially Katy Plowright. Its primary success, however, is attributable to the energy, vision, and organizational capacity of Ed Hess. It has been a great pleasure to work with and learn from Ed. I have certainly been inspired and informed by the insights of the authors in the book, but I have been motivated to perform by Ed's example and gentle prodding. Thank you for a great experience.

Introduction

This is not a standard book introduction. Usually co-editors produce an integrated explanation of the contents and the key lessons contained in the book. We have chosen to take another approach. We have written separately to introduce the book – not because we don't get along, and not because we have difficulty writing with one another. We have enjoyed many exchanges and have offered one another much editorial assistance in producing these chapters. We have written separately to illustrate the two kinds of stories and principles that you will experience as you read the chapters. One focuses on the practical lessons of leadership – how to be a better leader and how great leaders lead with values. The other focuses on an explanation of why the outcomes occurred, what might explain the success being described, and what key concepts must be kept in mind. That is, the book tells engaging and interesting stories, but it also adds substantively to our understanding of leadership, organizational success, and how they are related through values. We begin with Ed.

From Ed

This book is a symphony of wonderful stories about leaders and leadership. A particular brand of leadership – Values-Based Leadership – based upon certain universal, fundamental values, such as honesty, respect, trust, and the dignity and worth of every individual as a human being.

A values-based leader serves others in a positive way. A positive way includes the manner in which he or she leads; the way he or she treats his or her followers; and the ultimate morality of the objectives or results.

By studying the positive, that is leaders who have positive impacts, leaders who help others flourish, leaders who earn the trust placed in them, leaders who believe in stewardship, we follow the work being done in the areas of positive psychology, social psychology and positive organizational behavior.

We explore how values-based organizations are created and sustained by looking at highly successful, values-based, organizations: Synovus Financial Corporation; HomeBanc Mortgage Company; FedEx Freight; the Billing Department at Foote Hospital in Jackson, Michigan, and the United States Marine Corps.

Other issues examined in this book include devaluation of negative values; the role of mistakes and leader forgiveness; how values are translated or operationalized into action; how "sick" organizations can be revived and achieve spectacular results based on positive organizational design; and the role of values in crises. As the business world continues to recover from the recent scandals involving financial impropriety, fraud and unethical behavior, the fundamental message of this book is clear:

Businesses can act ethically and treat all stakeholders with respect and dignity, without sacrificing profits or performance.

Profits, values and ethics are not mutually exclusive. In fact, in order for an organization to sustain high performance, these characteristics may be a necessity.

This book is a blend of practice and academia. Academia has much to offer to the business world; but the opposite is also true.

The genesis of this book was a Conference sponsored by the Values-Based Leadership Institute of Goizueta Business School of Emory University in February 2005. Nine of the twelve authors presented at that conference. That conference brought together leading business executives and scholars such as:

Kim Cameron, University of Michigan; Joanne Ciulla, University of Richmond; Tom Donaldson, Wharton Business School; Tom Dunfee, Wharton Business School; Ed Freeman, University of Virginia, Darden; Charles Manz, University of Massachusetts; Laura Nash, Harvard Business School; Robert Quinn, University of Michigan; Gretchen Spreitzer, University of Michigan; Karl Weick, University of Michigan and Amy Wrzesniewski, New York University.

We were also fortunate to have four senior members of the United States Marine Corps University Leadership Faculty from Quantico, Virginia: Brigadier General Mel Spiese, Colonel John Toolan, Professor Paolo Tripodi, and Lt. Colonel Michael Parkyn.

Keynote speakers were: Dr. Roy Vagelos, former CEO and Chairman of Merck, Inc.; Jimmy Blanchard, Chairman of Synovus Financial Corp.; Dr. William Foege, former Director of the Centers for Disease Control and Gates Foundation; and Former Ambassador Andrew Young.

My co-editor, Kim Cameron, and I asked our authors to tell us stories about organizations and to drill down into the issues of how values are operationalized and how leadership is executed. This book resulted from those stories.

From Kim

Ed and I had three objectives in mind in producing this book – to inspire, to inform, and to affect behavior. The first objective is illustrated by a quotation by Nobel laureate Desmond Tutu (1999: 263): *"The world is hungry for goodness, it recognizes it when it sees it, and it has incredible responses to the good. There is something in all of us that hungers after the good and true, and when we glimpse it in people, we applaud them for it. We long to be just like them. Their inspiration reminds us of the tenderness for life that we all can feel."*

You will read about leaders who were dedicated to the good – their core values and their highest principles. By reading about these leaders' decisions and actions, we hope to inspire and motivate other leaders to follow suit, to be elevated in their thinking, and to aim to achieve similar results. We believe that we all hunger for that which elevates. In this book, examples of inspiring leadership are culled from a wide variety of organizations ranging from financial services and transportation industries, to open range firefighters, and the US Marine Corps. Regardless of their settings or circumstances, leaders are described who were successful because they held closely to and perpetuated tirelessly their core values. Their stories are moving and motivating for those who are inclined toward the good and true. We think you will be inspired as we have been by reading these chapters.

Our second objective is to inform. We want to expose you to a new set of leadership principles and practices that are based on virtues and positivity. Most research on leadership and management has emphasized problem solving, winning at the expense of others, and overcoming obstacles and challenges. Whereas we recount stories of similar situations in this book – for example, competition, mistakes, trauma, problem solving – the emphasis is always on the positive, the elevating, and the good.

This book builds on a recent and growing emphasis in social science research – based in positive psychology, positive organizational scholarship, and virtue ethics – which highlights positive phenomena. For example, recently published work has reported that extraordinary individual and organizational effects are produced by an emphasis on virtues, values, and positivity. These effects range from physiological health benefits (such as less illness), emotional benefits (such as resistance to depression), and psychological benefits (such as longer memories) at the individual level to organizational effects such as higher levels of profitability, productivity, quality, and satisfaction of both employees and customers. When leaders lead with values – that is, when they demonstrate virtues, values, and positivity – the effects are magnified because leaders serve as exemplars, vision creators, and sources of recognition and rewards. The chapters in this book highlight and illustrate some of these intriguing effects.

Our third objective was to affect behavior. This objective is addressed in two ways. One way is by offering practical advice and leadership prescriptions through the authors in the various chapters. You will most certainly uncover nuggets of advice and helpful hints that will be helpful in your own leadership roles. You may not run a company, fight a war in Afghanistan, or work in a hospital-billing department – each a setting described in a chapter – but the leadership principles that are described will nevertheless be applicable across many different situations.

A second way we hope to affect behavior is through the "amplifying effect" associated with virtuous and values-based behavior. Several researchers have described the dynamics of groups and organizations that experience virtuous actions and especially positive leadership. Under such conditions, people experience a compelling urge to build upon the contributions of others and to perpetuate the virtuousness that they see. When we experience an act of kindness, for example, we are inclined to reciprocate. Observing virtuousness tends to create a self-reinforcing upward spiral.

This amplifying effect can be explained by three different factors that occur when values-based leadership and virtuousness are displayed – positive emotions, social capital, and prosocial behavior.

First, positive emotions occur in people who experience virtuousness and values-based leadership. When organization members observe compassion, experience love, or witness spectacular performance, for example, they are inspired, their pride in the organization is increased, their enjoyment of the work is enhanced, and their satisfaction with the job is elevated. Several studies have demonstrated that this amplifying effect is disseminated throughout an organization emotionally by way of a contagion effect. That is, the entire organization is influenced positively when virtuousness and positive values are demonstrated, especially by individuals in leadership positions.

Second, the development of social capital results from this kind of leadership. Social capital refers to the development of positive relationships among employees. Building social capital reduces transaction costs, facilitates communication and cooperation, enhances employee commitment, fosters individual learning, strengthens relationships and involvement, and, ultimately, enhances organizational performance. Experiencing values-based leadership, with its emphasis on virtuousness, creates a sense of attachment and attraction towards virtuous actors. People experience an urge to join with and build upon the contributions of these exemplars. Organizations function better when members know, trust, and feel positively toward one another, and leading with values helps create the conditions for that to occur.

Third, prosocial behavior is the tendency to engage in helpful behavior toward others, or to want to make a contribution to others. Several authors have pointed out that almost all people have an intrinsic motivation toward helping others. Observing and experiencing virtuousness helps unlock the human predisposition toward behaving in ways that benefit others. Several studies support the idea that when people observe helpful or moral behavior, their inclination is to follow suit. Thus, helpfulness and an inclination toward helping others is fostered by values-based, virtuous leadership.

In this book you will read about many inspiring, virtuous, positively value-driven leaders. We hope that by presenting these examples, it will perpetuate this kind of leadership in others through an amplifying effect.

Now, let us jointly give you an overview of this work. In Chapter 1, "Synovus Financial Corporation: 'Just take care of your people,'" by Professor Robert Drazin, Professor Ed Hess, and Farah Mihoubi, a story is told of how founding families' values have been perpetuated for over 100 years by servant leaders. It is an in-depth look at the myriad ways an organization promotes certain values to its employees, and seeks their adoption of those values into their routine behaviors. It shows us that leadership is hard work and is a daily job; that an organization's values have to be promoted and reinforced by every human resources policy, and that every decision has to be tested against core values. The chapter illustrates how values are taught through stories and how good behaviors are memorialized in a culture.

Chapter 2 is "FedEx Freight – Putting People First," written by Fed Ex Freight executive, Gary W. Bouch. It recounts the story of one leader who thought his company was losing its values through growth and a merger and how his resulting actions reestablished a "People First" culture. It is a story of both personal courage and the step-by-step process of how a leader begins to build a culture based on values, including getting buy-in from top executives and hundreds of senior executives. Fed Ex Freight has been engaged in this change process for two years, and it is an insightful story for leaders trying to create a people-centric culture.

Chapter 3, "The Role of Values in High Risk Organizations," by Professor Karl Weick, is an analysis of high reliability, high-risk organizations such as air traffic controllers, nuclear power plants, and forest firefighters. Karl points out that in addition to promoting and teaching positive values, leaders must also spend time devaluing detrimental values such as hubris, arrogance, rigid mindsets, hierarchy, etc. Devaluing the negative is as important as promoting positive values.

The next chapter focuses on the role of spirituality in a high performance organization. Chapter 4, "Spirituality and Leadership in the Marine Corps," by Major Dan Yaroslaski and Professor Paolo Tripodi, discusses the role of spirituality in the United States Marine Corps culture. The authors explain that the success of the Marine Corps – historically as well as in the current world war on terrorism – is intimately tied to leadership values, core beliefs, and a commitment to spirituality.

Chapter 5, by Professor Ed Hess, also addresses the role of spirituality. "HomeBanc Mortgage Corp.: Quest to Become America's Most Admired Company," is the story of a major public company built upon common religious values. It tells how a minister at the age of 51 became the Executive Vice President of Human Resources at this Company in order to lead a quest for HomeBanc to become the country's most admired public company. Employees' statements reveal much about the impact of the change that occurred toward creating a caring, giving culture. Most importantly, employees created a "family" at work, which provided meaningfulness, a source of loyalty (low turnover), and high performance.

Chapter 6, "Leadership Lessons from Sarah: Values-based Leadership for Everyday Practice," was written by Professor Monica Worline and Sarah Boik, the leader of a staff unit in a hospital. It tells the impressive story of Ms. Boik who transformed a group of mostly single working mothers from a poorly performing billing department into a high performance organization by building a caring, people-oriented culture. This is an example of leading through values by a leader who never received formal leadership training. Rather, Sarah uses common sense, good judgment, knowledge and understanding of people, and firm personal values to teach, inspire, and create a meaningful, positive, high performance environment.

Professor Kim Cameron's Chapter 7, "Leadership Values that Enable Extraordinary Success," tells the story of an extraordinary organizational success, well beyond the level of performance achieved by any other similar organization in history. It describes the values that allowed leaders to overcome institutional and community hostility, employee apathy and negativity, and a contradictory culture to create a high performance environment. Leadership based on certain key values produced the closure and clean up of the largest nuclear waste dumpsite on the planet in one-sixth the projected time and at one-sixth the budgeted cost.

Many examples exist of leaders who espouse values but who do not translate those values into appropriate corporate behavior. In Chapter 8, "Principled Leadership: A Framework for Action," Professor MaryAnn Glynn and Heath Jamerson focus on the Enron debacle. They provide a perspective on why Enron – and other similar firms – have found themselves in such trouble, and they explain a set of principles to help leaders translate their values into actions. In a very clear and straightforward summary, the authors teach us that good intent is not enough but that intent must be translated into actions that produce intended results.

No matter how good the intentions, of course, and no matter how hard leaders try to stay committed to values and to good behavior, they always fall short. Mistakes are always made. In Chapter 9, "Forgiveness as an Attribute of Leadership," Professor David Bright discusses forgiveness in organizations. He identifies three different kinds of responses to offenses and harm in organizations, and he reports their effects on employees and organizational performance. The chapter points out key principles for enhancing a culture of forgiveness in organizations.

In Chapter 10, the theme of virtuousness and reactions to harmful events is continued. This chapter, "Values and Leadership in Organizational Crisis," explains principles of organizational healing after major trauma. Professors Edward H. Powley and Scott N. Taylor discuss the role of leaders and their values in helping organizations recover from a break-in, shooting spree, and hostage crisis in a university setting. In their explanation of recovery and resilience, they concisely summarize the essence of values-based leadership.

The last chapter (Chapter 11) focuses on how values-centered leaders are developed. "Making More 'Mike Stranks'-Teaching Values in the United States Marine Corps," by Marine Lt. Col. Michael Parkyn, illuminates how the US Marine Corps develops leaders through a career-long progression of leadership development. The Marine Corps is well known for transforming men and women to become leaders that do not resemble their former selves. As Brig. Gen. Mel Spies said, "We have learned how to take average people and teach them to perform spectacularly well under the most trying circumstances." Lt. Col. Parkyn's chapter shows us the different ways of operationalizing values in an organization and perpetuating them.

In summary, these chapters make several important points:

(1) Ethics, values, and high performance are not mutually exclusive.
(2) Positive values and virtuous leadership may be a necessity for sustainable long-term high performance.
(3) As important as the demonstration and perpetuation of positive values, is the devaluation of undesireable behavior.
(4) Positive leadership values and principles must be demonstrated, and leadership actions must be in harmony with the verbiage.
(5) The establishment of "family connectedness" – with its emphasis on virtuous principles and behaviors – is a strong prediction of loyalty and high performance.
(6) Leading with values enables a highly engaged workforce, which, in turn, becomes very loyal and very productive.
(7) Leading with values can produce success regardless of the organizational context, the industry or sector, or the nature of the workforce. Outstanding success depends more on the values being perpetuated than on the situation in which the leader is leading.

Edward_Hess@bus.emory.edu
CameronK@umich.edu

1 Synovus Financial Corporation: "Just take care of your people"

ROBERT DRAZIN, EDWARD D. HESS, AND FARAH MIHOUBI

Introduction

The Synovus Financial Services Corporation uses an extensive systems-wide approach to values-based leadership. By system-wide, we mean that values-based leadership permeates the entire company. Values are the basis for leadership, culture, selection, training and executive development. Values are used to shape the firm's strategy, its relationship to customers and to community. Senior executives consistently talk about values and culture among themselves and with employees at all levels. Values-based leadership is tangible – it is part of evaluation and promotion systems. Values are transformed into practices. While core values stay the same, senior managers are consistently updating practices. Values are discussed as much as strategy.

Our purpose in this chapter is to chronicle how these values extend back in history, what the values are now and how Synovus implements practices to support or operationalize its values. Synovus is an example of the founding families' values surviving four leadership successions, and a company flourishing financially because of its values-based people-centric culture. Some of the lessons to focus on while reading this chapter are: (1) you can achieve great financial results, create substantial shareholder value AND be an employee-centric company with values; (2) maintaining a values-based culture is hard work and can never be taken for granted; (3) senior leadership must live daily the values they want emulated and be role models for all levels of leadership; and (4) you have to back up the words by rewarding good values and recognizing cultural deviations.

History

The Synovus story began in the late 1800s, where it was founded in Columbus, Georgia. In November 1888, Mr. George Gunby Jordan

9

created the Third National Bank and the Columbus Savings Bank, Synovus' predecessor, by convincing seventeen wealthy patrons of Columbus to front $100,000 in investment capital to create a civic-minded bank. By 1900, a vice-presidency for the banks was created, and William Clark Bradley stepped up to the position. Over time, both Jordan and Bradley would work closely and in harmony together, cementing a friendship and investment partnership between the two families that would continue for five generations. Together, they helped to fund the construction of dams on the Chattahoochee River in Columbus for its hydroelectric energy potential. This led to the Columbus Power Company, which was later amalgamated into Georgia Power.

A wave of banking instability came in the late twenties and early thirties, with the Great Depression. On the heels of the two banks having merged into Columbus Bank and Trust (CB&T), the country was in the middle of a financial panic after October 29, 1929. Many banks collapsed during this period; meanwhile CB&T stockholders boasted an increase in the bank's assets. A phenomenal number of bank closures took place in 1931 (2,294), with half that many failing in 1930. Remarkably, job losses did not occur at CB&T during this difficult period, even as they were commonplace in the industry during this time. It was at this inopportune time that the bank's first president, George Gunby Jordan, passed away. The bank's directors credited him as a man of "vision, integrity, and business sagacity."[1] He was seen as a man "of unusual energy and intellect . . . wherever he touched the affairs of men, he was a leader."[2]

In 1947, W. C. Bradley passed away. As he had been a revered member of his community, the Board of Directors claimed that "this Board suffered an irreparable loss in the death of their president and beloved friend, William Clark Bradley . . . wise planning, cool judgment, integrity and square dealing marked his every endeavor."[3] As *A Trust to Keep* recounts,

As one of the foremost industrialists of the South, even the country, William Clark Bradley gave generously to the artistic, religious, and educational institutions of the city. This gentleman, born in the midst of the Civil War, knew

---

[1] *A Trust to Keep: The One Hundred Year History of Columbus Bank and Trust Company, 1888–1988*, Synovus Financial Corporation (1988), p. 43.
[2] Ibid.   [3] Ibid., p. 49.

the keen deprivations families faced for years in the South. By his great desire to improve the quality of life of the average Southerner and make that life affordable, he showed a moral dimension neither understood nor practiced by most people of means. For this reason, rather than for his monumental business achievements, he must be respected and recognized. A fair man of energy and unusual talent appears too infrequently not to be given appropriate commendation.[4]

After his passing, the torch was passed to D. Abbott Turner, Bradley's son-in-law. Turner also maintained the founder's high standards of personal integrity. According to *A Trust to Keep*,

Mr. Turner possessed the affection of the employees – even the citizens of Columbus. Respect and love present a formidable combination and Abbott Turner received them from a populace who appreciated his lack of pretense and his sensitivity to power, which he rarely used and never abused . . . along with his disarmingly keen sense of humor which endeared him to people. Abbott Turner had a natural gift for instilling trust. Individuals wanted to deserve his respect and worked to achieve it. He gave his best effort to his work and expected the same.[5]

Jim Blanchard (the current CEO's father) was appointed president of CB&T in 1957, and served until 1969. Blanchard's new energy, ideas and industry were just what the bank needed at the time.

From the time that Jim Blanchard came into the Bank, the operation began to change. He did not do it in a fast, quick, or rough manner. He very easily transferred people and began to build the organization without incurring the ill will of any employee. No one openly opposed him. He was the most unselfish man imaginable. Everything he did was for the people that worked with him; and from the day Jim Blanchard took charge, the Bank was a different operation. He was also interested in the community. A revival of public interest occurred in Columbus as a result of his being here. He became active in the Chamber of Commerce and all the other institutions, especially his church.[6]

Jim Blanchard, Sr. passed away on January 12, 1969, and finding someone to fill his shoes after his death "set off a frantic search for a successor who might possess his rare qualities of business acumen, religious convictions, educational interests, and dedication to community service."[7] Many in the organization wanted his son, Jimmy

---

[4] Ibid.   [5] Ibid., p. 54.   [6] Ibid., p. 78.   [7] Ibid., p. 85.

Blanchard, a lawyer at the time, to keep up his father's ethos and style, where he kept "his finger on the heartbeat of the city...for in the long run what's right for the community is good for the bank."[8] Jimmy Blanchard was understandably reticent about entering a profession for which he had no prior expertise. A well-known Columbus banker, Bill Curry, was enlisted to run the bank for two years, while Jimmy was groomed for the position, a role that at the outset he reluctantly fulfilled, a role that he has fulfilled for over thirty years. Mr. Jordan, Bradley and the Turner founding families are still involved today as investors, advisors and board members.

Strategy: growth by acquisitions

Synovus has grown into an $8 billion market bank by acquisitions. Its approach to acquiring banks is different from many of its competitors in the banking industry. According to Blanchard, "We don't have a quantity strategy or pins in a map. We're looking for targets where there's economic opportunity, where people mix and are compatible."[9] There must be synergy between the two banks in their cultural, social, and philosophical outlooks, and the "feel" must be right. The notion is that Synovus looks for "good banks, good markets, and good people."[10] As Blanchard explains, "This may sound corny, but we wouldn't want to acquire any bank where we wouldn't want to take the folks home to momma."[11]

Rather than subsume smaller companies under its umbrella, Synovus allows the small community banks it acquires to keep many structures intact, retain their autonomy, and "run their own show."[12] Unlike other bank mergers (especially during the period of banking instability in the nineties) which often generate a great deal of upheaval in the local communities, a great deal of volatility in jobs, and a great deal of apprehension among the employees of the acquired bank, Synovus acquisitions are much less disruptive to both employee morale and to customer loyalty.

The company usually acquires small-town banks that have a large market share in their respective communities, where a close

---

[8] Ibid., p. 85.   [9] Brannigan (1995).
[10] Personal interview at Synovus with Frederick L. Green, III, Vice Chairman, June 15, 2004.
[11] Brannigan (1995).   [12] Chambers (1997).

relationship exists between the bank and its customers. It also often chooses to have a presence in communities where there is a notable absence of larger, more competitive national banks.

Diversification into TSYS

TSYS was officially launched in 1959, as apart of CB&T and it processed credit cards. In 1973, the company unveiled Total System, a software product that would for the first time allow Synovus to electronically process credit card information and billing. By 1974, CB&T was processing paperwork for other banks' credit card operations and realized this could become a profitable long-term venture. Total Systems marked the beginning of the bank holding company's diversification efforts, and has proven to be a revenue-generating asset that is largely "recession-resistant," as credit and debit card usage has increased exponentially over the years. Today, 19% of TSYS has been spun off into its own separate public company, and is involved in processing credit and debit-card transactions and electronic payments for a variety of major financial institution clients worldwide, like Bank of America, Capital One and JP Morgan Chase (including their newest relationship with Bank One in 2003).

TSYS currently fills all the card-processing needs for five out of ten of the largest global card-issuing banks. Today, TSYS is the second largest credit-card transaction processor in the United States,[13] with 2003 revenues of $1.05 billion. At present, TSYS contributes about 30% of profits to the parent company's bottom line.[14] Over the years, the company has expanded to Great Britain, Mexico, Canada and Japan, and South America, Europe and the Asia Pacific region are next.

Performance

Synovus has done well based on standard banking metrics of performance. It has grown steadily from 1999 to 2003 in revenues, assets and earnings per share. Earnings per share compounded annual growth rate for this period was 13.0%.

[13] Synovus Financial Corp., Hoover's Company Profiles (2004).
[14] Boraks (2004).

Further, *Fortune* magazine has ranked Synovus one of the ten best companies to work for in America for five years in a row. In addition, Synovus has made it into the list's top 20 for seven years in a row.

In 2000 and 2001, Synovus also graced *Working Mother's* list of "100 Best Companies for Working Mothers." Citing their emphasis on human resources, CEO Blanchard noted,

> In a social and economic environment where so many things are uncertain, it is more important than ever that the team members of Synovus and the employees of companies throughout the country know that they are cared for. Enabling our working mothers to be productive, valued and rewarded while also caring for their families is one of our primary missions as an employer of choice.[15]

The magazine's criteria for comprising the list included "how 'deeply' benefits are available in addition to the traditional scoring for (a) percentage of women in workforce, (b) child care support, (c) flexibility, (d) leave for new parents, (e) work/life balance and (f) advancement of women."[16]

The *Wall Street Journal* awarded Synovus "No. 1 Bank in the South" for its shareholder returns over the years 1993–1998.[17] In addition, the company was named 49th among banks for the Fortune 1000 list. Synovus was winner of *Forbes* magazine's Forbes Platinum 400 index (for profitability and return on capital), ranking second among the 20 largest banking institutions listed, and ranked 10th out of 33 banks and 70th generally for *Business Week's* annual list of outstanding companies for performance on the S&P 500. Synovus' Investment Division was also ranked by *Pension and Investments* magazine as one of the country's top-ten money managers. Finally, TSYS was winner of the 1998 Georgia Oglethorpe Award (for performance excellence).

Certain key leaders at Synovus have also been singled out for exceptional achievement. Synovus' Chairman/CEO James H. Blanchard was ranked among the "25 Most Powerful and Influential Georgians" by *Georgia Trend* magazine. And, Synovus' CIO Lee James was named by *US Banker* magazine as one of the "25 Most Powerful Women in Banking."

---

[15] PR Newswire 2001.
[16] Ibid.   [17] Synovus Financial Corp. *Annual Report*, 1998, p. 13.

The culture

At Synovus, the culture can be summed as the Golden Rule and doing what's right, this expands into "treating others right, and treating others with kindness, and pulling for others. Decision-making follows from this, even when "right" may not be the most profitable avenue, the most expedient, or even the most popular. Outward from the company, this extends into the families of Synovus employees, others that Synovus come into contact with, and finally, out to the community. There is a sense of building a better family, a better community, and being a part of a better world. None of this is naive idealism, as those in the Synovus community know that they are performing meaningful work, and working for a higher purpose. This becomes contagious, and others realize, "I'd love to be part of that team."[18]

Operationalization of culture

The Golden Rule: Do What Is Right culture operates with the simplicity of a mere handful of founding principles, ones it is difficult to imagine *not* being able to resonate with.

At Synovus, the Golden Rule and 'Servant Leadership' – the notion that the boss is there to serve the organization and its people, not the other way around – are bedrock principles. The company's operations are centered around a well-defined set of expectations, graphically bisected by an ordered 'value chain,' that focuses first on people and culture, and places performance near the end of the list. Various committees and meetings constantly refine and reinforce the message. The latest addition, a "Customer Covenant" adopted last year, and carried on small cards in employees" wallets, codifies the company's goal of serving all clients "with the highest levels of sincerity, fairness, courtesy, respect and gratitude." All of this is wrapped up neatly in what officials like to call a "culture of the heart."[19]

The company pledges an "unwavering" commitment to its culture and its values. Synovus maintains, "Integrity. Service. Putting people first. Treating folks right, and doing the right things. This is not corporate rhetoric; this is our character. We won't compromise these values

---

[18] Personal interview at Synovus with Walter M. Deriso, Vice Chairman, June 15, 2004.
[19] Engen (2003).

under any circumstances."[20] Thus, within the company, the "we, not me" ethos reigns supreme.

The value chain begins with people, with performance being necessary, but people coming first. Performance comes from good people with good values. Management's role is seen as stewardship, since the company is seen as an asset borrowed from the shareholders, and one which must be maintained as if it were one's own. A distinctly non-secular approach to spirituality manifests as a belief in a "higher power," a belief in the inherent worth of every employee, and a commitment to developing the talents of each individual. While skeptical onlookers mock the company's Golden Rule, comically asserting that "He who has the gold rules,"[21] Synovus stockholders are laughing all the way to the bank, as profits and shareholder returns have steadily increased over the years.

Company culture

The company strives to maintain an atmosphere where employees grow "materially, spiritually, and intellectually," and where the customer sees the culture come "from the heart." For Synovus, there is a deep, embedded commitment to "walk the talk," unlike other companies for whom culture is merely paid lip service. For Synovus, its culture is firmly entrenched in the very fabric of its being, and it can be found from the highest levels of management all the way down the chain of command. Some have given this corporate philosophy an almost religious or cult-like status, recounting that "the atmosphere is hushed, reverential...attending an annual meeting...is almost like going to church."[22] Management meetings are decidedly not secular, as a recent management meeting began with Blanchard saying, "Thank you God, for the company we have to work for,"[23] and Biblical quotes are peppered throughout "pastor"[24] Blanchard's speeches. Weekly Tuesday morning meetings bring together local employees to hear the "sermon,"[25] and other Synovus employees may opt to hear it via conference calls or cassette tapes. Company meetings that involve meals begin with blessings, and executives explain, "We operate in a

---

[20] Synovus Financial Corp. *Annual Report*, 2001, p. 4.   [21] Engen (2003).
[22] Chambers (1997).   [23] Brannigan (1995).   [24] Engen (2003).   [25] Ibid.

culture where that is OK. It's not showy and people are comfortable with it."[26] At one time, it was considered whether to abolish this practice, but Synovus management was bombarded with pleas from their employees to retain it.

In addition, a "family-like" atmosphere permeates the culture. "Our culture is rooted in the notion that people are valuable. They're entitled to dignity and respect and appreciation," says Blanchard.[27] Employee evaluations are not threatening once-yearly encounters, but rather ongoing and interactive discussions. Servant leadership, or the notion that management serves the organization, rather than the other way around, translates into management-as-mentor or coach, rather than the traditional boss–subordinate relationship. According to Blanchard, "Supervisors who don't buy into that type of atmosphere – who want to be controlling and demanding and demeaning – we basically don't want them here. We want people who can coach and counsel and be concerned about a person beyond just what they do between 9 and 5 o'clock."

This approach translates directly into the company's success, as the company aims to follow the axiom that if we "take care of people, profit takes care of itself."[28] It is believed that an employee's life should not be "compartmentalized" into all its component parts, but that rather, the office environment should feel similar to all other parts of one's life. Thus, the workplace should also support all other parts of the employee's life such that "when one person at Synovus cries, everyone tastes the tears."[29]

Loyal customers palpably feel the warmth that emanates from the company as well. According to Chief Warrant Officer Four (Retired) Michael Novosel, United States Army, Congressional Medal of Honor recipient, and 31-year customer of a Synovus affiliate bank in Alabama, "Seeing the Synovus sign is like seeing the international Red Cross symbol – you know that behind it is an organization of dedicated people who are there to help."[30]

---

[26] Personal interview at Synovus with Walter M. Deriso, Vice Chairman, June 15, 2004.
[27] Engen (2003).
[28] Taken from Synovus public relations video entitled "Culture of the Heart."
[29] Ibid.   [30] Synovus Financial Corp. *Annual Report*, 2003, p. 21.

Walk the talk

For Synovus, living its values begins with compensating its employees adequately for their commitment and dedication. Employee benefits are grouped under the four broad categories of "health, wealth, well-being, and time" and include an 8% retirement match, an option to buy 150 shares of Synovus stock, an exceptional and comprehensive health-care plan, fitness center discounts, flex time, training programs, tuition reimbursement, child care centers, and adoption credits. TSYS employees are encouraged to enroll in the Columbus State University Masters of Information Technology program. Minority youth are also encouraged through internships at Synovus (INROADS), many of whom stay on for permanent positions with the company. REACH (Recognizing and Encouraging an Atmosphere of Community and Hope) is the company's volunteer arm, and employee participation in various community service projects is encouraged and enthusiastically supported by management. Whether it's building homes, caring for the homeless, feeding the hungry, or working on environmental clean-up projects, giving volunteer time *during work hours* is welcomed by management.

Living the culture then translates directly into superior customer service. In a competitive financial services market with largely undifferentiable products and services, employees "extending" themselves for their customers translates into greater consumer loyalty and higher product sales. In a push by the industry generally toward one-stop financial-services shopping, exceptional customer service is a key to success. The dedication of Synovus employees is a direct result of the trickle-down people-oriented approach the company applies to human resource management. Thus, "success is a by-product of the [bank's] culture,"[31] where employees are valued for themselves and not for the value they bring to the company. As mentioned in the company's 1998 *Annual Report*,

Some experts say a formula for success can't be that simple. Well, maybe it is. It's more than programs and benefits that make a great place to work. The challenge is teaching our leaders how to show genuine concern for each person they lead. People respond when they know someone really cares about them and appreciates them. They just do.[32]

---

[31] Chambers (1997).   [32] Synovus Financial Corp. *Annual Report*, 1998, p. 4.

Synovus also believes strongly in personal accountability. The company maintains,

Our values also describe a company at which every member is fully responsible for every loan, account, market trade, every client and every customer. That's 100 percent responsibility. No excuses when something goes wrong, just make it right. Mediocrity is never a solution. Every member of our team should have zero-tolerance for anything less than the best. That's us; that's our way.[33]

This becomes the foundation for the company's "mission statement," and can be found in the "Customer Covenant" as well. The Customer Covenant (see Appendix 4) was created in 2001, and is signed by every employee, which gives it unified company support.

Finally, living by its values can also be found in the company's approach to corporate ethics. The company has two fronts on which it addresses corporate ethics. The first, the Synovus Code of Conduct, covers proper operating procedures for most topics under the corporate umbrella. Further, there is a toll-free 24-hour ethics hotline, where calls are recorded anonymously, and employees may feel free to report any concerns about ethics violations anywhere within the company.

Keeping the culture alive

Keeping the corporate culture undiluted for a company that has been in existence for well over a century is admittedly difficult. While the founders believed with a passion in the core values they built the company on, it requires constant reinforcement to perpetuate over time. When the company was much smaller, it was obviously easier, and its critics often countered that once the company grew, it would be impossible to sustain the culture in such a fashion. Synovus' value-system is still firmly in place and very much institutionalized even at the lower ranks, with its 12,000-plus employees.

Toward this end, leadership at Synovus, even after its phenomenal growth, is deeply steeped in the company's core values. Leaders at the topmost levels are not content merely to "manage from this gorgeous office," and realize that "values will start to erode the minute you take

---

[33] Ibid., p. 18.

your eye off the ball."[34] Many Synovus initiatives have been born upon taking a closer look at the reality, and realizing with humility, that "we may not be as good at this as we think we are."[35]

Is it real?

Personal interviews with Synovus employees at all levels, from those who had been with the company less than a year, to those who were mid-level managers, to those on the executive committee, produced consistent stories. For these managers interviewed, arriving at Synovus for the first time felt like "coming home." For the mid-level managers, who echoed the same basic tenets as those in the executive committee, the "culture is just life to us, we live it everyday."[36] It is seen both literally and figuratively as a "fiduciary responsibility to our culture – which is both our privilege and obligation." Thus, it is "a trust to keep, whether to the customer, or to each other."

At Synovus, hiring is deemed highly important, since the company is only as strong as the weakest link (person) in its chain. "Chemistry" is the term often repeated in the company, where it is used for assessing fit and building relationships. For those in charge of hiring, the "chemistry" *must* be there, since at the end of the day, the biggest asset the company has is its people.

Management looks specifically for people with charisma, who have their priorities in the right order: family, spirituality, community activism, and who are leaders wherever they presently are. These kinds of people inspire others to be on their "team," where others would *want* to follow them, and they are also top performers by other traditional standards.

At Synovus, people take precedence over profits and performance. At the executive levels, this is especially apparent. Newcomers often spend

---

[34] Personal interview at Synovus with James D. Yancey, Chairman of the Board, June 15, 2004.

[35] Ibid.

[36] Quotations from personal interviews with J. Grantham, SVP, Customer Support Senior Manager, CB&T; Alison Dowe, VP, Director Corporate Communications, Synovus; Lee Sessions, VP, Financial Planning Manager, CB&T; Jon Long, AVP, Director of Organizational Effectiveness, Synovus; and Robin Grier, SVP, Director of E-Business, Synovus.

weeks and months developing relationships with Synovus affiliates, meeting other executives, employees, and members of the local communities. Meeting with everyone, regardless of their "rank" is seen as more important than "spending the day playing golf with the CEO."[37] As Mr. Yancey recalls from his days as a teller, "I know how it felt when the president shook everyone's hand."[38] With 41 different banks under the corporate umbrella, honoring the different nature of each member bank becomes a formidable task. Nevertheless, this is done with enthusiasm, and conversations revolve around people and communication issues and then numbers. This is based squarely on the Synovus ethic that "if you put the right people in the right role, you have faith that all the rest will work out."[39] Thus, the causality is first relationships, then performance, and not the other way around.

Personal growth is another important area, since Synovus likes to think of itself as espousing the *net exporting* of good people. Whether this means that good employees are "grown" within the company and moved higher in the organization, or whether their expertise is sought out by other companies, there is no monopoly on talent within the organization. Those who wish to understand their own career growth possibilities can feel free to talk to anyone in the company, at any level, and know that they will receive coaching, mentorship, and encouragement. The executives especially believe that "we take our jobs seriously, but we don't take ourselves seriously."[40] Thus, there is a notable absence of hierarchical boundaries among employees. It matters little where one falls on the traditional "organizational chart," as those "below" are just as important as those "above." Yancey comments, "people who promote me are below me . . . it is *they* who need to think I'm something special, and not the other way around."[41] It follows that employees who are most successful in climbing the organization's ranks are those who treat everyone with the same respect, regardless of their position in the company.

[37] Personal interview at Synovus with James D. Yancey, Chairman of the Board, June 15, 2004.
[38] Ibid.
[39] Personal interview at Synovus with Frederick L. Green, III, Vice Chairman, June 15, 2004.
[40] Personal interview at Synovus with James D. Yancey, Chairman of the Board, June 15, 2004.
[41] Ibid.

At the customer level

At Synovus, the focus is not on commission-based selling of financial products and services. Instead, the concern is to first understand the needs of the customer, and only then suggest products that fill that need. The focus is on relationships, and employees first attempt to discern whether or not they can meet a client's needs. If they truly cannot, they will suggest that the client seek assistance from a potential competitor. The ethic is then, "Do your best to make your fellow team members successful and your customers successful in their financial lives, rather than push a product or live from one [sales] campaign to the next."[42]

To rejuvenate the culture

The People Developing EveryONE (PDE) initiative was created in 1996. PDE came about as a response to a company survey, which identified key areas in which Synovus could improve. Among the initiatives that PDE spawned include: Cultural Trust Committees, a new Orientation Program, Re-Orientation, Leadership Education, Foundations of Leadership, The Leadership Institute, the Performance Management Process, a Team Member Survey, Evaluation of Officer Criteria, and Continuous Review of Work/Life Issues.

PDE is a people-development initiative, and as such, rests on four fundamental ideas: "We pledge to respect the fundamental worth of every individual. We treat people right. We do what's right. We will safeguard our 'culture of the heart.'"[43] Thus, PDE is based on the Company's

most enduring value: Every person has great worth. We will invest in every member of our team just like we save money for the future. We should build people. Teach them. If team members know their part in the plan – why they are important, regardless of their roles – then their attitudes are brighter. They want to serve. Our returns are hearty. Working here is better. PDE is a key part of our success.[44]

[42] Personal interview at Synovus with Richard E. Anthony, President and COO, July 6, 2004.
[43] Synovus Financial Corp. *Annual Report*, 1999, p. 12.
[44] Synovus Financial Corp. *Annual Report*, 1998, p. 14.

The use of stories

In the Synovus tradition, the corporate culture and values are often passed on via storytelling and the recounting of parables and anecdotes, which help to maintain the essence of the culture for newcomers. Storytelling ("what's in your heart that you want to share?"), or the recounting of personal triumphs of the human spirit, are used especially for teaching at the Leadership Institute. Via "teachable stories," managers each humble themselves by presenting a story of something they have learned along the way.

The following two stories are examples, which are used repeatedly by senior management to teach key lessons.

Gandhi

This is a story of the great Gandhi of India when he was a student in South Africa. Gandhi had heard so much about Christianity, and he wanted to know more. One day, he slipped into the back of a church in South Africa and sat on the back row. An usher came to him and very courteously informed him that there were no "coloreds" allowed in the church. In a speech years later, Gandhi declared that the usher was only doing his job, thinking he was simply ushering a colored man from the church. In reality, what he was actually doing was ushering India out of the British Empire.

So often we think that we don't make a difference. But the words that we speak, the looks we give, the actions we take, are all incredibly powerful. There is somebody around you right now that with just a single word of encouragement would be what it took to get them over a hump. There is somebody at your office for which a harsh word could be the last straw. You and I make a difference as a common thread in a business sense. There is no question that the common thread is how you treat folks. You can make a difference.[45]

Waldorf-Astoria

Many years ago, an elderly man and his wife entered the lobby of a small Philadelphia hotel. "All the big places are filled," the man said. "Can you give us a room?" The clerk replied that with three conventions in town, no accommodations were available anywhere. "Every guest room is taken," he said, but then added, "but I can't send a nice couple like you out into the rain at one o'clock in the morning. Would you be willing to sleep in my room?"

---

[45] Synovus Financial Corp. *Connections* Magazine, "Synovus Stories," Fall 2002, p. 24.

The next morning as he paid his bill, the elderly man said to the clerk, "You are the kind of manager who should be the boss of the best hotel in the United States. Maybe someday I'll build one for you." The clerk laughed and forgot about the incident. About two years later, however, he received a letter containing a round-trip ticket to New York and a request that he be the guest of the elderly couple he had befriended.

Once in New York, the old man led the clerk to the corner of Fifth Avenue and Thirty-Fourth Street, where he pointed to an incredible new building and declared, "That is the hotel I have just built for you to manage." The young man, George C. Boldt, accepted the offer of William Waldorf Astor to become the manager of the original Waldorf-Astoria, considered the finest hotel in the world in its time. You can make a difference.[46]

Leadership institute and foundations of leadership

The Leadership Institute and Foundations of Leadership were established in 1998 to allow for all Synovus management to "constantly and consistently deliver our most important message – that people come first in every decision we make – to every member of our team."[47] These two company innovations help ensure consistency in the company's core message of making human resources a true priority and in keeping with the notion of a company as a "ministry." In these two forums, the culture and values of the company are passed on to all those in management levels (both in Synovus companies and in their affiliates), in a holistic manner, embodying the idea that all members are part of the entire whole and essential to its functioning. The notion of stewardship and servant leadership is stressed, and leaders are expected to value and ensure the success of their teams in order to carry out the grand vision of the larger company. The concept of "averaging up" in promoting from within, such that the new person should exceed his predecessor in every way, is also stressed. It becomes apparent that with management symbolically at the bottom of the hierarchy, providing foundation and support, it becomes easier to develop a common vision that is "owned" by all within. Foundations of Leadership seminars train via four "action requirements." These are: "live the values, share the vision, make others successful, and manage the business."[48]

---

[46] Ibid., p. 38.   [47] Synovus Financial Corp. *Annual Report*, 1998, p. 6.
[48] Synovus Financial Corp. *Annual Report*, 1998, p. 16.

Through the Synovus story, it can be seen that corporate responsibility and ethics need not be merely a "flavor-of-the-month" management strategy. Indeed, it is possible to speak of a corporate values-based culture and more-than-adequate shareholder returns in the same sentence. Whether the culture is deeply entrenched and maintained from the outset, as has been the case at Synovus, or whether it is brought in later as an all-encompassing ethic, such a values-based style is indeed a viable alternative. From servant leaders to personally fulfilled employees to well-served customers, a holistic vision toward a company's day-to-day operations is not mere fanciful idealism, but rather a new and necessary direction for future leaders and managers.

The future

One of the unique properties of Synovus is that it continuously updates and rethinks its programs on leadership and culture. Where warranted, Synovus collects data to determine if its practices are meeting its core values of putting people first. By all means Synovus is not a company that rests on its past achievements. It recognizes that environment and strategies are constantly changing and seeks to change itself to keep up with new challenges.

The Jordan, Bradley, and Turner family values have been perpetuated and passed on through the Blanchard family to create a Synovus values-based culture made up of thousands of employees who have had the opportunity to contribute and participate in the business, their community, all the while being able to take care of their nuclear families and find meaning in life. Synovus is an example of a Company that believes that fundamental values of human decency can go hand-in hand with making profits. To Synovus, values-based leadership and cultures are employee- and customer-centric. And as Jimmy Blanchard says: "It is pretty simple: Just take care of your folks."

References

Bills, S. 2002. Synovus on Consolidation Units' CRM Was Suffering. *American Banker*, 167 (119), 20.

Boraks, D. 2004. Hybrid Synovus' Plan: Evolve but Don't Budge, *American Banker*, 69 (61), 1–2.

Brannigan, M. 1995. Synovus Goes Courting – Very Quietly – US Firm Prospers by Buying Small Banks and Leaving Them Alone. *Asian Wall Street Journal.*

Chambers, R. 1997. The Georgia 100 – The Best of Business, *Atlanta Journal Constitution*, retrieved online.

Christie, R. 1990. Have the Klingons Taken Over Banks? It Sounds Like It – Some People Look Askance at Names Like 'Imtrex,' 'Avantor' and 'Synovus, *Wall Street Journal*, A1.

Connections Magazine (published for Synovus family team members), Spring 2002, Fall 2002, Spring 2003, Winter 2004.

Crockett, B. 1993. The Back Office: Systems (Synovus at Crossroads After Decade of Growth), *American Banker*, 158 (30), 1A.

Engen, John. 2003. Sizing up Synovus' Cult of Personality, *US Banker*, 113 (7), retrieved online.

Frick, D. M. and Larry, C. S. (eds.) 1996. *On Becoming a Servant-leader: the Private Writings of Robert K. Greenleaf*, San Francisco, CA: Jossey-Bass.

George, D. A. and Jaycee, D. G. 2004. Synovus Financial Corporation, A. G. Edwards Analyst Report, retrieved online.

Greenleaf, R. K. 1977. *Servant Leadership: A Journey Into the Nature of Legitimate Power and Greatness*, Mahwah, NJ: Paulist Press.

Greenleaf Center for Servant-Leadership, 2004. What is Servant-Leadership? taken from website www.greenleaf.org/leadership/servant-leadership/What-is-Servant-Leadership.html, June 23.

Greer, R. 1996. The Georgia 100 – Best of Business, *Atlanta Journal Constitution*, retrieved online.

Groeller, G. 1998. Synovus Financial Corp. CEO Mulls Firm's Community Role, Expansion Plans, *Knight-Ridder Tribune Business News*, retrieved online.

"Keeping it in the Family," 2000. *Private Banker International*, March 10, retrieved online.

Kitchel, R. 1999 Forbes Names Columbus, GA-based Synovus Best Place to Work, *Knight-Ridder Tribune Business News*, retrieved online.

"Lots of Banks, No Slip in Service," 2002. *Bank Technology News*, 15 (10), October 4, retrieved online.

Personal interviews at Synovus with James D. Yancey, Chairman of the Board, Walter M. Deriso, Vice Chairman, Frederick L. Green, III, Vice Chairman, Elizabeth R. James, Vice Chairman and Chief Information Officer, and Margaret Amos, Director of Talent Management, June 15, 2004. Richard E. Anthony, President and COO, James H. Blanchard, CEO, Margaret Amos, Director of Talent Management, and various

mid-level managers (J Grantham, SVP, Customer Support Senior
Manager, CB&T; Alison Dowe, VP, Director Corporate Communica-
tions, Synovus; Lee Sessions, VP, Financial Planning Manager, CB&T;
Jon Long, AVP, Director of Organizational Effectiveness, Synovus; and
Robin Grier, SVP, Director of E-Business, Synovus) and various other
employees new to the company, July 6, 2004.

Servant Leadership: Expand Your Circle Of Influence by Living Authen-
tically, 2004. taken from website www.teamchrysalis.com/AC/V2/
AC24_Servant_Leaders.htm, June 23.

Sisk, Michael. 2002. Power to its People, *US Banker*, 112 (9), retrieved
online.

Smyre Appointed Chairman, CEO of Synovus Foundation; Succeeds
Wellborn in Directing Synovus' Corporate Giving, *PR Newswire*,
April 11, 2001, retrieved online.

Spears, L. C. 2004. On Character and Servant-Leadership: Ten Characteristics of Effective, Caring Leaders, Greenleaf Center for Servant-
Leadership, taken from website www.greenleaf.org/leadership/read-
about-it/articles/On-Character-and-Servant-Leadership.html,

Synovus CEO: Focus on Community Banking Gives Co. Edge, *Dow Jones
News Service*, December 22, 1998, retrieved online.

Synovus Financial Corp., 2002. Canadian Shareowner, 15 (6), 34–37.

2004. Hoover's Company Profiles, April 21, retrieved online.

2004. History, Datamonitor Company Profiles, April 14, retrieved online.

2004. Major Products and Services, Datamonitor Company Profiles,
April 14, retrieved online.

Synovus Financial Corporation, *Annual Reports*, 1998, 1999, 2000,
2001, 2002 and 2003.

*A Trust to Keep: The One Hundred Year History of Columbus Bank
and Trust Company, 1888–1988*, Columbus, GA: Synovus Financial
Corporations.

Various company materials, including videos entitled "Culture of the
Heart," "Our Customer Covenant: Words to Lead By (Day 4)," and
transcript of Bill Turner's speech at the Leadership Institute, September
28, 1998. Also various compact disc transcripts of "Tuesday Morning
Meetings."

Synovus Goes the Extra Mile, 1999. *Financial Modernization Report*, 1
(11), April 12, retrieved online.

Synovus Named to Working Mother Magazine's List of "100 Best Companies for Working Mothers," 2001. *PR Newswire*, October 9, retrieved
online.

Total System Services Inc. 2004. History, Datamonitor Company Profiles,
January 26, retrieved online.

Turner, W. B. 2000. *The Learning of Love: A Journey Toward Servant Leadership*, Macon, GA: Smyth & Helwys Publishing, Inc.

Van Dusen, C. 2001. "No. 1: Synovus, 8: TSYS Growth of Payments Processor Like Money in the Bank for its Financial Services Parent," *Atlanta Journal Constitution*, May 20, retrieved online.

2 | *FedEx Freight – Putting people first*

GARY W. BOUCH

As the Senior Vice President of Operations and Transportation for FedEx Freight, Gary W. Bouch faced a life changing vision of leadership, and unlike many executives, did something. The result would be a leadership environment called "People First," the design of an experiential learning model that can be measured, engaged the workforce, and did prove positive results. The FedEx Freight story is a good example of how even a very successful company has the potential to lose their values because of success, and a merger, unless a senior leader takes ownership of consistently and repetitively championing the values. It is a story of personal courage, meaning, corporate political risk, how values are operationalized and measured, and a story of how powerful values can be resonating deeply inside of people. It is also a reminder that leadership is hard work, that leadership and putting people first is an everyday job, and that success can bring complacency unless it is countered by leadership.

History

October 25, 1982, was the birth of what would become the nation's leader in less-than-truckload (LTL) transportation. Sheridan Garrison started the operations of Arkansas Freightways by opening twenty centers with next-day transit times in mind. The industry laughed at Sheridan (he preferred first names), saying, "He must be crazy." After a very short time of operations, the competition's tone changed from laughter to pensive concern. "How is he doing this?" At the time, Sheridan would answer that in some very concise statements: *"If you are going to be successful in this business, it is all about people. People with principles to live by and a common goal of working together to satisfy customers each and every day. People are the tiebreaker. You don't hire people for their backs; you hire them for their minds and their winning spirit."*

29

Arkansas Freightways grew quickly, spreading its aggressive transit time system throughout the Southeast and Midwest. Sheridan Garrison knew that he must be the change leader in the industry, employing the best people, running the best equipment, and embracing leading-edge technology. After over ten years as Arkansas Freightways, in 1993 Sheridan and his team took a bold step and re-branded his company for a more national appeal as American Freightways, with his people and six business principles:

- Take care of our customers.
- Take care of our people.
- Honor our commitments.
- Work hard, smart and safely, and work together.
- Make the most of resources.
- Have fun!

It was upon review of these principles that all business decisions should be made. While simply stated, each principle has a more detailed statement behind it to explain its meaning.

Sheridan set out to revolutionize the LTL industry. He embraced his people, had a great long-range vision and loved change, not for change's sake, but in order to keep the competition off balance and the customer always on the radar screen. Change was a requirement to create differentiation and give the customer a reason to use our company.

In early 1996 I was hired, along with a team of five others, to help Sheridan not only maintain growth, but ensure the company's infra-structure was rock solid, and that we had not lost sight of his single most important asset – his "People."

It's important for readers to know that Sheridan constantly traveled throughout our network of centers to visit with our employees infor-mally – in break rooms, on docks, or wherever people were and wanted to talk. I spent many weekends during my first three years traveling to off-site employee breakfast meetings followed by a lunch meeting in another city that same Saturday afternoon. Sheridan loved his people, and he thanked them regularly and told them how proud they made him. His "passion" for the business and his people was truly an inspi-ration for me and others.

Success is hard to ignore, and many companies began to notice us. As Sheridan would often point out, *"When you are on the top of the hill, there is always someone wanting to knock you off!"* And somebody wanting to knock you off can happen a couple of different ways. Competition is always after your position and your people, but sometimes great companies become attractive to greater companies for acquisition targets. This is where FedEx comes in, or at least in my version. While we were busy planning our final Western expansion at American Freightways, we had also been talking with FedEx about offering them some premium freight services, moving some of their shorter length of haul freight over the road. As discussions continued, our Western expansion projection costs seemed to be higher than desired and, for the first time in my knowledge, Sheridan started to think about acquiring a carrier rather than expand internally. This was a huge decision for him to even consider because acquisition was never an option for discussions, and I have a vivid recollection of being scolded for suggesting it at one point. He strongly believed in maintaining the culture he had established and protecting his people and that would be very difficult through acquisition. Anyway, FedEx owned a well-established Western less-than-truckload (LTL) carrier named Viking Freight Systems that would match our expansion plans very well. To make the longer story short, instead of American Freightways acquiring Viking Freight from FedEx, the acquisition turned around, and in 2001, FedEx Corporation purchased American Freightways, aligning us with Viking Freight. FedEx Freight became our combined new name, servicing the entire United States. It was a perfect fit for us freight guys, and even a better strategic fit for FedEx Corporation.

Do I have a problem?

October 2003 I was now Vice President of Operations and Transportation, recently promoted from Vice President of Transportation, where I spent the previous seven years. The change in responsibilities meant that, in addition to leading our over-the-road linehaul systems and expedited products, which encompassed about 4,800 people, I now had responsibility for all our field operations (256 service centers), Fleet Maintenance, Claims Prevention, Weight and Research, Operations Support, Operations Planning, etc., meaning another 12,000-plus people. We were operating very strong, beating all our revenue, profitability and efficiency goals. I was adapting well to my new responsibilities, learning about my new team, giving them lots of room and empowerment as we learned together and worked through challenges, and I was thinking about what we could do to make further improve-ments on great results. After all, our belief was always to seek contin-uous improvements. In other words, things were going GREAT, and that's the best time to facilitate change, so what next? Well, all was great except these occasional e-mail notices I would receive, called *InTouch*®.

In order to keep our finger on the pulse of our people, we have an 800 number that our people can call to give us suggestions, comments, and complaints or really just say anything they want to say. They can leave their name, or they can give us an anonymous message. The "InTouch Voice of Americans" system, as it was originally named, was and is extremely effective. While compliments sometimes come through on calls, the more typical comments tell us where people see "smoke" allowing us to address issues before they become fires.

During a two-week period, I received at least four or five of these messages, which are summarized by category monthly, and it just hap-pened to be that time. So there I was in my office reading the most recent summary of *InTouch*® communications from our people when I became very emotionally disturbed. I saw what I viewed as a new trend as I read claims from around our company of employee favoritism, poor leadership and lack of communication, resulting in employee dis-satisfaction. I couldn't believe stories that supervisors were ignoring seniority to work a favored less senior employee, or that a favored city driver was getting their choice of city routes over a less favored driver. Another *InTouch*® was saying that their manager never communicated with them; they never had pre-shift meetings, which are supposed to be daily, and, as a result, he didn't know the deadline had passed for submitting his daughter's information for a Sheridan Garrison Scholarship.

Yet another message stated that the employees at a certain center never saw their manager and those drivers were locked out of and forbidden to enter the office area without an appointment. But the one that finally set me off was an *InTouch*® alleging that a supervisor asked a driver to drive another driver's tractor and trailers outside the property gate so that a late driver dispatch would not be recorded against that center's dispatch performance goals. If true, this was a pure integrity breach to falsify production numbers where a leadership person was essentially telling an hourly employee that it was okay to be dishonest to achieve efficiency targets. This one really angered me because if there was any point I had ever repeatedly made clear to all leadership, it was that we cannot tolerate dishonesty or theft in our operations, and that no one should ever play with the numbers to produce false results.

Pondering my internal conflict, I asked myself, "How could we be having these problems? Are they real, and, if so, why are we having these problems? Have I been misunderstood? And why would we not communicate with our people; why would we play favorites?" Our Business Principle #2 says Take Care of Our People, and we stress that we must openly and regularly communicate with our people, so why this new trend?

After contemplating where we might be failing in our communications and/or expectations, I worked myself through the analysis. It could not be my Division Vice President level because they clearly knew what I expected, so my Division Vice Presidents must be failing with their Managing Director Operations. Then I found myself in a little bit of a circular argument, thinking to myself that if my Division Vice Presidents mirror my leadership style, then the Managing Director Operations should mirror the Division Vice Presidents, so the problem must be the Division Vice Presidents... which meant it had to be ME! I wanted to find what level of my leadership team I could blame, and suddenly the answer smacked me right in the face... It was my fault! It was my reflection in the mirror...

Could it possibly be true that I was not demonstrating what I expected from my leadership team, and I was accepting the status quo because I thought things were going well? Certainly not me! After some further reflection I realized the fact was that our leadership styles were not consistent because we had never agreed upon what expectations we were going to lead by. Their styles, based on personal experiences, were producing good results, so I never truly defined leadership expectations. Sure, we had our Six Business Principles as defined by our founder of American Freightways, Sheridan Garrison, but now we were FedEx Freight, and there was some uncertainty about those Business Principles. So maybe it was time to develop some clarity.

Ok, now what do we do?

It was clear to me that my leadership beliefs were not as clear to my leadership team as I had thought. It was my responsibility to the

Company, and ultimately to myself, to make sure we had clear expectations to lead by, right? But, I wondered, does anybody else really see
this? I mean we're producing good results and nobody has asked me
about these *InTouch*® messages, so . . . do I need to act? Why rock the
boat if it's not really an issue to anyone but me? Suddenly, it dawned
on me. "Gary, what are you thinking here? If you consider yourself a
good leader, then isn't it your obligation to proactively take action, to
do something, to lead yourself rather than be told by somebody else to
take action? If you were a true leader, you would recognize that you
have but one choice – to act. But at that same time, you also recognize
that you have an opportunity to change our leadership expectations."
So, I challenged myself to step out to make a difference, try to effect a
change of beliefs to create more consistency in our leadership approach.
In hindsight, is this not the goal of many, to simply want to make a
difference in life? Well, at least for me it has been and will continue to
be, as that is my value to the Company – to help differentiate us from
all others.

Perhaps another less philosophical reason was my simple belief that
leadership all boils down to having the right attitude and building
relationships with your people. Sometimes we just lose sight of those
facts and think we have to be some "super-person" who must know
all; that must control everything. We forget it's the people who got us
where we are, that it was their belief in us at one time which made
them want to produce for us and made us successful. I just honestly
wanted to believe that it could be that simple, that basic. It had worked
for me in my past experiences with much smaller groups. Couldn't it
work here?

Initially, I took a cautious approach, unsure how it would be
received. I thought it best to ease into the idea of a leadership style
change and set forth some of my beliefs so people could get a better
sense of where I was coming from. I started with a series of messages
about trust and integrity and talked about communication and empowerment, not totally sure where I was headed and unsure of how much
acceptance I would have. I knew to foster change that I could attempt
to impose it upon my team as their superior, or I could seek a desire for
change from them by building belief in needed change. For long-term
success, I knew that if I were them, I would only change if I "wanted
to," so that became my challenge – how to move my leadership team

from a "have to" attitude to a "WANT to" change attitude. Only then could I succeed at moving their direct reports and so on.

First step

Each year, beginning about mid-January, we conduct a series of three divisional annual management meetings, which include all leadership from the service center level up, including our account managers and sales leadership. These meetings include about 1,200 people in total, so we reach a good sample of our company. I decided that I would use an hour of these meetings to take a more aggressive path and begin to speak out about my leadership beliefs in a town hall-type setting. I planned on stating my leadership expectations, seeking feedback, and hoping that we were more aligned than not. While it's hard to have an informal setting with 400 people, I sat on the edge of the stage with a microphone in my hand and just spoke about my leadership beliefs; how I learned and forged them over years of experience, sharing stories that impacted me – pretty much straight from the heart and unrehearsed. Several people asked questions, many offered supportive statements, but many others just sat and listened. I struggled with how my discussion was interpreted by the captive participants. Perhaps it did not apply to some of them because the Sales folks don't report to Operations, but I received good feedback from many, suggesting that we were more closely aligned than I had thought. I left them with the clear message that I would have more to share with them in the near future, and if anyone had thoughts they preferred to share one-on-one to reach out to me at their convenience.

Second step

From the confidence I gained from the three informal meetings and the message I left with them, I knew I needed some kind of vehicle or event to draw the senior leadership closer together to build trust, share thoughts and exchange some beliefs about control or micro-management. After some discussion with our Managing Director of People Development, John Sherman, the event suggested by his team was a ropes course. My initial reaction was "WOW!" My question was, "Are you sure that's the *'best'* vehicle? It seems a bit radical, doesn't it? The premise was to provide an atmosphere where we had to learn to trust and rely upon each other, and to challenge our beliefs (with the hope for change), so that we could build a cohesive team prepared to take us to the next level – in Jim Collins' term, move from *Good to Great*. John Sherman could read in my face that I was taking a leap of faith, and he sought to comfort me. He told me of a place his team had found called Victory Ranch in Bolivar, Tennessee, about two hours east of Memphis. After some discussion, and trusting in John's judgment, I agreed we should schedule this ropes course in the face of huge risk to pursue a change of beliefs with what I hoped had greater benefits.

To be frank about it, the challenge scared me to death. I felt I was really reaching, and it could destroy my credibility if we failed. So again, with the support and help of John Sherman, we recruited help from our sister company FedEx Express, because their leadership development folks were familiar with ropes courses and the ability of these courses to change beliefs.

Off to Memphis we went to meet with Ross McAllister of FedEx Express. Ross offered himself and two other members of his team (David Fitzgerald and Sam Haskins) as facilitators to support our needs. We further discussed some learning objectives, leadership text ideas, course recommendations, pre-evaluation tools, and Ross recommended a pre-visit to Victory Ranch so I could experience what I would be asking our people to experience, as well as get a layout of the area. It was also to help relieve some of my fears and apprehensions.

We scheduled our pre-planning visit, determined the list of potential attendees, the random team assignments, and all the other agenda ideas after walking through the site. Ross thought it might be a good idea for our small planning team to try several of the actual obstacles to get a real feel for the learning opportunities. I was certainly not ready for that. I didn't imagine that I would be challenged that day to climb rock towers, jump 60 feet above the ground on a wire cable and zip line, perform trust falls, walk through an actual high ropes course, and several other uncomfortable events. He put me way outside my comfort zone: Heck, I had no idea I could do the things I was asked, nor did I want to do them – but WAIT! Something happened to me. I did things I never believed I could do, and suddenly I realized that my beliefs had not only been challenged, but had been changed...I DID THINGS I NEVER WOULD HAVE TRIED IF NOT CHALLENGED! After one and a half days, I was totally convinced this was the right vehicle. It could change beliefs that we would relate to leadership challenges, and I immediately became super-charged to try and prepare our team for change.

Creation of a "people centric" culture

So what were we trying to do? It was simple, insuring we were focused on our people and understanding that our people operate all this equipment and perform all the duties that make us successful. Perhaps more than anything else, our people need validation that this type of leadership is okay; that it is the way to lead our people and we can achieve not only equal results, but more than likely superior results, if we will believe it possible. The trucking industry is not known for having engaged and empowered employees, but rather it is known for micromanagement and control-dominated leadership styles, so there is much of the old mindset to overcome. While our internal Company culture and beliefs may not have been as harsh as trucking management historically, we are still a relatively new Company at 23 years old, and our leadership pool is typically from the older established styles. It takes courage to change leadership styles when financial results are hanging in the balance and short-term (next quarter) thinking prevails. Not many are willing to take that risk.

The moment of truth

The first day of Victory Ranch was perhaps one of the most emotionally cold days of my life. Each person that arrived was very quiet and very skeptical. In retrospect, they probably each said, *"Why are we here? Why are you wasting my time? My people love me, and there is nothing you can teach me about leadership."* In addition, I'm sure they were thinking, *"You're forcing me to be away from my family, and you plan to strip me of my privacy by making me sleep in open quarters. How dare you!"*

I would sum up the prevailing attitude going into Victory Ranch as, *"Gary must not think we have a very good team, or else why did he think this week was necessary?"* While all were physically present because they had to be, mentally they wanted to tune out Victory

Ranch. In reality, my belief was that we had a good team, but that
we needed something to move us to want to become a great team.

Sunday night was really more of an introduction program that
started with some basic opening comments, which led into a video presentation from two critical people: the President and CEO of FedEx
Freight Corporation, Doug Duncan, and the President and CEO of
FedEx Freight East, Pat Reed. Both spoke from their heart about the
importance of engaging our workforce and the leadership styles necessary to take our Company forward. I felt these presentations would
answer the questions about how serious our support for our Leadership Summit was. The remainder of the evening was to just get briefed
about the rules and housekeeping type issues, let them all get settled
in, and a name game to break the ice, so everybody could put a face to
names. We handed out a checkbook-looking pad of something called
"Emotional Deposit Slips" and vaguely told people they could give
these to anybody they felt performed some task or feat that was worthy of recognition. On the Deposit Slip you would write the person's
name who performed the worthy act, describe the act and why it caught
your attention. Whether you signed your name as the author or not
was optional. When complete, the Deposit Slip was to be placed in
a mailbox in our meeting room. That's all that was said, and it was
purely optional. Then, we told everyone that they were expected to
participate fully, openly and give it their best efforts, not leaving anything on the playing field. Finally, we sent each of them off to bed with
the message that Monday would start early and be a long day, as would
every day that week.

Monday morning was welcomed with Reveille blasting from the
boom box at 5:30 a.m. While I thought this would add a little humor
to start the day, most didn't seem to appreciate it. Breakfast each day
was at 6:00 a.m. and calisthenics were scheduled for 7:00 a.m. Most
were quiet, but in wonderment of what was ahead, which was soon to
be FAILURE.

The first obstacle was a large platform on a fulcrum point, or what
I'd call a low impact balance platform. The task was simple – get
everybody on the platform, keeping it balanced without the platform
touching the ground. There was absolute chaos with 36 egos all trying
to talk and have control at once. After each failure, the temporary
speaker was tossed aside as the new voice was heard. Soon, several
small groups broke off and had their own ideas, planning and waiting

for the next failure. Some just totally disengaged and stood alone, just waiting for it to end. But as the exercise continued, there were some people who actually started planning and working together, adjusting their plans as they moved forward. As we (I was a participant) got closer to success, you could see others re-engage and pay attention or offer advice. Finally, time ran out, and we failed because we couldn't work together and function as a cohesive team. This was probably the bottoming out for the team, as they did not expect failure.

During the debriefing, some brutal honesty came forward as we acknowledged the fact that we didn't work together as well as we thought we would. We began talking about why we failed, what we could have done better, that we needed to have just one or two people in charge, create a plan and build a strategy on the next challenge. As we wrote our individual experiences in our journals, you could see most knew that we had to get committed to the future tasks if we were going to succeed. I wrote in my journal that I was fearful about whether we could set aside the egos and be successful.

The next challenge placed us into our six-person teams and separated us from the whole team. My team succeeded in the next challenge because we planned and worked together. Everybody was asked for input to develop the plan and we executed it, making a few adjustments along the way. I can tell you, we felt much better after tasting success and were committed to work together going forward. Other teams found mixed results, depending how well they released control and worked together, and the results presented great lunchtime discussion. Monday afternoon the teams had more successes than failures, and that felt good. But there were still some long faces in the crowd, and either titles or egos seemed to be a factor. Monday night this issue was addressed with a silly game called "Bunny-Bunny" that related to "commitment." Let me try to explain . . .

Sometimes as leaders, we are asked to do things we may not always agree with, and our lack of commitment usually shows through to our people. Because we are the mirror for our people, if we expect success with new ideas, projects, initiatives, policies, procedures, then our commitment behind the implementation is critical. Without commitment, we won't succeed. So, with this established as the premise, the objective of Bunny-Bunny is for three people working together to be the *best* bunny they can possibly be. Visualize three people standing together with the middle person hopping and wiggling their fingers under their nose as whiskers saying "bunny, bunny, bunny"; the person on the right uses their left arm in a raised "L" position to represent the bunny's right ear; and the person on the left uses their right arm in a raised "L" position to represent the bunny's left ear. The whole team is in a big circle, and once started, the middle bunny person randomly points to the next group of three people who must immediately jump into bunny mode, and so on at a very quick pace. Here's the catch: it's not easy to figure out who is being pointed to as the next middle person to be the bunny face, so you have to pay very close attention. If you don't focus, what occurs is bunny mutilation, meaning multiple left or right ears, multiple whiskers, etc., and if you are one of the extra parts, then you get eliminated. The game continues until only three people (one bunny team) remains, and they are crowned the best bunny and thanked for being the model of commitment.

As silly as it sounds, Bunny-Bunny was phenomenally successful. While the intent is "commitment," the benefit we found was that all egos and titles went out the door. I mean how can you perform in this game unless you have checked your ego? The game created a moment for fun and laughter, for bonding, and took all the tension away.

As Monday night came to an end, the facilitators distributed the small handful (maybe a dozen) of Deposit Slips written that day. The simple recognition provided by these few forms nearly brought tears to some, one of whom was me. With all the tension and stress that I had built up in anticipation of this event, I choked up when a teammate wrote a simple statement: *"Thanks for believing in me and giving us this opportunity."* It was from somebody who recognized the risk I was taking and offering encouragement. That's all I needed; my day just became wonderful. But more than that, it made me think of how receiving such simple words of encouragement could be so powerful and that I must remember that we all have the power to encourage others who just need a little help to make their day outstanding! I learned an important message, and so did the other few who received Deposit Slips that evening.

The first real life challenge

Without going into more detail, Victory Ranch did change our beliefs and has established a solid foundation of cohesiveness from which we have continued to build. It gave us common goals, which began with consistency in our leadership approach. Victory Ranch also gave us our first real challenge as a single-focused team, the disappearance of our founder, Sheridan Garrison. During our final days, we received an emergency message that Sheridan was missing, that it appeared he may have fallen from his boat while fishing, but it was not confirmed. This was very disturbing news, and it was unclear to me how our team would respond to this. I had two very different thoughts pop into my mind: (1) I expected that all would say that they must return to their domiciles to communicate with their people, and (2) is there some sick irony in Sheridan's disappearance as we are discussing how to differentiate ourselves in the industry by making "Take Care of Our People" our number one Business Principle, refocusing on something he held so near and dear to heart? Was this potentially a passing of the torch, if you will? While I quickly criticized myself for such a thought, I knew Sheridan would have been proud of the huge progress we had made as a leadership team that week.

As news spread among the facilitators and our Vice President of Human Resources, the initial direction sought was to pack up and go. Perhaps being a little pig-headed and insensitive, I questioned whether we could really make a unilateral decision to go when our discussions all week focused on working as a team, not making decisions without input. After some further discussion, it was decided to discuss the circumstances with the team and seek their input. Wow! What a surprise and revelation came forth from doing so. The team had several questions about how they could communicate with their folks back in their respective centers and develop a plan with the input of their subordinates. Having clarified this for them, one team member who knew Sheridan well voiced his opinion, stating that we should stay and complete our leadership summit. In his mind that is what Sheridan would want because Sheridan did not like people fussing over him. A few others voiced similar support when I stopped speaking. What I put in front of the team was that we had a serious issue that needed to be communicated very well and very carefully. Could they trust their people in the centers to convey the proper message of Sheridan's disappearance in their absence? Furthermore, before we debated that, I was going to ask for a show of hands on a three count to determine whether we should just go and not prolong debate. I said the vote would have to be unanimous, a single vote would send us home. So, if you think we should go home, then raise your hand. One, two, three, not a single hand went up. Thinking I confused them, I asked a second time. If you think we should STAY, then raise your hand. Immediately everybody, without hesitation, raised his or her hand high. It nearly brought tears to my eyes; we were unified, right or wrong.

The unanimous vote was that we could trust our subordinates to communicate with our people until we could join them upon return. This was from a team that only four days earlier hotly contested that we could place so much trust in our people and relinquish control. Again, wow! I was awestruck. We immediately began to brainstorm and discuss the basics we needed to accomplish during a brief conference call communication between the leaders at Victory Ranch and their leaders back in their centers so as to ensure a consistent message would be conveyed. This was a huge demonstration that we could trust our people if given a new opportunity to do so.

Top-level validation

When I returned from our Victory Ranch Leadership Summit, the buzz from the week had already been circulating throughout our Company. Our Executive Committee had been briefed prior on our plans, but was not fully informed, because, honestly, I wasn't confident how much we'd accomplish. I was taking some risks. Once fully updated on the events and on our team experiences, our Executive VP Operations and Chief Operating Officer, and President and CEO of FedEx Freight quickly expressed their desire to take proactive charge of what we were now calling our 'People First' strategy (since we were making Take Care of Our People Business Principle number 1). John Sherman spent some reflection and visionary time with our FedEx Freight President and CEO, Doug Duncan, and was given the privilege of designing a "FedEx Freight Commitment" model, of which People First would be the foundation (a pyramid model People First base, followed by Quality, then Certainty, and a pinnacle of World Class Customer Experience). I'll speak more about this later.

Declaration of leadership expectations

In our July 2004 Management Meetings, we scheduled time to follow up on the Declaration of Leadership Expectations assignment from Victory Ranch. During the month of June, we passed several drafts among the team members from their submitted ideas with the intent to finalize them at the July meeting. The name and format were no accident. The Declaration format carried a historical theme, which honors our founder, Sheridan Garrison, who had a talent for tying our products and marketing to American history and patriotic themes. As the process would unfold over time, I liked the idea of each service center as a local team "ratifying" or adopting the Declaration of Leadership Expectations, agreeing to be bound by the tenets on the original Declaration that was signed by senior leadership. These signatures would indicate 100% unanimous commitment to these tenets, which was the condition established for each of the tenets to appear on the Declaration.

Further, each senior leader agreed to be held accountable by any person in our Company to these tenets and specifically asked others to hold us accountable; that is our promise to our people, and they would honor us by holding us to our word, by making us walk the talk.

Having the local centers ratify the Declaration and then post both the original and their adopting versions side by side in the centers for all to see would make a powerful statement to our people. I didn't have a time-table for this to be completed; it's a personal local leadership choice; and the Managing Director of Operations for their particular region would be required to challenge and validate the ratification as genuine for this adoption process by speaking and seeking input from the local center people.

Why the process described above? I firmly believed the symbolic use of the Declaration imposed a slightly different commitment from the local centers and leaders because they did not participate in the process my team did, nor did they have a hand in drafting these tenets. My sincere request from the center was to commit with their leadership Team as soon as they would become comfortable to commit to these tenets. I believed this request was fair because I believe that as senior leaders we are their mirror for leadership, meaning that if we lead in a fair and just manner, then local leaders would, in turn, lead this way.

Their local team would also mirror their leadership so each individual leader clearly sets the tone at their location and is the example that their people will follow – a responsibility that requires courage.

Our commitment to local leadership is to provide educational and leadership support to make their thought process consistent with ours. When their people see consistency and are ready to voluntarily commit to the tenets that would be the right time to adopt the Declaration.

Our first outward support in the field operations began by holding individual operation regional meetings to introduce our People First learnings and to discuss the Declaration of Leadership Expectations. Each of the 17 regions held meetings across our Company between mid-July and October to spread our refocus. I personally attended many of these two or three day meetings to offer further clarity, some history or other support. The plan was to complete this series of meetings prior to our next Division Vice Presidents/Managing Directors joint meeting in mid-October to assess our next steps. At each meeting I attended, I would personally read the detail behind Business Principle "Take Care of Our People" so as to link our efforts to our past culture and more a refocusing effort than a new "flavor of the month" project. In other words, use our founder's own words for credibility. That Business Principle developed more than 20 years ago says it all:

Take care of our people.

When we started this company we said we wanted a living, breathing fire-belching company – but one that still had feelings. What we wanted was a company with a heart – and a soul. And that translated to people **with a pioneer spirit, people with open minds and "can-do" attitudes.** We did not have to look far. Good people heard what we were doing, and they came to us.

These people shared our belief that we could build a different kind of company, one not afraid to take risks or make mistakes. One that would embrace an operating environment which was non-political, or of making mortal enemies. **One, where people have the freedom to think and propose ideas without fear of ridicule.** One, where people would believe in the future of their company but also would understand and practice the principle that when it comes time to get things done, there is no tomorrow.

If you plan to build a business, you have to believe in people. You have to like people. People and principles are the proven building blocks of a successful business. At our Company we do not want our people to all come from the same mold. We do not want our people to become numbers. We want individuals. We recognize that all people have strengths. Our job is to identify and accentuate those strengths, combining them in pursuit of common goals.

We owe our people opportunity, trust and respect. They need to know what we expect of them and they need the tools, the education and the freedom to do their job. As they succeed, and they will succeed under these circumstances, we share that success with them in the form of better wages and benefits and opportunities for growth as individuals. The development of people through personal growth and betterment of their lot in life are primary aims of our Company.

It is routine and almost fashionable for a business organization to say it is "people oriented." But saying it and being it are two different matters. People relationships of any type are a very fragile thing. Treating people decently and fairly has to be a way of life. It has to start from the top down. As a leader, if you want your people to respect you, then you have to respect them first. What you say, how you say it, and what you do all count. The people of our Company are all leaders, respectful and helpful to each other and their customers. They are not whiners and groaners. They are unique in this business, and they get the job done.

People – Get the best, expect a lot, and take care of them.

The meetings went very well and were generally well accepted. Most service center managers wanted to carry back and deliver their own special messages to their centers. To support them we provided handouts, history, copies of the Declaration, reading materials/books we used, PowerPoint presentations, and essentially anything else they felt would help.

New people in our life and validation

It was also during this period that I met Ed Hess after reading and sharing some of his published articles. Don Hinkle (one of my key Victory Ranch initiators and supporters) reached out to Ed and Ed graciously offered us an opportunity to meet with him in Atlanta. During our

Figure 2.1 FedEx freight commitment

meeting, Ed offered some great advice to Don and me, as well as some additional books to consider which I did put to use later. I honestly credit Ed Hess for validating our ideas and direction, and he gave me courage to continue on what I felt a very worthwhile, but somewhat risky path.

At the same time, we had two other efforts going: (1) John Sherman and his small team continued work on the Freight Commitment model with particular attention to developing the full educational support behind that foundation... People First, and (2) detailed planning for our upcoming Division Annual Management Meetings (AMM) that were scheduled for January 2005 through early February 2005. Below are illustrations of the two models:

People First is a leadership methodology, and way of life.

- The model starts at its foundation, "Leader Awareness – Knowing You." The theory behind this beginning is that "you" as a leader must know and admit to who you really are based on what others perceive you to be. Also, the experiential learning exercises in our

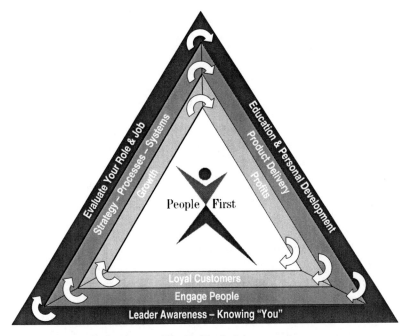

Figure 2.2 People first layer of the FedEx freight commitment

People First Leadership Experience will reveal many of our fears, and shortcomings. Only a leader who knows him/herself will gain the most success from their team.

- The next step going clockwise is "Evaluating Your Role & Job." Through various personality profiles and skills evaluations the course reveals if you are doing the job that makes you happy, or performing because you have to perform.
- Step three is "Education & Personal Development." Throughout the leadership course are education steps needed for development. Followed by assignments for further growth.

Based on the first three steps, the rest of the model becomes a result of People First behaviors:

- ➤ People First leaders produce "Engaged Employees"
- ➤ Engaged Employees produce the "Strategy– Processes – Systems" needed for a world class successful business
- ➤ These "Strategy– Processes – Systems" produce for FedEx Freight a world class service "Product Delivery"
- ➤ With world class service come "Loyal Customers"

➤ Loyal Customers produce "Growth"
➤ Growth along with all of the above produce "Profit"
➤ Tie it all together, and you have a "People First" culture…

People will be our competitive advantage

Another reason for People First is that I truly believe our service products will become commoditized as further consolidations occur within the transportation industry. Recent evidence demonstrates the trends such as Yellow-Roadway-USF and UPS-Overnite, following the footprints of FedEx-American-Viking. My personal opinion is that three or four global giants will prevail; hence, our products become commodities. At that point, differentiation becomes difficult but I believe that our people can be the differentiator, giving customers the reason to choose our services. I believe as Gallup reasons, that customer service and loyalty are all based on emotional bonds (relationships) with our customers and people. Therefore, if our people do not differentiate us in the eyes of customers, then customers will move their business to another carrier with whom they have better relationships. People do business with people they like. People are more productive when they are happy and that typically correlates to a good leader/employee relationship. I believe this because of what my lifetime experiences have taught me. I believed this *before* the Gallup research validated it for me, but I will use such data to help support my personal experiences.

Our pathway becomes solid

Thanks to the energy spreading throughout our leadership teams, and probably somewhat related to promoting our founder's legacy of Take Care of Our People, our Executive Committee decided that our Annual Management Meetings (AMM) theme would be "First Class to World Class." Now if you think about the elements of the Freight Commitment model mentioned earlier you would remember that to provide the World Class Customer Experience which builds customer loyalty that we must first establish the People First foundation, then Quality and Certainty. In other words, the primary focus of our Annual Management Meetings in early 2005 was People First.

Assignments, measurement and results

People First works... The results of the curriculum and follow-up assignments and measurements are life changing. The sections below are assignments given to each participant:

"People First" Assignments
Know Yourself
Know Your Role
Educate and Develop Yourself

1. **Mend relationships**
   a. Report via email any and all relationships you have mended or attempted to mend:
      i. No names, just situations
      ii. Done within the next two weeks
      iii. Permission to forward to either the facilitators or other members of the group
2. **Select accountability partners**
   a. Name them
   b. Let others that influence our life know who they are
   c. Continue to add Accountability Partners as you need them. You cannot have too many...
3. **Select/seek/mentor**
   a. Name them
   b. Let others that influence our life know who they are
   c. Continue to add Mentors as you need them based on your situations. You cannot have too many...
4. **Live and "walk the talk" people first tenets:**
   a. **communication** – Increase your communications at your center. Measurement for ROI:
      i. Improvement in the People/Gallup Survey
      ii. Improved productivity
   b. **expectations(s)** – Insure that each person in your center has reviewed their job expectations. Measurement for ROI as follows:
      i. Lower HR incidences
      ii. Lower OS&D
      iii. Improvement in the People/Gallup Survey
      iv. Fewer errors
   c. **education/development** – Measurements for ROI as follows:
      i. Fewer mistakes
         1. Lower OS&D incidences or claims

       2. Improved productivity resulting in:
         a. Improved transit time
         b. Fewer billing errors
       3. Fewer safety issues or incidences
     ii. Engaged and confident employees
   d. **encouragement & recognition** – Measurement of success:
     i. Improved People/Gallup Survey results
   e. **Right seat on the bus ...** Measurement of success:
     i. Lower HR incidences
       1. Measurable turnover
     ii. Improved People/Gallup Survey results

5. **100% full responsibility** – Recognizing that everything is a choice and you are responsible for the choices you make
6. **Servant leadership** – Recognize and "walk/do" the following:
   - Servants lead through relationships, not coercion
   - Servants lead by support, not control
   - Servants lead by developing others, not by doing all the work themselves
   - Servants guide people, they do not drive them
   - Servants lead from love and caring, not domination
   - Servants seek growth, not position
7. **"please" & "thank you" & "why"** – Make these kinds of verbal gestures a part of your vocabulary going forward. Measurements of success:
   a. Improved People/Gallup Survey results
8. **conflict = positive outcome**
      "Good for the Many ... Sometimes the Few ... Never the One ... "
   a. Do not walk past problems
   b. Approach all potentially negative situations with a positive outcome
   c. Use your "Emotional Braking System"
9. **emotional braking system** – Behavioral device for you to use during potentially negative situations. Measurement of success Improved People/Gallup Survey results:
   a. STOP – Do not blow up ...
   b. Think before you speak
   c. Do not take things personally
   d. Listen more than talk
   e. Try to empathize with the other's point of view
   f. Look between the lines to their personal "feelings"
   g. Do the right thing for the good of the many
10. **people first in everything you do; positive and compelling "attitude"; total employee "engagement"** – Measurements for ROI are extensive. Gallup Survey – HR – Operations – Systems – Processes etc.

a. If you are People First, your people will get the task completed . . .

b. Take Care of Your People, they will take care of the customer

The following are just a small selection of statements/testimonies from People First participants:

I just completed my 35th year in the industry, of which most were spent in leadership. In 35 years I have attended several management courses, but none that stressed leadership as much as this. Victory Ranch . . . I had my concerns about attending, but found by the second day I was really into this . . . I came back to the center and held meetings with confidence on "People First." I would like to thank all involved for the opportunity and the fact that this "old dog" can still learn new tricks. (*Steve Wood*)

When I came to Victory Ranch, I said that there was nothing you could teach me about leadership. I was wrong . . . I am going to take back to my people a new appreciation for listening to their ideas. I am going to let nothing frighten me in the future, let nothing stop me from being successful for my company, and always have respect and trust for my people. (*Bob Fennell*)

It really doesn't matter how strong you are personally, as long as your team is pulling together in the same direction, at the same time. (*Bill Cherry*)

This final excerpt is from a young leader as he followed up on his first assignment: Mending Relationships:

I gave this a lot of hard thought, and initially had a hard time with this. I kept telling myself that I really did not have any relationships to mend, but after I thought about it a while I really did have a lot of opportunity. I did not really have any relationships that were "bad," but had some gaps in some relationships that needed mending.

(1) In my opinion I have a great relationship with my family, and we have always been close even though we live many miles apart. I have never had a very emotional "touchy feely" type relationship with my parents just because this is the way it has always been. I realized mainly through our coat of arms exercise at Victory Ranch that I really needed to let them know how I really felt. At Victory Ranch when we were going over our coat of arms we had 3 out of the 7 presentations that were really touching and opened up my eyes. 3 people had lost a loved one and had really not closed the gap, and felt they had left something on the table that they wanted to share or experience with that person. I have started, and will continue to work on this "process" with my parents for the rest of my life. I want to be one of those people who, when I lose a loved one, can say I had the best relationship I could have had, and did not leave anything out there.

(2) My wife and I have been married for 9 years and as of a couple of months ago now have 3 children. We have a very good relationship, but have really started to let our relationship dwindle because of so much focus on our children. After Victory Ranch we had a long talk about our relationship and I feel really good in the direction we are going. It does not take a lot to sustain a loving relationship, but it is something that I have to remind myself of on a daily basis. The little things are what count and I have to realize that it takes these little things to make it work. Also a large part of what I thought I was doing to help out, and what I thought I was doing to show my love and commitment my wife did not perceive as the same. She realized that I was helping with the kids giving her some time to herself or cleaning the house to help her out, but she wanted family time or words of affection or a loving touch etc. I have learned a lot and will continue to as long as I continue to look out for her needs.

(3) I do a good job of communicating, but sometimes I do not communicate enough. I know we have the right people on the bus here in South Bend IN, but felt we did not have two supervisors on the right seat. About 5 months ago I realigned some duties within the center for 2 supervisors. For one of the supervisors it did not change much and only gave him more time to plan, but for the other it changed a lot of what he does. Both of them knew how to perform the job functions that they were going to be doing, but for one of them it was a big change. I set the minimal expectation and sat down with them and talked very briefly about the change. What I realized after VICTORY RANCH is that I did not really communicate the expectation and get the buy-in that I should have before making the change. I spoke to this supervisor for a couple of hours about this last week, and I feel like a weight has been lifted off of my shoulders. I also believe that he is more engaged now, and has a sense of ownership of his duties. Also because of this change I know our business in South Bend IN. has increased because people are in the right seats now. (*Aaron*)

Today

As you can see, I believe we're making progress and have a good top-down plan. I'm still concerned about the bottom-up plan and will continue to work on that. In the meantime, we have just finished the Gallup Q12 Survey company-wide, to establish a baseline for employee engagement so we now have a good idea of where we are...plenty of opportunity but not bad, with some truly bright spots to examine and perhaps model. I have certainly had my ups and downs and some passive top leadership challenges to meet. There are always the questions of when will the productivity improvements from this engaged style reflect in the financials, are we sure we can hold people accountable with this style to ensure desired results, etc., etc.... Again, most publicly held companies are focused on the next quarter's financial results, so long-term commitments are always a challenge to keep on track and transition is not a fast path. At the same time we just completed a record-breaking performance year in all areas. Morale is high, retention is great, best claims performance, best injury rates, best service performance... I would argue that we're already seeing the results but aren't quite ready to admit that our People First focus is the reason. To do so would challenge the beliefs of some that want to remain within their comfort zones and take credit for successes with little or no personal involvement. The heck with them, our people are performing because our leadership cares, and time will only further document that fact.

One final note... In November 2006 all the corporate and executive officers of FedEx Freight (East, West, Corp, Systems) will be attending a leadership challenge course at Team Trek in Heber Springs, AR. *All* means all officers. I believe this session will do more to unite and bond our leadership than any other event we could experience together. This is an absolutely huge step for our team. I just hope that I will survive to join them with the "contracts" I'm sure some have taken out on me... HA! HA!

Summary

In this chapter we have shared with you a little of our rich history; and the reasons why we needed to revisit our most important asset, our "people." For some this might be seen as a program that will wear out its welcome over the course of time. For us "People First" helped us realize a new beginning that must be maintained for a lifetime.

It is easy to direct and or command that change take place. The "thinning out" process is actually quicker, but more costly from a people point of view. With "People First" the job is harder; takes more courage; takes extraordinary leadership; stretches the leader beyond what they think is safe; but more importantly for most, the process sticks. The truth is simple, People First works.

We will maintain that our industry, (Less Than Truckload Trucking) will be come more competitive each moment we are in business. We will also maintain that we will be a world-class company with "people" being the only sustainable competitive advantage.

3 | The role of values in high-risk organizations

KARL E. WEICK

I want to approach the issue of values by focusing on a set of organizations that strive to be high reliability organizations (HRO). Organizations such as nuclear power-generation plants, naval aircraft carriers, wildland firefighting crews, and emergency departments in hospitals aspire to produce high reliability performance under trying conditions with fewer than their fair share of accidents. Usually their aspirations succeed; occasionally they fail. For our purpose what is important is that the fate of these organizations often can be traced to the strength of their attachment to values or general principles concerning patterns of behavior that they hold in high regard. But what is crucial to this strength of attachment is the way in which it was achieved. In organizing for high reliability, values are the last thing to be crystallized, not the first. And it is this departure from conventional treatments of value driven behavior that has the potential to help us understand the mechanisms by which values-based leadership gains its legitimacy and effectiveness.

The following discussion is grounded in several studies of HROs including the collision between two 747 aircraft on Tenerife island that killed 583 people (Weick, 1990); wildland fire tragedies at Mann Gulch (Weick, 1993), South Canyon (Weick, 1995), Dude Fire in Walkmore Canyon (Weick, 2002), and the Los Alamos/Cerro Grande fire (Keller et al., 2004); excess pediatric surgery deaths at the Bristol Royal Infirmary (Weick and Sutcliffe, 2003); the grounding of the carrier *Enterprise* on Bishop Rock (Roberts, in press); the chemical plant explosion at Bhopal (Weick, 1988); and successes of alertness associated with groups such as the Polish Solidarity movement (Weick, 1999), Paul Gleason's effective firefighting crew called the "Zig Zag hot shots," the carrier *Carl Vinson* (CVN 70) under the command of Tom Mercer; and the Diablo Canyon nuclear power-generation plant close to San Luis Obispo California. Events in all of these settings replay many of the same scenarios of alertness that you run into every day. Your own scenarios might not have the sweep or complexity of these larger dramas, but I will argue that your scenarios do have a similar form. And that similarity makes it possible for all of us to learn from the hard-won lessons embedded in these spectacular events.

The nature of high reliability organizations

To understand the role of values in HROs is to understand how such organizations work. Part of this understanding involves the adoption of three unconventional assumptions about organizations. The first assumption is that organizations are hubris-inducing places (the phrase is Paul Schulman's, the meaning is a place that induces excessive self-confidence and arrogance). Organizations are places that make it possible for surgeons to cut into people, air traffic controllers to make life or death decision for 250 people at a time, firefighters to face down a 30-foot wall of fire, and dispatchers to direct electricity toward or away from people hooked up to life-saving electrical medical devices. The trouble with hubris is that it is hard to contain and it is tough on alertness. When people experience a near miss, they can treat it either as safety in the guise of danger or danger in the guise of safety. Under the sway of hubris, people tend to treat a near miss as safety in the guise of danger (March, Sproull, and Tamuz, 1991). The blunt lesson of hubris, in Martin Landau's words, is that optimism is arrogant. To be alert is to take that message to heart.

The second assumption is that it is hard to make strong responses to weak signals. Machiavelli summarized this problem neatly: "As the doctors say of a wasting disease, to start with it is easy to cure but difficult to diagnose. After a time, unless it has been diagnosed and treated at the outset, it becomes easy to diagnose but difficult to cure" (Hock, 1999, p. 117).

And the third assumption is that core competence is not the advantage it used to be. Competitive advantage has all but disappeared because it is easier to copy core competence more quickly, which means that the advantage of knowing something, anything, declines faster than it used to. The advantage previously bestowed by knowledge has shifted to one that favors those who have a well-developed capability to detect and learn from and improvise on small changes.

I want to talk about organizations that have less than their fair share of accidents even though they operate under trying conditions. They put a premium on reliability as well as efficiency, but the way in which they do this carries important lessons for everyone interested in values.

A further part of understanding HROs is that they live in a context where they are thrown into the middle of unknowable, unpredictable events that don't play by the rules. Here's an example of that context. This is a comment by the naval commander of a nuclear aircraft carrier whose job is to make sense of 6,000 people who daily face a million accidents waiting to happen. Here's how he described life on a carrier:

Imagine that it's a busy day, and you shrink San Francisco airport to only one short runway and one ramp and one gate. Make planes take off and land at the same time, at half the present time interval, rock the runway from side to side, and require that everyone who leaves in the morning, return the same day. Make sure the equipment is so close to the envelope that it's fragile. Then turn off the radar to avoid detection, impose strict controls on the radios, fuel the aircraft in place with their engines running, put an enemy in the air, and scatter live bombs and rockets around. Now wet the whole thing down with seawater and oil, and man it with 20-year-olds, half of whom have never seen an airplane close-up. Oh, and by the way, try not to kill anyone. (Weick and Roberts, 1993, p. 357)

A carrier is a million accidents waiting to happen, yet almost none of them actually occur. What's interesting is that challenges on a carrier are not that different from the challenges you face when you are thrown into several overworked, multi-tasking teams that find themselves in the midst of situations not of their own making. What's the role of values under these demanding conditions?

The nature of high reliability values

Reliability, defined as "lack of unwanted, unanticipated, and unexplainable variance in performance" (Hollnagel, 1993, p. 51) is a central value. A good illustration of threats to this value was the persistent, puzzling variance associated both with the Challenger (Starbuck and Milliken, 1988) and Columbia (Weick, 2005) space shuttles. For example, the original design requirements for the Columbia precluded foam shedding by the external tank (CAIB, 2003, p. 122) and also stipulated that orbiter should not be subjected to any significant debris hits. Nevertheless, "Columbia sustained damage from debris strikes on its inaugural 1981 flight. More than 300 tiles had to be replaced"

(CAIB, 2003, p. 122). And it continued to shed foam on 65 out of 79 missions (CAIB, 2003, p. 122) with an average of 143 divots taken out of the shuttle's body on each mission (CAIB, 2003, p. 122). Foam shedding was an unwanted, unanticipated, unexplainable variance in performance, but over time, NASA got comfortable with foam coming off the tank. This history is troublesome because it means that foam shedding was no longer seen as a threat even though it remained unexplained. The trouble was that people started to anticipate it. And if the shedding becomes anticipated, then it is easy to mistake this anticipation for understanding and to wind up forgetting that foam shedding was something fundamentally unwanted right from the beginning. This gradual acceptance of the unreliable is hastened or stopped by the values a firm has.

The values of HROs have some interesting properties. Recall that part of their world keeps changing. Since impermanence is a constant for them, their relationships, understandings, and structures need to be reaccomplished over and over. Since their previous successes are not bankable, they have to keep re-doing their practices and outcomes to keep them from unraveling. A history of failure-free performances does not insure against the next error. And the organization is only as reliable as its next error. This means that "Unless continual reinvestments are made in improving technical systems, procedures, reporting processes, and employee attentiveness, those performance standards that have already been attained are likely to degrade" (Schulman, 1993a, p. 35). This is where values come in. They either animate continuous learning and attentiveness or they allow complacency to prevail.

The value placed on sensemaking

HRO values focus on quick size-ups, frequent updating, and candor regarding their doubts and mistakes. The important values in HROs center around sensemaking, not decision making. The reason for this is that decisions often make it hard for people to learn and think on their feet. This subtle point was made clearly by Paul Gleason who is one of the world's foremost wildland fire supervisors. Much of Gleason's fame comes from his work in over 500 serious fires, as Crew Chief leading a 19 person Interagency Hotshot Crew (the Zig Zag crew). Gleason said that when fighting fires, he prefers to view his leadership efforts as sensemaking rather than decision making. In his words, "If I make a decision it is a possession, I take pride in it, I tend to defend it and not listen to those who question it. If I make sense, then this is more dynamic and I listen and I can change it. A decision is something you polish. Sensemaking is a direction for the next period."

When Gleason perceives his work as decision-making, he feels that he postpones action so he can get the decision "right" and that after he makes the decision, he finds himself defending it rather than revising it to suit changing circumstances. Polishing and defending eat up valuable time and encourage blind spots. Gleason is on solid ground here. There is good evidence that when people choose to do something and that choice is public and irrevocable, they feel strong pressure to justify it. Because the decision is public and irrevocable, it's hard to argue that it never occurred. And because you chose to make the decision, it's also hard to argue that it is not your responsibility. Since you did it and since it's your responsibility, then presumably you must have acted that way for good reasons. As you justify the decision to yourself and others you make it that much harder to change it, see its flaws, or consider a better line of attack. This is precisely what Gleason is sensitive to when he worries about polishing a decision, defending a decision, taking pride in a decision, and ignoring those who question it. If, instead, Gleason treats an unfolding fire as a problem in sensemaking, then he gives his crew a direction for some indefinite period, a direction which by definition is dynamic, open to revision at any time, self-correcting, responsive, and with more of its rationale being transparent.

Gleason's commitment to sensemaking is striking. When crews fight fires, they post a lookout whose job is to monitor the relationship between the oncoming fire and the crew and to warn if the distance between the two gets too small. On some of Gleason's especially hazardous fires, where there is danger of rolling rocks or windblown spot fires, he has assigned as many as sixteen people to be lookouts, leaving only four people to actually fight the fire. In the Dude fire near Payson, Arizona, which was an active, dangerous fire, Gleason worked part of the time without gloves so he could get a fuller sense of the weather conditions. He clothed himself as if he didn't know for sure what his surroundings were. It paid off. The first day of fighting this fire, around 1:45 in the afternoon, he felt a few drops of rain on the back of his hands. He knew there were no thunderstorms in the area, inferred that he must be feeling "virga" from a huge column of smoke that had iced over on top and was about to collapse, and he now knew that it was time to act. He moved firefighters into a safety zone just before the column collapsed. When it collapsed, it pushed fire in all directions and six people who were located some distance from his safety zone were killed.

The value placed on mistake avoidance

Values affect how people arrive at what Gleason calls, "a direction for the next period." In the case of wildland firefighters, that direction for the next period tends to be framed in terms of mistakes they *don't* want to make. Three mistakes are uppermost. First, they don't want to entrap their crews when a fire suddenly explodes or changes direction. Second, they don't want to confuse their crew by keeping them in the dark about the intent behind their attack on the fire. Third, they don't want to misjudge a dynamic, complex situation. There are specific ways that they reduce the likelihood that these mistakes will occur. They *avoid entrapment* by insuring that, before they engage a fire, they have in place four things: lookouts, communication, escape routes, and safety zones, a structure that is preserved by the acronym LCES. They *avoid confusion* by doing their sensemaking in public. They give their people a clear idea of what is happening by covering five key issues: the situation, here's what I think we face; the task, here's what I think we ought to do; the intent, here's why we ought to do that; concerns, here's what we should keep our eyes on because if that changes we're in a whole new situation; and calibration, now talk to me, what can't you do, what don't you understand, what do you see that I've missed? This protocol is preserved with the acronym STICC, which stands for situation, task, intent, concern, calibrate.

And underlying all of this concern with entrapment and confusion are efforts to *avoid misjudgment*. Here's where we reach what is probably the most central value in any effective HRO, the value of mindfulness. The value of mindfulness is best put in a sign I have above my desk. The sign is yellow, with greasy fingerprints on it, and it was taken from the wall of a machine shop of the old New York Central Railroad. The sign says, "Be where you are with all your mind."

To value mindfulness is to be alert to mechanisms that create blind spots and then to undo them. Here's the key point. People often fail to see developing problems when they pay too much attention to their successes, require people to keep it simple, focus on the big picture, spend time trying to anticipate consequences, and equate expertise with a person's position in a hierarchy. What is striking to me is that those five hallmarks of efficiency are the very things that HROs treat as *mistakes they don't want to make.* When HROs put mindfulness into practice they scrutinize small failures, refine and complicate the categories they use to understand events, concentrate on operations and their current situation, strengthen their capability to bounce back when things invariably go in unintended directions (resilience), and search out sources of expertise independent of hierarchical position (Weick, Sutcliffe, and Obstfeld, 1999; Weick and Sutcliffe, 2001). The ways people handle failure, simplification, operations, resilience, and expertise are the ways in which they take the value of mindfulness seriously and put it into action.

The value placed on wisdom

Here's an example of a mindless moment that was later transformed into a mindful guideline that placed a high value on wisdom. Six firefighters burned to death at the Dude fire in Payson, Arizona (e.g., Johns, 1996) when a change of command was botched at 1:00 p.m. on a hot, windy day with temperatures in the high nineties while the fire was making spectacular runs. When this flawed change of command was investigated, it resulted in a mindful maxim we'd all do well to practice: "Never hand over a fire in the heat of the day." What this maxim means is that when a departing crew hands over a fire to an incoming crew, they should do so when it is easiest for the incoming crew to understand what is happening and to step in and continue the strategy used by the departing crew. The easiest transitions in firefighting normally take place at night when the combination of low winds, high humidity, and cool temperature makes fire behavior more predictable. In the heat of the day, by contrast, the fire is at its most dynamic and most volatile, which makes it harder for the incoming crew to catch up with its rapidly changing character. When there is an attempted hand-off in the heat of the day, the incoming crew is always behind, its grasp of what is happening lags behind what is actually happening, and when the incoming crew fails to synchronize their actions with a rapidly developing situation, the level of danger increases dramatically.

Failure to synchronize actions during handoffs is also visible in medical settings. Carthey et al. (2000, pp. 117–138), for example, describe adverse medical events that occur in conjunction with neonatal cardiac surgery as the patient is handed over from pre-operative to intra-operative teams, and from intra-operative teams to post-operative care. When the operating team hands the patient over to people in ICU, incorrect information may be communicated (e.g. team says blood loss during the operation was insignificant when it was actually massive, and ICU team is not prepared for related problems); or, no information may be communicated at all (e.g. surgeon starts next case immediately which leaves ICU staff in the position where they have to take people away from patient care at a key moment in order to get the information they need); or, the surgical team may communicate information too early while the ICU team is trying to set the patient up, and the ICU people fail to hear most of the key information. Recipients never learn what they need to know, and problems compound. The same thing happens in wildland firefighting.

The advice to avoid hand-offs in the heat of the day reflects a shrewd awareness that a relatively small moment in an otherwise complex event has an important bearing on the success or failure of the mission. It is *not* at all obvious that when a tired crew leaves a fire and is replaced by a fresh crew, things will get worse. The addition of fresh resources normally would mean redoubled effort and faster suppression. The maxim alerts people that precisely the opposite could occur. That is an example of the wisdom that can flow from mindful action.

But, the maxim also reminds us that wisdom works a little differently than most people assume. "The essence of wisdom...lies not in what is known but rather in the manner in which that knowledge is held and in how that knowledge is put to use. To be wise is not to know particular facts but to know without excessive confidence or excessive cautiousness...[T]o both accumulate knowledge while remaining suspicious of it, and recognizing that much remains unknown, is to be wise" (Meacham, 1990, pp. 185, 187). Thus, "the essence of wisdom is in knowing that one does not know, in the appreciation that knowledge is fallible, in the balance between knowing and doubting" (Meacham, 1990, p. 210). The more one knows, the more one realizes the extent of what one does not know.

Think back about the advice "never hand over a fire in the heat of the day." That advice reminds firefighters that fires in the heat of the day are the hardest to understand, which means that this is the period when the firefighters' knowledge of the fire will be most fallible. The maxim reminds people that they don't know and can't know midday fires as well as they can know midnight fires, even though they are perfectly free to ignore that fact. And firefighters may ignore that fact if they have to accept the midday fire anyway and continue the efforts to suppress it. What remains true is that the fire can still be fought more or less mindfully.

Remember the LCES acronym mentioned earlier: lookouts, communication, escape routes, safety zones. What's interesting about a LCES design is that it is a blend of knowledge and doubt. The lookouts and communication capabilities imply that one knows what is going on and how the local conditions are related to the big picture. The attention to escape routes and safety zones, however, implies that what one knows may be incomplete and that this potential ignorance needs to be recognized and hedged. The crew is simultaneously confident and cautious.

Here's what a wise organization looks like. No routine in an HRO is beyond the reach of re-evaluation and critical reassessment. HROs have a "consistent, preventative preoccupation with failure" (Schulman, 1993a, p. 36) and the people within them are said to act with "prideful wariness" (LaPorte, 1996, p. 65). The reason for the preoccupation and wariness is the "widespread recognition that all of the potential failure modes into which the highly complex technical systems could resolve themselves have yet to be experienced. Nor have they been exhaustively deduced. In this respect the technology is still capable of surprises. In the face of this potential for surprise, there is a fundamental reluctance among higher management to put decision or action frameworks in place that are not sensitive to the possibilities of analytic error" (Schulman, 1993b, p. 364). Awareness of the possibility that analytic error is embedded in ongoing activities and that unexpected failure modes and limitations of foresight may amplify those analytic errors, dominates attention and learning in HROs.

The value placed on disvaluing

The final and most crucial way to describe valuing in HROs is to observe how much effort people put into preventing misspecification, misestimation, misunderstanding. The relevant background for this assertion is Paul Schulman's (personal communication, June 25, 1997) research on reliable performance at the Diablo Canyon nuclear power generation plant. His two most important findings about how this plant

attained nearly error free performance were, *first*, that the major deter-
minant of reliability in an organization is not how greatly it values
reliability or safety per se over other organizational values, but rather
how greatly it *disvalues* the misspecification, misestimation, and misunderstanding of things. And his *second* important finding was that,
all else being equal, the more things that more members of an organization care about misspecifying, misestimating and misunderstanding, the higher the level of reliability that organization can hope to
attain. Notice how all of this ties back to the value of mindfulness. If
you mindfully examine simplifications, operations, and the locations
of experts, then you effectively disparage misspecification. If you mindfully focus on small failures, operations, and strengthen the capability
to be resilient, then you reduce the likelihood of misestimation. And
if you engage in all five of these activities of mindfulness, you readily
disvalue misunderstanding.

Much of the discussion about values up to this point has focused on
their opposites. The important lesson that can be learned from HROs
is that they focus on "disvaluing." To disvalue means to disparage or
to regard something as being of little or no value and typically harmful. We often talk about what we value, but remain silent about what
we disvalue. That's one reason why statements of values often sound
hollow and have little effect. They are silent about what we want to
avoid. That is what we can learn from HROs. In essence their search
for values starts with "mistakes I don't want to make." As Roberts
and Creed (1993, p. 254) put it, "reliability-enhancing organizations
identify sets of outcomes they continually work never to experience."
Once HROs identify crucial outcomes that they fear, they then ask
"what values would prevent those mistakes?"

When it comes to values, *HROs work backward*. First, they identify
mistakes they don't want to make. Then they identify practices that
prevent those mistakes, then principles that generate those practices,
and finally values that generate those principles. For example, a mistake that fire supervisors don't want to make is to entrap their crews.
One practice that helps prevent this mistake is for firefighters to wear
thin clothing. This practice is found much more often among Aus-
tralian firefighters than US firefighters. The reasoning is that, if you are
wearing thin clothing, you'll feel the heat of an active fire sooner and
will keep a safe distance from it. With thicker protective clothing people take more chances and move deeper into active fires, which leaves

them no escape route if the fire blows up. The more abstract principles that support safer practices are assertions such as "small discrepancies conceal larger problems" and "reliability necessitates making strong responses to weak signals." These principles, finally, are generated and supported by at least two values that are held in high regard: resilience and mindfulness. Resilience is the capacity for *recovery* or continued adaptive behavior following an initial retreat or setback (Sutcliffe and Vogus, 2003, p. 10). Mindfulness is a rich awareness of discriminatory detail.

Conclusion

To summarize, the "role of values in high risk organizations" is to provide a direction for people who are thrown into the middle of unknowable, unpredictable events that don't play by the rules. The direction is supplied by the value of mindfulness and by the imperative "be where you are with all your mind." What is noteworthy about HROs is that their values focus both on things that are disvalued and things that are valued. HROs disvalue misspecification, misestimation, and misunderstanding. In addition, HROs are wary of people who pay too much attention to success, simplicity, strategy, anticipation, and hierarchy. All of this disvaluing is achieved when people live the value of mindfulness. They live mindfulness on a daily basis every time they scrutinize small failures, refine the categories they use to understand events, concentrate on operations, strengthen resilience, and search out sources of expertise independent of hierarchical position. The Mission Management Team at NASA did not live mindfulness when they had oversight for the Columbia shuttle that disintegrated over Texas on February 1, 2003. As the Columbia accident investigation board noted, "Shuttle managers did not embrace safety-conscious attitudes. Instead their attitudes were shaped and reinforced by organization that, in this instance, was incapable of stepping back and gauging its biases. Bureaucracy and process trumped thoroughness and reason" (CAIB, 2003, p. 181).

If you want to restore thoroughness, reason, stepping back, and gauging biases, one way to do so is to take seriously the values of mindfulness and resilience and be clear about the mistakes you don't want to make. HROs take these values seriously. There are good reasons why we should take them seriously as well.

References

CAIB 2003. *Columbia Accident Investigation Board: Report*, vol. 1. Washington DC: US Government.

Carthey, J., de Leval, M., Reason, J., Leggatt, A., and Wright, D. 2000. Adverse events in cardiac surgery: The role played by human and organizational factors. In C. Vincent and B. De Mol (eds.), *Safety in Medicine* (117–138). Amsterdam: Pergamon.

Gleason, P. 1991. LCES: A key to safety in the wildland fire environment. *Fire Management Notes*, 52 (4), 9.

Hock, D. 1999. *Birth of the Chaordic Age*. San Francisco: Berrett-Koehler.

Hollnagel, E. 1993. *Human Reliability Analysis: Context and Control*. London: Academic.

Johns, M. 1996. Dude fire still smokin'. *Wildfire*, 5(2), 39–42.

Keller, P., Weick, K. E., Sutcliffe, K., Saveland, J., Lahey, L., Thomas, D., and Nasiatka, P. 2004. *Managing the Unexpected in Prescribed Fire and Fire Use Operations: RMRS-GTR-137*. Fort Collins, CO: USDA, Forest Service, Rocky Mountain Research Station.

LaPorte, T. R. 1996. High reliability organizations: Unlikely, demanding and at risk. *Journal of Contingencies and Crisis Management*, 4, 60–71.

March, J. G., Sproull, L. S., and Tamuz, M. 1991. Learning from samples of one or fewer. *Organization Science*, 2(1–13).

Meacham, J. A. 1990. The loss of wisdom. In R. J. Sternberg (ed.), *Wisdom* (181–211). New York: Cambridge University Press.

Roberts, K. H. 1990. Some characteristics of high reliability organizations. *Organization Science*, 1: 160–177.

(In press). Bishop Rock dead ahead: The grounding of the U.S.S. *Enterprise*. *Naval Institute Proceedings*.

Roberts, K. H. and Creed, W. E. D. (1993). Epilogue. In Karlene H. Roberts (ed.), *New Challenges to Understanding Organizations* (249–256). New York: Macmillan.

Schulman, P. R. 1993a. The analysis of high reliability organizations: A comparative framework. In K. H. Roberts (ed.), *New Challenges to Understanding Organizations* (33–54). New York: Macmillan.

1993b. The negotiated order of organizational reliability. *Administration and Society*, 25(3), 353–372.

Starbuck, W. H. and Milliken, F. J. 1988. Challenger: Fine-tuning the odds until something breaks. *Journal of Management Studies*, 25, 319–340.

Sutcliffe, K. M. and Vogus, T. J. 2003. Organizing for resilience. In K. S. Cameron, J. E. Dutton and R. E. Quinn (eds.), *Positive Organizational Scholarship* (94–110). San Francisco: Berrett-Koehler.

Turner, B. A. and Turner, P. N. F. 1997. *Man-Made Disasters* (2nd edn). Oxford: Butterworth-Heinemann.

Weick, K. E. 1988. Enacted sensemaking in crisis situations. *Journal of Management Studies*, 25(4), 305–317.

Weick, K. E. 1990. The vulnerable system: Analysis of the Tenerife air disaster. *Journal of Management*, 16: 571–593.

1993. The collapse of sensemaking in organizations: The Mann Gulch disaster. *Administrative Science Quarterly*, 38, 628–652.

1995. South Canyon revisited: Lessons from high reliability organizations. *Wildfire*, 4 (4), 54–68.

1998. Wildfire and wisdom. *Wildfire*, 7 (1), 14–19.

1999. Sensemaking as an organizational dimension of global change. In J. Dutton and D. Cooperrider (eds.), *The Human Dimension of Global Change* (39–56). Thousand Oaks, CA: Sage.

2002. Human factors in fire behavior analysis: Reconstructing the Dude Fire. *Fire Management Today*, 62 (4), 8–15.

2005. Making sense of blurred images: Mindful organizing in Mission STS-107. In W. H. Starbuck and M. Farjoun (eds.), *Organization at the Limit: Lessons from the Columbia Disaster* (159–178). Malden, MA: Blackwell.

Weick, K. E. and Roberts, K. H. 1993. Collective mind in organizations: Heedful interrelating on flight decks. *Administrative Science Quarterly*, 38: 357–381.

Weick, K. E. and Sutcliffe, K. M. 2001. *Managing the Unexpected*. San Francisco, CA: Jossey-Bass.

2003. Hospitals as cultures of entrapment: A re-analysis of the Bristol Royal Infirmary. *California Management Review*, 45(2), 73–84.

Weick, K. E., Sutcliffe, K. M., and Obstfeld, D. 1999. Organizing for high reliability: Processes of collective mindfulness. In B. Staw and R. Sutton (eds.), *Research in Organizational Behavior*, 21 (81–123). Greenwich, CI: JAI.

4 | Spirituality and leadership in the Marine Corps

DAN YAROSLASKI AND
PAOLO TRIPODI

In the Marine Corps, values and virtues acquire a special meaning, and they combine with several other elements to become part of a strong spirituality. Spirituality and the Marine Corps would seem, on the surface, to be incompatible concepts. Battles, killing, and warfare – activities in which Marines excel – do not seem to have a place in discussions about spirituality. This chapter, however, explains in what ways spirituality is an integral part of the Marine Corps identity and is crucial to the success of the organization.

Values, spirituality, and the Marines

Marines believe that they enjoy a unique and special relationship with the American people. Marines have a strong perception that they are the "most" American institution and are proud to serve the American people, particularly in times of trouble. In the late 1950s Brigadier General Victor Krulak offered at least three main beliefs or values held by American people toward the Marine Corps.

First, they believe that when trouble comes to our country there will be Marines, who, through hard work, have made and kept themselves ready to do something useful about it and do it at once. They picture these Marines as men – individual components of a lean, serious professional outfit. Second, they believe that when the Marines go to war, they invariably turn in performance that is dramatically and decisively successful – not most of the time, but always. Their faith and their convictions in this regard are almost mystical. The mere association of the word "Marines" with a crisis is an automatic source of encouragement and confidence everywhere. The third thing they believe about the Marines is that our corps is downright good for the manhood of our country; that the Marines are masters of a form of unfailing alchemy which converts unoriented youths into proud, self reliant stable citizens.[1]

[1] Victor Krulak, *First to Fight*, Annapolis: Naval Institute Press, 1984, p. xv.

As pointed out by General Krulak, Marines have a clear sense that they are performing a broad task that goes beyond fighting and winning the nation's war. They are committed to doing *good* for the American people. This pursuit of doing good motivates the Corps to play a key role in protecting and strengthening American society. Stated another way, Marines have a unique task. They are America's key organization in dealing with crises and conflicts that affect the country. They do not "compete," rather they face and deal with deadly threats by applying the necessary amount of force. Marines pride themselves in being mentally prepared to deal with any potential enemy, and they are ready to sacrifice their own lives if necessary. It is the foundation of spirituality in the Marine Corps that enables individuals to deal with death and extreme sacrifice. When using force on the battlefield, they use *decisive* force, but they place great importance on always respecting the rule of law. That is, they value human life, whether that life is an enemy combatant's or a civilian's, and they become immersed in a value system that focuses strongly on doing the right thing.

In this chapter we highlight spirituality as a key element that helps Marine leaders at all levels do the "right thing," particularly in situations in which it is increasingly difficult to draw a clear line between right and wrong. This sense of right and wrong contributes to a strong sense of spirituality that characterizes the Marine Corps.

In the following pages, we explain how spirituality affects the organization and its members. We believe that spirituality emanates first and foremost from individual Marines and it makes an impact on the everyday life of the Corps both during peacetime and, more importantly, on the battlefield. We begin our analysis by explaining some of the relevant features of Marine Corps culture. Indeed, our approach considers spirituality as a combination of several factors ranging from an individual Marine's understanding of his or her role to Marine Corps culture and tradition. In order to explain the practical implications of spirituality, we rely on some distinguished leaders in the Corps. A sampling of their experiences in Vietnam and in the war in Iraq is included in this chapter. We begin by addressing the culture of the Marine Corps as a fundamental building block in explaining spirituality. We then explain the meaning of spirituality in the Marine Corps and illustrate its role in producing the excellence that characterizes this organization.

Marine Corps culture

The military has a unique culture. In the words of two retired Air Force senior officers: "Men and women entering the military know that it will be different from the lives they left. Those who are in the military know that they are set apart from the rest of society."[2] Although the armed forces are a component of society, military culture with its distinctive rituals, symbols, and traditions emphasizes elements of distinction from that same society. The perception is that this culture is like a single all-encompassing entity. The reality, however, is rather different. Every service has its own features. The Marine Corps, maybe more than any service, is the one that nourishes strong cultural features. As pointed out by Thomas Ricks, culture plays a key role in the Marine Corps: "Culture is important in all the US military service, but nowhere so much so as in the Marines."[3]

The unique nature of Marine Corps culture requires that it must be learned.[4] While there are many cultural aspects of human society that are transmitted genetically or are accepted without thought, the culture of the Marine Corps is different. A Marine cannot simply adopt it unknowingly or through osmosis. When an individual becomes a Marine, he or she begins to act differently, think differently, and relate differently to others. Individuals consciously and willingly adopt a unique Marine Corps culture. This culture is maintained by a special system of meaning. Although it shares a great deal with its sister services, the truly unique motto of *Semper Fidelis* (Latin for "Always Faithful"), the Marines' formal traditions and ceremonies like the annual Birthday Ball, which has not changed in any significant way since it was prescribed by the 14th Commandant, Major General John A. Lejeune in 1921, and the war fighting structure[5] of the Corps provide Marines with a unique identity separate from other armed forces. The organization of the Marine Corps is a society. The Marine Corps identifies itself as unique in the armed services, largely

---

[2] Robert Taylor and William Rosenbach (eds.), *Military Leadership*, Boulder, CO: Westview Press, 2000, p. 74.

[3] Thomas Ricks, *Making the Corps*, New York: Touchstone, 1998, p. 188. Ricks identifies several feature of USMC culture. He also points out the differences from other services.

[4] Karen Dunivin, "Military Culture: Change and Continuity," *Armed Forces and Society*, 20 (4), Summer 1994, 531–547.

[5] The Marine Corps Air Ground Task Force.

due to a sense of being elite within the Department of Defense, which has historically been summed up in the motto: The Few, The Proud, The Marines. This unique identity can be attributed to the distinctive technique used by Marines to acculturate new inductees and the characteristics of the product produced by that technique. The distinctive technique used by the Marine Corps is a "zeroing" of all individuals entering the Marine Corps. Whether a man or a woman becomes an enlisted person or an officer, he or she must first pass a test of character and capabilities. While other services tend to emphasize the immediate specialization of individuals within a career field, the Marine Corps focuses first and foremost on creating a transformation within individuals, making them Marines first and only afterward members of a specialized occupational field. The results are that all Marines proudly describe themselves as, first and foremost, riflemen, and all believe that there is no greater honor than to wear the Eagle, Globe, and Anchor and be proudly called "Marine."

Five essential elements of Marine Corps culture may be identified. First, the Marine Corps is expeditionary in nature; second, it focuses on survival; third, it maintains a strong sense of accountability within the current and former membership; fourth, it utilizes maneuver warfare; and fifth, it must be ready to use violence when called for.

Expeditionary in nature

The Marines often refer to themselves as "America's 911." In order to maintain this motto, the Marine Corps is heavily focused on maintaining equipment that is readily deployable aboard various forms of strategic lift – US Navy warships, Merchant Marine cargo vessels or US Air Force cargo aircraft. Consequently, Marine units focus on Marine personnel and equipment mobilization readiness as well as the readiness of the individual Marine's family. The spartan appearance of most Marine barracks and housing has long been an indication of a distinctive lifestyle.

Focused on survival

Although the Continental Congress signed the Marine Corps into existence, it was not until the 1950s that the Marines were legally secured a place within the Department of Defense. Consequently, the Marine

Corps leadership and even the individual Marine has come to understand that in order to survive he or she owes the American people their
best effort – "be good or be gone." Marines have distinguished themselves in countless battles and, throughout their history, have secured
a place in the hearts of the American people.

Accountability

The Marine Corps, as a smaller service than the other branches of the
military, has developed a greater degree of family feeling which directly
translates into increased accountability. A Marine is accountable for his
or her actions to all other Marines both past and present. Being small
also provides Marines with a sense of being elite, although at 175,000
Marines on active duty and no real commando mission, it truly is "an
elite of the ordinary." This belief manifests itself not just in the often
used recruiting slogan "The Few, The Proud," but it lives within the
minds of individual Marines who understand and constantly attempt
to live up to the hard fought reputation of Marines who have served
in past battles and conflicts.

   This sense of inter-generational accountability weighs heavily on
Marines' mindset in both peacetime and, more importantly, on the
battlefield. Recently, retired Lieutenant General Paul VanRiper told a
group of Marine majors that, as a former Marine, he takes great pride
in the actions of current Marines, but he is also not shy about commenting when he sees the need for a course correction.[6] He stated that
since he was older than any Marine still on active duty, and he would
most likely be guarding the streets of heaven sooner than any of them,[7]
any Marine who strays can expect to answer to him in the afterlife as
well. Clearly, Marines understand that they have a place in the universe, and maintaining that place means they can never forget their
accountability.

---

[6] Stated in a class presented by Lt. Gen. Paul K. VanRiper to the students at the
Marine Corps School of Advanced Warfighting, August 16, 2005, Quantico,
VA.

[7] As stated by the third verse of the Marines Hymn: Here's health to you and
to our Corps Which we are proud to serve In many a strife we've fought
for life and never lost our nerve; If the Army and the Navy ever look on
Heaven's scenes; They will find the streets are guarded By The United States
Marines.

Maneuver warfare

In maneuver warfare, the Marine Corps leaders must both empower and trust their subordinates in a way that is unique when compared to other services and civilian organizations. The Marines rely on combat orders focused on expressing the "Commander's Intent" rather than volumes of meticulous detail. This implies an extremely close working relation between leaders and followers. The subordinate trusts the leader's judgment, while leaders trust that, left to their own devices, the subordinates will understand their place in the universe and perform their assigned duties. That trust is implicit to the Marine Corps culture.

The use of violence

Throughout its history, Marine Corps leaders have placed enormous emphasis on the moral, ethical, and spiritual aspects of warfare across the spectrum of violence. This unique and deep understanding of the use of violence was expressed by Lt. Gen. Mattis, who, in March of 2003, led the 1st Marine Division into Iraq. His most fundamental values were expressed in two phrases: "No Better Friend, No Worse Enemy," and "First do no harm." These "passwords" served as the basic ground rules for all personnel assigned under his command. Lt. Gen. Mattis' now famous statements fit perfectly into the Marine's culture. Thomas Ricks noted that one of the main components of Marine Corps culture is "about avoiding making enemies, but not treating them gently if you do."[8]

Lieutenant General Mattis explained that "Going into Iraq, I wanted discrimination but I wanted to give whoever fought us a bruising they would never forget. I wanted a shockwave to move through the country." When the Marines returned to Iraq, Mattis added one more concept: "'First Do No Harm,'" which meant that if they could take a shot across a crowded marketplace to kill a terrorist but put a woman or child in danger, then they did NOT take the shot. They had to try and stay friendly one minute longer, one second longer, so that we could try to win the people over."[9]

---

[8] Ricks, *Making the Corps*, p. 187.
[9] Yaroslaski interview with General Mattis, August 30, 2005, Quantico, VA.

Summary

Marine Corps culture is the foundation of a high performance organization. The expeditionary nature of Marines leads them to maintain a light force, capable of conducting operations across the spectrum of conflict. The focus on survival and accountability to each other helps to encourage Marines toward excellence even in the most difficult situations. The trust necessary during the execution of maneuver warfare requires that Marine leaders provide useful and ethical guidance, so that the individual Marine is capable of applying violence to the situation in an effective yet controlled way.

The meaning of spirituality in the Marine Corps

The most common notions raised by the term *spirituality* are the ideas of a creator or the practice of a particular religion. Since the Marine Corps is made up of individuals from a wide variety of backgrounds and religious beliefs, the term, as it is used in the Marine Corps, cannot imply adherence to any particular religion or notion of God. Indeed in the words of General Krulak, the 31st Commandant of the Marine Corps:

it is difficult that a chapter on spirituality can "duck" the role of a Supreme Being, the role of some foundation upon which to base a value system, the sense that in talking of spirituality, you are talking about an overarching view of life and how we live it. It makes no difference what religion we are talking about . . . Jewish, Christian, Muslim, Buddhism, bushmen, American Indian, etc., etc. All start with some belief in some "power." It could be found in the rocks and trees, in a person, in a serpent, in whatever. But to try and define spirituality without some mention of a higher order is, in my opinion, intellectual gamesmanship.[10]

We recognize that a belief in a Supreme Being or higher power beyond our self is critical to explaining Marine Corps spirituality. While this belief is crucial, on its own it could not explain the excellence in leadership that has been demonstrated by Marine leaders for over 200 years.

In conjunction with the core belief of a supreme being and as a means of explaining actions taken by Marine leaders, we adopt Kanungo and

[10] D. Yaroslaski email interview with General Krulak, August 29, 2005.

Mendoca's definition of spirituality as "the experience of reality at a deeper level, or at a higher level of abstraction. It is experiencing the incorporeal, or the symbolic reality underlying the mundane phenomena."[11] As a means of amplifying Kanungo and Mendonca's definition, Gilbert Fairholm adds a sense of self to spirituality. "Spirituality connotes the essence of who we are, our inner self, separate from the purely physical, but including the physical. Spirituality includes issues of ultimate values. It describes those essential human values that teach us how our basic humanity fits within the overall scheme of things and how we can attain harmony in life and in our work."[12]

For Marines, spirituality is a strong source of motivation and inspiration to make decisions that are morally sound. This becomes absolutely clear in the Marine Corps' first Leadership Principle: Know Yourself and Seek Self Improvement.[13] According to Lieutenant General Martin Brandtner, an outstanding leader has a good grip on himself and is able to identify his strengths and weaknesses. His skill is in knowing how to effectively transition among different leadership styles for different situations. Lieutenant Brandtner maintained that

Such leaders will possess the ability to inspire subordinates to achieve lofty goals, to innovate, to improve performance and productivity, while adhering to the principles and ethics that drive the Corps. The Marine Corps style of warfare requires intelligent leaders with a penchant for boldness and initiative down to the lowest levels. Boldness is an essential moral trait in a leader, for it generates combat power beyond the physical means at hand. Moreover, a good leader understands that good leadership is about who you are – not so much about what you do or can do. Anyone can seek out persons with specific skills to address a deficiency or provide a capability, but they can't infuse that so-called "expert" with character and heart. It has to already be there. Knowing who you are suggests a sense of spiritual awareness and knowledge of one's place in the universe and purpose in life. Knowing who you are also bespeaks the fact that you understand reality – that you have to deal with what is happening now and with who you really are at this moment, not what you were ten years ago, or who you would like to have

---

[11] Rabindra Kanungo and Manuel Mendoca, *Ethical Dimensions of Leadership*, Thousand Oaks, CA: Sage, 1996, p. 88.

[12] Gilbert Fairholm, *Capturing the Hearth of Leadership. Spirituality and Communality in the new American Workplace*, Westport: Praeger, 1996, p. 78.

[13] *Marine Corps Values: A User's Guide for Discussion Leaders*, MCRP 6-11B, Quantico, VA: Headquarters Marine Corps, 1998, p. 15–2.

been or would like to be ten years from now. You cannot change the past nor predict the future. You can think about what you would like the future to be, but it is this very moment that counts, and for which you are being held accountable.[14]

According to Lieutenant General Brandtner, there can be no separation between good leadership that follows the accepted Marine Corps traditions and practices and a fully developed sense of reality and place in the universe. Even in the basic concept of spirituality, the essential elements of Marine Corps culture are already being indicated. Paralleling the definitions of spirituality presented by Kanungo, Mendoca and Fairholm, Lieutenant General Brandtner has indicated that a Marine Corps leader must be able to recognize the possibilities within even the mundane circumstances of either daily life or combat operations. This recognition must be in harmony with an understanding of who he or she is right now, and eventually lead to the best decision, in concert with the ethics and standards of the Marine Corps. In other words, Marine leaders, with an appropriate understanding of who, where and when they are, must constantly attempt to achieve inner harmony in their daily lives and work.

This harmony has been expressed by both outside observers and Marine leaders. Robert D. Kaplan, in his book *Imperial Grunts*, writes:

The US Marines came from the East, from the orient. That was their spiritual tradition. It was the legacy of their naval landing throughout the pacific, of the Marine legation guards during the Boxer Rebellion in China, of the China Marines in the 1920s, and, most of all, of the very didacticism of the Navy itself, the Marines' sister service, which fit well with Eastern philosophy. The Army had Clausewitz, the Marines Sun Tzu.[15]

Lieutenant General Mattis parallels Robert Kaplan's statement by attributing one of the most commonly recognized expressions of the Marine Corps to the influence of Eastern thought: "If you look at the China Marines, they made the connection that nothing exists in a vacuum; that no man is an island. From them we get the motto, 'Gung Ho,' which means 'work together' and comes from the Chinese

---

[14] Presented by Lt. Gen. Brandtner to the students of the Marine Corps Command and Staff College, May 6, 2005, Quantico, VA.

[15] Robert D. Kaplan, *Imperial Grunts*, New York: Random House, 2005, p. 311.

Communist Route Army, and more importantly, the Confucius concept of body, mind and spirit."[16]

As a result of this Eastern influence, Marines possess a spiritual awareness that places them in harmony with the universe and provides them with a mechanism to better understand themselves in the context of emergent phenomenon. The culture of the Marine Corps helps Marines demonstrate their understanding of spirituality and then provides them with the physical guidance they require for excellence in execution of their duties. General John Lejeune, a veteran of countless combat operations ranging from the Spanish American War, Nicaragua, Panama and as a Division Commander in World War I, describes his understanding of the guidance provided by an acute sense of spirituality in the following way:

> To be a really successful leader, a senior officer must avoid aloofness...He should not place himself on a pedestal and exercise command from a position far above the heads of his men, but he must come down to the ground where they are struggling and mingle with them as a friend and as a father. A word or two of sympathy and of praise spoken to . . . men exhausted from the stress of combat may change depression into exaltation and, being spread about among the men, may cause them to feel that their chief has their welfare at hear and that he is full of human sympathy for them.[17]

Spirituality enables Marine leaders to demonstrate excellence in combat operations through the creation of the bond felt between fellow Marines. Although Major Yaroslaski never lost a single member of his unit in combat, his every waking moment during his experience in OIF was spent ensuring that every effort was made to ensure the safety of his personnel while still accomplishing the mission of ensuring that if a Marine was killed or wounded, it would not be for a lack of preparation or training. Unfortunately, after he departed his previous command, one of his Marines was killed in a roadside explosion. While attending his funeral and delivering the Marine's eulogy, Major Yaroslaski faced the reality that his bond was broken with that Marine, and that he had to ensure that his death and the death of other Marines would not be in vain. Another Marine, Lieutenant Colonel Howard A. Christy, now retired, describes his sense of spirituality as being made

[16] Interview with Lt. Gen. Mattis.
[17] Gen. John A. Lejeune, *The Reminiscences of a Marine*, Philadelphia: Dorrance, 1930, pp. 307–308, 277. See also pp. 374–375.

manifest in an overwhelming sense of responsibility while serving in Vietnam as the commanding officer of A Company 1st Battalion, 9th Marine Infantry Regiment. "The first bloodletting came within minutes of entering battle, and after several days of long company-sized combat patrols in enemy-infested country, with few exceptions the men, officers and enlisted men alike, exhausted and still reeling from the first day's events, just stood there looking at me, silently and, as it seemed, dumbly, asking for leadership. The utter loneliness, the fear that I might fail, that we might all die, was staggering."[18]

Colonel Toolan, the Commanding Officer of the 1st Marine Infantry Regiment during Operation Iraqi Freedom and during the first assault on Fallujah, stressed this bond between Marines by stating: "The reality of sharing combat and the associated hardships brings about a huge bond, because you really get to know people. The memories last a lifetime and often give you an appreciation for life. There have been times when you wonder why some were saved and others were not. As a leader you are responsible for everything that happens. It is a sense of responsibility that gives you the satisfaction to press on and enjoy the life you are blessed with. For those who didn't survive, you have an obligation to never forget them."[19]

Spirituality and leadership in the battlefield

In February of 1968, then Captain Ron Christmas was deeply embroiled in the battle for Hue City, Vietnam as the Commanding Officer of Company H, 2nd Battalion, 5th Marine Regiment, 1st Marine Division. The attack into Hue had begun and Company H was heavily engaged in the fight for the bridge over the Phu Cam Canal. The company had fought bravely and effectively against a numerically superior force and when Marine reinforcements finally arrived they still held the bridge. During the fierce fighting the company had taken numerous casualties to include the deaths of two popular squad leaders. As a result of their superb efforts the battalion commander had

---

[18] Howard A. Christy, "Imperatives of Real Military Leadership", *Marine Corps Gazette*, November 2004, p. 79.

[19] D. Yaroslaski interview with Colonel John Toolan, September 8, 2005, Quantico, VA.

ordered the company out of the fight for a few days and provided them with some much needed rest and recuperation.

As the company moved into its reserve position in the Christian Brothers' School, the Chaplain approached me to lend assistance. He had recognized the signs of sagging morale. Telling me that he had found a chapel in the school, he asked permission to offer a memorial mass for those Marines of the company who had been killed in recent fighting. I agreed, but stated that attendance must be strictly voluntary.

When I entered the chapel, at the announced time, I found it filled by every Marine of the company except those posted for security. The Father began his mass by stating that he was offering a memorial mass, not just a common service, because he was a Catholic priest and saying mass was what he knew how to do best. It was an appropriate honor for our dead. As the service progressed, he asked me to read the gospel. Then, when it came time to offer the sacrament, he invited *all* who wished to partake, no matter what their religion, to come forward to honor his fallen brothers – Jews, Catholics, Protestants, and some who had never seen the inside of a church before. As the Marines left the chapel they seemed changed. There was a spring in their step; *esprit de corps* had returned; morale was high![20]

In the late winter/early spring of 2003 Lieutenant General Mattis provided his Marines with the following spiritual guidance: "No Better Friend, No Worse Enemy." In 2004 when the Division was ordered back to Iraq, Lieutenant General Mattis added the expression: "First Do No Harm." Since Vietnam, there has been a focus on ensuring that the actions taken by the combatants are understood by each individual so that when hostilities end, he or she can understand and live with the results of their actions. Lieutenant General Mattis' comments reflect this modern understanding of ethics in combat operations which require a leader to not only provide guidance germane to the concepts of proportionality and discrimination,[21] but which also promote the

---

[20] Lt. Gen. Ron Christmas, USMC (RET), "The Chaplain and Marines", *The Marine Corps Gazette*, July 1975, p. 47. This text was provided to the authors in lieu of an interview. With Lt. Gen. Christmas' permission, the original article has been placed in the first person.

[21] For a discussion on proportionality and discrimination see Michael Walzer, *Just and Unjust Wars*, New York: Basic Books, 2000, and James Turner Johnson, *Morality and Contemporary Warfare*, New Haven: Yale University Press, 1999.

psychological survival of the individual Marine after the combat action is complete. Under the concept of proportionality combatants must apply no more force than what is required to defeat the enemy, thus preventing any additional and unnecessary harm even to an enemy combatant. Discrimination limits the use of force only to enemy combatants, additionally, if an enemy combatant surrenders, then they too become an illegitimate target. In other words, every possible caution must be taken in order to ensure that noncombatants in the area of military operations are not harmed, even if that means the risks are greater for the combat forces.

By adopting the "passwords" of, "No Better Friend, No Worse Enemy," "First Do No Harm," Lieutenant General Mattis not only demonstrated a sophisticated understanding of discrimination and proportionality, but he emphasized to his Marines the value of human life whether civilian or enemy combatant. One "password" was worth long hours of tedious legal training in a long detailed list of carefully crafted do's and do not's. The spiritual connection between leaders and followers becomes particularly effective when the leader knows and succeeds in directly touching a Marine's mindset and motivation. Through this password, the cause of violence rested squarely on the shoulders of the enemy combatant. If the enemy decided against the use of violence, Marines could respond through non-violent means and either take belligerents captive or turn toward a focus on caring for the needs of the Iraqi people. Yet if violence was the choice of the enemy, the Marines were ready to respond with violence. By stating that Marines would "First Do No Harm," Lieutenant General Mattis made it clear that the mission was not to spread death and destruction across Iraq; rather, violence would be applied through the filters of proportionality and discrimination. Adherence to proportionality and discrimination were not seen as hindrances to the use of "decisive force" or the force necessary to accomplish the mission, but no less and ideally no more.[22] General Mattis remembers that:

---

[22] E-mail interview with Lt. Gen. Mattis on September 13, 2005, Quantico, VA. Lt. Gen. Mattis wanted it made clear that he authorized his subordinate commanders to use decisive force and not think in terms of minimum or maximum force. In his estimation, if the situation called for air strikes, then that was the right decision, is the situation called for less, less should be applied. Lt. Gen. Mattis believes that it is an error to confuse the concept of no more force than the situation requires with the concept of minimum force.

I was also concerned for my subordinates. I wanted them to be able to come home and be proud of what they had done. If they had done things they weren't proud of, if they had murdered people or were too quick on the draw, then there was going to be a problem. I couldn't give them a little card that said, first step A then B then 2B. They had to be reactive and not reflective; the time for reflection is before you cross the line of departure. We have an obligation to ourselves and others that we have to live up to an ethical, moral standard. If we don't recognize that just because you put on the uniform and went to boot camp ten years ago doesn't really make a difference, it is what you do each day.

We were morally justified in our actions – we did not go there to "kill ragheads." I have been in more than one fight and it is not an insignificant moment to live through, you don't want to look into the mirror years from now and not be able to live with what you did. All this life is about choices, sometimes bad things happen but how do you deal with them? Some guy goes to war and nobody in his unit dies or is injured, another guy goes and 75 of his guys are killed or wounded, so life is not fair. The Greeks saw the gods as not necessarily on our side, but we expect our God to be on our side all the time, so if you don't understand your place in the world and operate within a moral framework then you can create some horrible results.[23]

While commanding the 1st Marine Division throughout OIF, Lieutenant General Mattis observed Marines first hand. He witnessed countless examples of Marine leaders who understood their mission and their spiritual role in relation with humanity and in the end exemplified virtuous and excellence in the performance of duty.[24]

I came up behind some of the Marines who were heavily engaged in the fighting, and a young Marine, who had not seen me, yells, "Don't shoot the house on the corner, the guy has women and children in there, we have to get around behind so we can just get him." So to hear that from one of the youngest Marines in the most junior battalion, you can just imagine what had gotten through to the rest of the division. So it is a spirituality that translates into not only action but to virtuous action and does not leave you having to justify some horrific action by saying "I was only doing what I thought was right."

There was a Marine patrol that came across a funeral procession. The patrol leader, a corporal, stops his patrol, lines up his Marines against a wall

---

[23] Interview with Lt. Gen. Mattis.
[24] Ibid. All three vignettes that follow were from the same interview.

with their back to it and tells them to take their helmets off and hold them over their heart in respect. A small thing but an example of spontaneous but studied expressions that were possible because of a sense of spirituality.

One day in Najaf we were getting a lot of hate and discontent directed toward us even though we had been getting along with the people, but when it is 125 degrees things get rough and about a thousand people pour out into the streets, and began confronting the Marines. The Marines have their bayonets fixed and the scene gets very confusing and we had been getting along so well – they didn't know what had changed. It is hotter than hell. So Commander Devine [Chaplain Corps, United States Navy, Regimental Combat Team 7 Chaplain] grabbed some US Navy petty officers and Marine Staff non-commissioned officers and some water bottles and took the group into the crowd and started handing out water bottles. Now I never would have thought of that; the Marines found out the crowd was mad because they had no power and no air conditioners. The Marines said they were in the same situation and didn't like it any better! The Marine leaders asked for some of the city leaders to come forward and talk about what they could do together. This was the perfect example of diffusing a situation without a shot being fired or a single injury being incurred.

Colonel Toolan worked directly for Lieutenant General Mattis. His experiences with the Marines reflect the deep spiritual understanding Marines possess even when faced with the unpleasant task of being a supporting effort designed to distract the attention of the Iraqi Army. The fierce fighting along a barren stretch of Highway 7 in eastern Iraq became a killing field as countless Iraqi units threw themselves in vain against the 1st Marines. With these horrific scenes fresh in the minds of his Marines, Colonel Toolan still observed countless examples of Marines acting with virtue and Marine leaders clearly acting from a sense of spirituality enabled by Lieutenant General Mattis' passwords.

During OIF 1, after we had crossed the Dyala River, we came into contact with Iraqi fighters along the eastern edge of Sadr City. We lost two Marines very quickly from small arms fire, coming from several houses that were located at the corner of a major intersection. The city appeared boarded up, as they all disappeared into their homes. Taking the two casualties so quickly prompted me to act and I immediately called artillery support from the 1st Battalion of the 11th Marine Artillery Regiment to respond to a fire mission on the selected target houses. While I was calling for fire, one of my subordinate commanders explained to me that the building appeared to have other civilians in the houses nearby. In order to avoid any harm to innocent civilians we opted to abort the fire mission and clear the houses without fires or grenades. It proved to be the right thing to do: the houses were full of civilians, kids and women. There were, however, fighters with weapons, who were holding the families hostage.[25]

Upon his unit's return to Iraq in 2004, Colonel Toolan was faced with a situation that had degraded into Improvised Explosive Device attacks on his convoys and heavy insurgent activity. Even in the face of all the injuries and uncertainty, he was able to witness the impact of spirituality at all levels among Marines.

A platoon from 1st Bn 5th Marines while sweeping through a town east of Fallujah looking for caches of weapons near a local market, were confronted by some sporadic fire. They proceeded to clear the building and came upon a young mother with her children. As they were following up with a search they came upon a child who had a huge set of rashes and blisters on her face and neck. They weren't sure what was wrong with the infant, but they assessed the situation with their corpsman and their interpreters and decided to take the child to the Abu Ghraib medical facility. The platoon took the father and the child together to see if something could be done. The medical facility personnel decided to take a look, which resulted in a doctor from the Army medical unit contacting a personal contact back in the states to see if surgery was possible. The platoon adopted the child and the family. Eventually the platoon's leaders contacted a Non-Governmental Organization in Baghdad who in turn contacted a hospital in Kansas City and they agreed to conduct the surgery, and to bring the father along. The end story is the child's life was saved and she is now back with her family. The town where many caches were found, Nasr wa Sahlan, is now one of the most cooperative cities in Iraq.[26]

In 2003 Major Jason Smith, a captain and a Company Commander within the 1st Marine Regiment, was able to observe the front-line application of Lieutenant General Mattis' passwords. Major Smith led his company from the initial Kuwait border crossing, through the death and destruction of Highway 7 and finally into the fight for Baghdad and the subsequent stability operations once hostilities dissipated. His insight into the spirituality based actions of individual Marine leaders is both intense and enlightening. It was his job to make sure each Marine carried out Lieutenant General Mattis' intent and, in the end, was able to live with what he or she had done. The complex issues faced by

[25] Interview with Col. Toolan.   [26] Ibid.

Marines in the urban settings of Iraq required subordinates who could think on their feet and apply the necessary force for the situation at hand.[27]

As a company commander I was more concerned with dealing "with what is happening now . . . " instead of "experiencing the incorporeal, or the symbolic reality underlying the mundane phenomena." I bring this up because too often Rules of Engagement (ROE) seem to be written using the first definition as a guideline. Lawyers and even some commanders will say that the ROE are very specific but unfortunately most, if not all, riflemen view ROE as some vague, "incorporeal" burden to be endured. Speaking in the abstract is not wrong in a classroom but, while it may make sense to discuss the reasons behind something, it does nothing to make the job of the Marine rifleman easier.

I was concerned with spirituality only in that I wanted Marines to think about themselves a certain way and I wanted them to think about others a certain way. I wanted them to think about themselves as the biggest, baddest, guys on the block who were in Iraq to provide a safe place for people who wanted a better life. One of the analogies I used was a bouncer in a bar. Good bouncers are big strong guys who don't feel the need to show off how big and strong they are by bumping into people. Good bouncers aren't looking to start trouble but aren't afraid to stop it. They don't hesitate to get involved when there's a problem and they're not afraid to put themselves in the middle to solve the situation.

Knowing the reality on the ground was very important in giving the Marines a quiet sense of determination to do the job instead of surviving the job. I wanted them to know the reality that they were the guys with all the guns, armor, comm, and vehicles and could easily crush anyone that needed crushing, but I also wanted them to know that it wasn't necessary to crush everyone.[28]

---

[27] D. Yaroslaski correspondence with Major Jason Smith, September 9, 2005. As an example of subordinates applying only the necessary force, Major Smith provided the following vignette: "I had a Lt. during OIF that was on a night patrol in Baghdad and came across a guy standing in front of a mosque with an AK-47. The patrol saw him from a distance, kept patrolling and waited for him to display hostile intent. The Lt. went up and spoke with him under the cover of the Marines and found out through the interpreter that he was there to prevent looting – a huge concern in Baghdad during April '03. The Lt. told the man who he was and why he was there and told him what would happen if the Marines were threatened. The Lt. then kept patrolling while the Marines kept their collective eye on the man.

[28] Ibid.

The vignettes provided by Lieutenant General Christmas, Lieu
General Mattis, Colonel Toolan and Major Smith all demonstra\
through the ages Marines have come to see themselves and thei
roundings in a unique way. They understand that they must be me\
women of action and that their actions will have not just significant
but perhaps permanent consequences. While these comments perhaps
sound extremely heady and even clichéd, Marines take their calling
seriously and take the application of their spirituality as a way of life
rather than as just a guideline.

Conclusion

Because of the Marine Corps culture, the Marines maintain a strong
and practical sense of spirituality. This spirituality is based largely on
an understanding through which leaders see themselves in the context
of the greater world around them. While the concept of a Supreme
Being is central to most Marines' understanding of spirituality, it is the
individual Marine's ability to translate belief into action that matters
the most. Ask Marines what the motto of the Marine Corps is, and
they will tell you *Semper Fidelis*. Ask them what that means, and while
you will hear "Always Faithful," you will also hear *Semper Fidelis*
means that fellow Marines need never worry about who is looking out
for them, that they will keep faith with those Marines who have gone
before, and that Marines know their priorities of God, Country, Corps,
and will act accordingly when the time comes. Finally, you will hear
that *Semper Fidelis* means Marines will do what is right according to
what they believe their spirituality calls them to be.

It is only fitting to end the chapter the way it began, with a quote
from a Marine Corps leader. This time, though, the quote is provided
by a much younger officer, Major Jason Smith, who is speaking 48 years
after Lieutenant General Krulak spoke, and he vividly demonstrates the
fact that Marine spirituality is as timeless as ever and is still providing
the basis for excellence in performance:

Spirituality requires us to be men of action. Marines are expected to take
action to resolve situations, regardless of how dangerous, difficult, or incon-
venient those situations may be. Marines (and people) generally view Rules
of Engagement as restrictive and as a tool by which the command can both
cover their ass, and punish Marines who mess up. The understanding of

spirituality that comes from a complete understanding of the authorized uses of deadly force and from a complete understanding that we are there to help is liberating. That understanding gives us so many more options with which to affect a situation and doesn't confine a Marine to the two mutually exclusive options of shooting or not shooting.

I would explain Marine Corps spirituality to civilians by saying that Marines have a purpose in this world. Our purpose is to make things right. We are not able to sit idle when bad people act with impunity and we're not able to watch passively when bad things happen. We will default to action – instead of hiding behind the excuse of not being told to do something we expect that Marines will, using the commander's intent, positively act until told otherwise. "No better friend, no worse enemy" implies that a choice has been made and that we will *act* accordingly. Friend and enemy are on different sides of a fence that we have to climb or jump over. We don't expect to be sitting on the fence watching what happens and avoiding trouble. It doesn't say, "No better fence sitter" for a reason.[29]

[29] Ibid.

5 | *HomeBanc Mortgage Corporation: quest to become America's most admired company*

EDWARD D. HESS

HomeBanc Mortgage Corporation ("HomeBanc") is a residential mortgage lender headquartered in Atlanta, Georgia. HomeBanc went public in July of 2004 and is one of the Southeast's largest home mortgage originators, employing over 1,300 associates. HomeBanc closes about $6 billion in loans a year and services a mortgage portfolio in excess of $3 billion. HomeBanc originates its business primarily through retail outlets and commissioned sales people who are among the most productive in the industry. HomeBanc's "corporate scorecard" places employee satisfaction first, believing all other important business metrics – customer satisfaction, market share, and profitability in that order – will follow from building a workplace to which employees are thrilled to come to every day.

This chapter will strive to explain the special features of HomeBanc, its values-based leadership, and what employees think of the firm – that is, how HomeBanc has captured the hearts of its employees. To this end, I will include many illustrative quotes taken from their 2003 Employee Survey:

HomeBanc is special because we live daily what we have written on our walls...our vision, mission, and credo are not decorations for the boardroom or well-written script for marketing materials, but they are the definition of our culture. We all strive to become "America's Most Admired Company" by becoming the type of individuals Americans admire – honest, professional, respectful, courteous, truthful, humble, compassionate, giving, enthusiastic, and caring. Our vision was generated in the heart of our executive team but would have died there had it not been lived out daily and delivered in actions to managers and leaders and carried on to the people that fulfill the daily operations. (HomeBanc Center, 2003 GPTW Survey, "Comments")

What differentiates HomeBanc is that: (1) It is a young company; (2) Its CEO and leader is young (aged 43); (3) It is a spiritual corporation – that is, faith plays a large role in its culture; and (4) its Chief People Officer is a former minister, with thirty years' experience building two churches in Atlanta. His first corporate job began at age 51, and was at HomeBanc. Dr. Dwight "Ike" Reighard, as Chief People Officer, reports to the CEO and is a member of the Senior Executive Team.

The HomeBanc story raises two obvious questions: (1) Why did a young company with a young CEO adopt a "people-first" values system? and (2) How do they execute or implement the system? We will explore these two issues in this chapter by highlighting many unique attributes of HomeBanc.

To understand the *why* question – why they created a company that places values related to people and faith as the highest priority – one has to understand HomeBanc's CEO, Patrick Flood.

The CEO

Pat Flood is, as he is quick to point out, an average man who, by choosing to be extraordinary, became a sales superstar, and eventually a leader of a publicly traded company. Pat has been in the mortgage origination business for over 20 years and was a top sales producer at HomeBanc prior to entering top management. Being an extroverted salesman causes many people to think Pat's business philosophy may be another sales pitch to motivate employees to work harder.

What makes him effective is the fact that he "walks the talk." That is, he not only believes in what he says, but acts on it by providing Home-Banc employees with extensive training, benefits, perks, and opportunities to grow and reach their professional and personal potential. He treats them as owners. When HomeBanc went public, every HomeBanc associate received restricted stock or stock appreciation rights. Every associate was given ownership in the company.

Pat Flood's journey to the CEO's seat was not preordained. When Pat was a young boy, the family lost a younger son to illness at the age of four. The loss of his brother drove Pat's mother to alcoholism and eventually to abandon Pat, his two surviving brothers, and his father. Pat's father did more than support his boys. He created an emotional environment that was positive, and he infused his sons with love and the belief that they were special and even exceptional. Pat's father taught by example, and he told Pat, "You have something exceptional to offer to people," and "You can be extraordinary."

Pat's love was athletics, not academics. Raised in inner-city Miami, Pat learned at an early age how to play and work with people of different races and ethnicity. During high school and most of college, as Pat would say, he "talked the talk" when it came to values, but his actions sometimes varied from the values his father taught him. This reality hit him at age 23, when he became a Christian and vowed to become a true servant leader. Pat's faith and values became a dominant part of his life. They led him to take courageous business stands with his superiors and ultimately drove him to build a company and culture that mirrored his values.

Pat deeply believes that his employees are owed dignity, respect, opportunity, and an environment that is like a family – supportive, caring, loving, and encouraging. The results speak for themselves: (1) HomeBanc in 2005 was ranked No. 20 on the *Fortune* magazine list of "The 100 Best Companies to Work For"; (2) its employee turnover is very low by mortgage industry standards; (3) it is performing well as a public company; (4) it has over 24,000 applications annually from people wanting to join the company; (5) its customer satisfaction ratings exceed 75%; (6) its training programs at HomeBanc Academy set the industry standard; and (7) its employees are diverse – 43% are minorities, 47% are female, and all religions are represented in its workforce, as are non-believers (agnostics and atheists).

Pat's values-based leadership approach is illustrated by his own descriptions of his philosophy:

First and foremost, I am a Christian. All my decisions are made taking that into account. When I meet my maker, I don't believe He is going to be impressed by my financial statement. However, He is going to hold me accountable for how I treated my people. I have a responsibility to help them be all they can be.

The two most important relationships people have are their marriages and their jobs. People want stability and want to feel valued in both.

A CEO has to make choices – money or people. Our first choice is people. Money is a byproduct or result of treating people right.

Although not all our people share my religious beliefs, what we do share is a fundamental belief in certain core values – truth, loyalty, character, and hard work.

There is a great sense of pride working for an organization that is making a difference in an industry that is typically less than admirable. (HomeBanc Center, 2003 GPTW Survey, "Comments")

Athletics also had a big influence on Pat. Through sports, he learned that the best talent does not always win and that "average talent can perform exceptionally well." "Teams win – not individuals." And "my role is like a coach – to create an environment where the best happens – to create an enjoyable environment."

How does HomeBanc implement this philosophy?

Mission and values

At HomeBanc, the mission and values put people first; serving employees, customers and communities, while fulfilling the dream of home ownership. This value is a guiding force within the company, and the sentiment is included in almost all company-wide communications and corporate graphics. In the elevator lobbies of each floor of HomeBanc's Atlanta headquarters is a floor-to-ceiling HomeBanc Mission Statement featuring photos of associates and their families. These images also appear in HomeBanc's branches throughout the Southeast. No one who comes to visit HomeBanc can miss the central importance of the company's mission, which states:

Our mission is to enrich and fulfill lives by serving each other, our customers, and communities...as we support the dream of home ownership.

That is, while profits are required to stay in business, at HomeBanc, putting money first is not a formula for success. The winning formula flips the traditional "money-first" structure and puts associates first.

I appreciate Pat Flood's beliefs. It means a lot to work for a company with such values. I also believe that the associates and management make Home-Banc a great place to work. It is evident that family is important to our CEO and other management. This means a lot to me because my family is so important to me. I could go on and on but this is truly just a great place to work. In 23 years, I have never worked at an association that I have been so pleased to be a part of as much as HomeBanc. (Central Atlanta, 2003 GPTW Survey, "Comments")

The company's corporate metrics associated with its mission include four measured components:

$$\text{Associate Satisfaction} = \text{Customer Satisfaction}$$
$$= \text{Market Share} = \text{Net Income}$$

Stated that way. In that order.

When I first started with HomeBanc, I found out I had cancer. I remember going to my manager and my team leader. I expected some fake words of encouragement followed by why they would have to replace me. Instead, I got a closed-door meeting for my privacy and the biggest hug and support I can remember throughout my whole ordeal. I was able to do something I hadn't done, which was let go and let it all out. I was so scared walking into that office because I'd just started with my HomeBanc family and did not know if I would have job security through what might be a long process. To top it all off, I signed up for the insurance policy with a high deductible. I chose the high deductible insurance because I was NEVER ill. I did not know how I was going to pay the deductible for the surgery that may be required.

Well, I finally found out that the cancer had spread. Luckily, it was contained in one area but I would need surgery and cancer treatment afterward. Thanks to my managers, I knew I would have a job afterwards. I still had many questions and concerns. Another HomeBanc "guardian angel" stopped by the office to ask me questions about any HR issues and asked how I was doing. We talked for a long time. Later that week while at a luncheon, she came over to update me on the things she had checked on with HR and slipped a piece of paper under my arm and walked away with a wink and a smile. I opened that paper and was immediately overwhelmed with tears of joy. It was a check from the HomeBanc Associate Emergency Fund to pay for my deductible. While working on a special project with another HomeBanc Associate, she found out about the cancer and so was supportive. She introduced me to someone at the company whose family member had the exact same type of cancer. She formed a short meeting (out of her very, very busy day) with all of us so I could ask whatever questions I might have.

Well, that was a few years ago, but I will NEVER forget what HomeBanc did for me and how they helped me get over the hardest thing I've ever had to face in my life. Pat Flood has employed some of the BEST people as employees at HomeBanc. I am so PROUD to be part of such a GREAT HomeBanc Family! (LaTonya Stains)

Values card

When associates join HomeBanc, they are provided with a HomeBanc Values Card and are asked to carry it in their wallets. By having the Values Card close at hand, they are reminded to provide the best service possible – to each other and to every customer. One side of the card contains the mission statement and the vision.

The vision is: "to become America's most admired company."

The other side of the card outlines the "HomeBanc Values," which are:

- Have integrity . . . do the right thing, always!
- Deliver world-class service . . . serve all customers as they wish to be served.
- Deliver results . . . good enough never is.
- Invest in the best people . . . yourself and others.
- Represent HomeBanc . . . live the credo.
- Give back to the community . . . from the heart.
- Have faith . . . in God we trust.

The dream of home ownership is HomeBanc's focus, and it helps its own associates realize their personal dream of home ownership. Every associate whose family annual income is less than $86,000 receives a $5,000 check when they buy a home. Helping people achieve dreams is one of the core values that characterize HomeBanc.

HomeBanc symbols

HomeBanc has numerous symbols that represent the meaning of its mission, vision, and values. Associates wear the HomeBanc logo on their clothing, encouraging the general public to ask questions about the company on a regular basis. For example, when associates join the company, one of the items in their welcome package is a HomeBanc license plate. This gift is a symbolic gesture to remind associates that the company cares for them not only when they are in the office, but also when they are in the community and with their families. Additionally, each meeting at HomeBanc with three or more associates begins with the group restating the company motto, "The only sustainable advantage in business is world-class service," reminding all participants of the foundation for business decisions. In addition, at each HomeBanc store, where available, a HomeBanc flag is raised as a symbol that HomeBanc believes in the company and its associates as members of its greater community.

The values are uncompromising, and Pat practices what he preaches. For the most part, the entire organization agrees with our values. The company's priorities are in the proper order and help to perpetuate our values and success. Every time I have the privilege of telling others about HomeBanc, they are impressed at how proud I am of our company. (HomeBanc Center, 2003 GPTW Survey, "Comments")

The HomeBanc credo

Every associate participating in HomeBanc Academy's Professional Sales Development Institute (PSD) is required to memorize and recite the credo, "The Spirit of HomeBanc." The credo, which is another representation of values, ends with these words:

"We are motivated by desire to serve each other, each customer, and our community. What comes from our heart – enthusiasm, willingness, sincerity, a caring way – will show our valued customer – *A Better Way Home*."

HomeBanc is built on true core values of integrity and quality and lives the values it possesses. Also, there is opportunity for anyone to showcase their skills regardless of position and be considered for career advancement. HomeBanc focuses their number one priority on associate satisfaction through development and by giving them a voice. (HomeBanc Center, 2003 GPTW Survey, "Comments)

HomeBanc Academy

In 2003 HomeBanc started HomeBanc University. Upon reviewing the components in the University, the company determined that its training programs were actually better aligned with a military academy-style education. HomeBanc's educational courses instill discipline and loyalty similar to a military academy rather than the traditional liberal arts feel of university-style courses. In 2004, therefore, the HomeBanc University officially changed its name to the HomeBanc Academy.

While education has always been a cornerstone of the HomeBanc culture, there is now a formal program to develop world-class associates. From the nine-week, 12-hour-per-day, nationally acclaimed Professional Sales Development class to the customer service training that is the foundation of the company's rallying cry: "The only sustainable advantage in business is world-class service," HomeBanc is committed to furthering associates' job knowledge and enhancing their ability to perform to its consistently high standards.

It is the focus of the company to "grow our own" talent through the HomeBanc Academy. HomeBanc offers its associates opportunities to challenge themselves and develop alongside their teammates. All associates receive regular communications regarding course offerings and schedules within the four Institutes that make up the Academy. HomeBanc's philosophy is to grow both its revenue and its product base organically. Its top producer for many years now spends his days as the Producer Coach, mentoring young producers.

The resources provided make HBMC a better workplace. Computer technology, internet access, and informational reading materials are all provided to help you perform your duties and assist your personal life. (Central Atlanta, 2003 GPTW Survey, "Comments")

Hiring process

HomeBanc begins its cultural indoctrinization in the hiring process – a detailed, extensive testing and interviewing process as evidenced on its website. Every applicant is given a battery of tests that have been proprietarily developed to test values and cognition. Thirty percent of the applicants self-select themselves out by not completing the tests.

HomeBanc receives over 2,000 applications a month for employment. HomeBanc's Chief People Officer has built a sophisticated values testing program under the direction of Dr. Courtney McCashland, who recently joined HomeBanc as an executive vice president. HomeBanc selects employees based on character and compassion.

New associate orientation

Assimilating new associates into HomeBanc's corporate culture is one of the most important elements of its people-first value system. Home-Banc wants each associate to understand what makes HomeBanc such a great place to work and to welcome them to the family. HomeBanc's orientation offers its newest members an opportunity to learn more about the company at which they have chosen to continue their career. Held monthly, the day begins as attendees share breakfast with a HomeBanc executive team member while discovering the company's history, vision, mission, culture and how their new roles will affect the company's future success. Throughout the day, associates interact with leaders from each business group learning "How HomeBanc Makes Money," following the "Life of a Loan" from real estate to investor portfolio, and discovering marketing and community involvement opportunities. Interspersed with the business-related information are teambuilding activities, videos, and stories that exhibit the unique culture and serve to pass corporate folklore on to the next generation. Equally important to the curriculum is the opportunity for current and up and coming leaders to interact together in an informal setting. Orientation is a vital piece of an associate's assimilation. Beyond sharing business needs and plans, orientation is the foundation for HomeBanc's camaraderie. From this shared knowledge of HomeBanc's beginnings, shortcomings, successes and stories, HomeBanc passes on its future.

I was given such a great opportunity right out of college to work for Home-Banc. They have taken me under their wing and provided me with a home away from home and a caring, spiritual influence to help me be the best that I can be. I will be working with them for as long as I can. (East Atlanta, 2003 GPTW Survey, "Comments")

HomeBanc is a great place to work because despite the demanding work-loads, they still believe in their core values. I enjoy working for a company that promotes both professional and personal growth, and facilitates an environment where both are possible. (Central Atlanta, 2003 GPTW Survey, "Comments")

There are a lot of opportunities here for growth. The fact that we have a leader with genuine concerns for his employees as well as our families makes me feel really proud to be a part of the organization. (Central Atlanta, 2003 GPTW Survey, "Comments")

HomeBanc's training program was developed by studying in detail what real estate brokers thought made the best loan officers as well as studying its own best performers. With respect to its best performers, HomeBanc examined two aspects: first, personal traits and secondly, competencies. HomeBanc built into its recruiting process a trait selective process and developed an industry-leading nine-week, 12-hours-a-day skills and competencies training program based on its best practices model.

HomeBanc's detailed approach to training was carried over to hiring. Cultural fit and job fit are the two recruiting goals. Will the person like and fit into the values-based culture while liking the disciplined accountability and production goals? HomeBanc's Dr. Courtney McCashland spent years developing HomeBanc's recruiting tests designed specifically to meet these two fit tests.

HomeBanc tests for seven key behaviors and uses layers of test screens to identify competencies. The goal of HomeBanc's hiring process according to Dr. Ike is to change hiring from a "possibility of success to a high probability of success" both for HomeBanc and for the hiree.

HomeBanc continues to iterate and improve on the science and rigor of its hiring and training processes. It is also turning to the more difficult issue of investigating the ROI on its "people first" philosophy. The whole HomeBanc system is predicated on finding the 3 C's – people chemistry, competency, and cultural fit. HomeBanc is not satisfied with the facts that its loan officers are 2–3 times more productive than industry averages and that its turnover is half the industry average. It knows that better employee retention encourages deeper employee enjoyment and productivity.

HomeBanc is looking for more proof that its system works. Mortgage Originator Magazine, a leading industry magazine – annually names "Top Rookie Loan Officers" This past year, 45 people were chosen nationally. Fourteen of those 45 rookies were HomeBanc employees with the next highest concentration in one company being three employees.

Clearly, HomeBanc is doing something right. But it is striving to become as sophisticated in outcome measurements as it is in hiring and training.

Associates' appreciation celebrations

During 2004, HomeBanc showed its appreciation to its associates with several celebrations, starting with the Fourth of July, which featured "Sweeten Your Fourth of July Barbeque" with HomeBanc Barbecue Sauce. Later in July all associates received a "Weekend Family Fun Package" including Blockbuster gift certificates, candy, popcorn and movie treats. In August, HomeBanc held a "Chill-Out in August" day with a family Baskin Robbins ice cream gift certificate bundled with an afternoon off from work. During the summer HomeBanc also offered

Health Fairs at its store locations promoting work/life balance and wellness.

WOW! cards

WOW! cards are blue and white printed 5×7 cards that HomeBanc associates complete and give to other associates, recognizing them for going the extra mile, exhibiting HomeBanc spirit and attitude, or sacrificially serving one another. The original WOW! cards are kept by receiving associates to display in their offices while a copy is sent via fax or interoffice mail to the Office of People and Culture. On the 5th of each month, a WOW! card winner is randomly selected and awarded a $50 gift certificate. E-mail is sent to all employees announcing the month's winner as well as list of all the nominees. WOW! cards are also a factor in promotion to leadership positions.

Associate recognition

Each month, associates nominate their peers for the Ron Hicks World Class Service Award. Ron was an Associate who was killed in a car accident in 1999. He personified the ultimate in customer service and is remembered by this award. The award has several monthly nominees, a monthly winner, and a runner-up. The winner is someone who has shown world-class customer service to an internal or an external customer. Each month, the winner receives $250 and a world-class service pin embedded with a jewel. The runner-up receives $100 and a world-class service pin. At the Annual Meeting, a roulette-style wheel is brought onto the stage and each of the 12 monthly winners is invited to "take a spin." Participants win a total of $49,000 in increments of $25,000, $10,000, $5,000, and nine $1,000 prizes.

Tenure awards

HomeBanc presents each associate with a glass award based on length of tenure and a gift as indicated in the list below. The associate's proudest moment is when the CEO recognizes him or her during the monthly All Hands Call. The associate's HomeBanc story is recounted: perhaps how he or she came to the company, what positions he or she has held over the years, and what an asset he or she is to the HomeBanc family. The glass awards are as follows:

- *5 Years*: A $500 American Express gift certificate.
- *10 Years*: A $1,000 American Express gift certificate, a framed letter and a book, currently *Built to Last*, with an inscription from the CEO.
- *15 Years*: A $1,500 American Express gift certificate, a framed letter and the book *HomeBanc Choice*, with an inscription from the CEO.
- *20 Years*: Same as above with $2,000 American Express gift certificate.
- *25 Years*: Same as above with $2,500 American Express gift certificate.
- *30 Years*: Same as above with $3,000 American Express gift certificate.

Associate Emergency Fund

At HomeBanc, the core value is to serve others. The HomeBanc Associate Emergency Fund (AEF) is a prime example of how this value is brought to life, beginning at home with HomeBanc's own associates. The sole purpose of the fund is to care for each other in times of need. The fund is financed entirely by donations from HomeBanc associates. Whether the donation is small or large is not an issue; the issue is to serve others. The AEF is available to all associates whether they choose to contribute or not. Examples of AEF distributions include: those burdened by financial problems due to illness, unmanageable medical bills, death in the family and funeral service expenses, as well as personal disaster such as fires, floods and accidents. Often the fund covers the cost of travel to visit an ill family member. In 2004, 94% of associates contributed to the AEF and the fund assisted about fifty associates with a total payout of $150,000 in benefits.

Appreciating uniqueness

In 2005, HomeBanc provided diversity awareness training to all associates promoting the value of people in their role as individuals, associates, and customers in order to maximize business objectives. HomeBanc believes that diversity is about:

- learning new behaviors to develop relationships;
- breaking down barriers to effective communication;
- recognizing our biases and how they impact work decisions;
- appreciating the whole person; and
- including all people.

No layoffs

HomeBanc Mortgage Corporation has never had a layoff. The mortgage industry tends to have volatile production increases and decreases due to swings in interest rates. HomeBanc makes a conscious effort not to over-hire. Instead, hiring is based on planned growth. When production is heavy, all associates boost their efforts to go the extra mile rather than forcing the company to hire additional associates who may be laid off when production returns to normal levels. Associates will often look to the person in the next office for assistance and support in order to maintain this hiring philosophy. All associates know they are part of a family, a family that is interested in helping them build a career for the long run.

The focus on the employee helps to distinguish HomeBanc. While the job pressures at times can be great, the company tries to offset that with various benefits to the employees. In addition, there is a real spirit here that each employee gets caught up in. While some outside may view this as over-the-top, it does help to focus the employees to the mission of serving customers, each other, and the communities we live in. Pat [Flood] has done a great job of defining and delivering the message. In addition, opportunities abound for people wishing to change their career focus. In other companies I've been involved with, you would have rarely been offered opportunities to participate in events outside your designated job. It's all one focus of improving HomeBanc that drives people around here. (HomeBanc Central, 2003 GPTW Survey, "Comments")

Stock options

When the executive team contemplated taking HomeBanc public in 2004, one thing Pat Flood and the team wanted to ensure was that associates were rewarded for their efforts in growing HomeBanc and that they had a stake in HomeBanc's future. Through a stock appreciation rights program, every HomeBanc Associate who had been with the company since March 31 of 2004 received stock in the company as a result of HomeBanc's July 2004 IPO. It is extremely rare for companies going public to grant all of their associates a stake in the company. According to Hewitt Associates, a global human resources consulting firm that assisted HomeBanc in designing their plan, only about 30% of companies going public provide all of their associates with stock grants.

Further, according to Hewitt, only about 9% of companies going public made any kind of stock grant to salaried non-exempt associates and only about 6% of companies going public made any kind of stock grant to hourly associates. With recent changes in the rules and regulations related to stock plans, about 44% of public companies are now restricting all stock grants to upper management associates and executives. HomeBanc, on the other hand, made stock available to all associates whether hourly, upper management, or executives.

Time off with pay

Seven years ago, the CEO recognized that one of the most precious benefits HomeBanc could provide to associates was "time." To that end he established a series of HomeBanc holidays in appreciation for their contributions, augmenting national holidays and personal vacation time. This allowed each associate to take advantage of at least 30 full days off during the calendar year. A committee of HomeBanc associates selects the company's corporate holidays, which change each year to support the needs of the company's business and its associates. The formula for determining the 30 days or holidays each year is the following:
- 6 Federal Holidays
- 6 HomeBanc Holidays
- 2 Personal Days
- 2 Volunteer Days
- 10 Vacation Days (minimum)
- 4 Sick Days

In addition to federal holidays, sick days, and paid vacation, HomeBanc also offers its associates two days off per year with pay to perform volunteer work with their teams. Every associate also receives one personal day off and one additional day off during the month of their birthday.

Volunteer days

HomeBanc offers associates two days of paid time off to participate in volunteer activities. For at least one of the volunteer days, management determines with their team where to focus their contributions. Associates always have the option to select their choice of location to individually volunteer.

Corporate chaplains

Corporate Chaplains of America (CCA) is a confidential service for all associates and immediate family members regardless of the associate's religious or non-religious preference. This organization was founded in 1996 and supports 72 different companies in over 100 locations in nine states. All CCA chaplains have a minimum of 10 years' workplace experience and at least one master's degree. There is no discrimination on the basis of religious affiliation, gender, race, or position in the company. The CCA chaplain visits each HomeBanc office at least once a week, and is available via a custom voicemail data pager system 24 hours a day, 7 days a week, 365 days a year to care for associates or their family needs.

Customer service guarantee

HomeBanc is unique in its industry, offering an unconditional 100% customer service guarantee. HomeBanc is absolutely committed to excellent customer service, and the company backs up that commitment. If, at any time during the home investment process, Home-Banc service does not meet the customer's needs, the company gladly refunds the application fee. The organization is determined to make the customers' home-buying experience outstanding! HomeBanc was initially told by their peers in the mortgage and real estate industries that it would "go broke" by offering this guarantee. Redemptions on the program today are less than 1%, customer satisfaction surveys are good and revenues are at record levels. Associates believe in exceeding the customers' expectations.

Community affairs

The HomeBanc Foundation was established in 2001 as a 501(c)(3) non-profit corporation with two community goals:
• To support the American dream of home ownership for those who might not reach it on their own; and
• To provide support to organizations funding cancer research and prevention programs.

HomeBanc encourages all associates to financially support its two designated charities – Habitat for Humanity and the American Cancer Society – and promises to match all eligible charitable contributions at a 1:1 ratio up to $100 per associate. In 2000 HomeBanc committed to build 100 homes in partnership with Habitat for Humanity. HomeBanc has also motivated other groups within the communities with whom they do business to participate in building homes. These groups include real estate partners and homebuilders. The company has also shared its community focus with college athletes, having partnered with football teams from the University of Georgia, Georgia Institute of Technology, University of Miami, University of South Florida and Florida Atlantic University to build Habitat homes.

The HomeBanc Foundation also supports the American Cancer Society through corporate donations and fundraising events. With dedicated associates and business partners, in 2000 HomeBanc pledged to raise $1 million for the American Cancer Society by 2010. One of the more popular fundraisers is the art and wine auction at the home of the CEO.

The positive attitudes of every associate make it a joy to work here! The fact that "management" really cares about each and every associate, that Home-Banc is built on strong ethics and values, that we give to the community in so many ways (Habitat, ACS, Corporate Volunteer Days, Fundraisers) – all of these things make HomeBanc such a good company, built on a solid and logical business plan. (HomeBanc Center, 2003 GPTW Survey, "Comments")

HomeBanc celebrates together

The HomeBanc Associate Satisfaction Survey indicates that 91% of its associates believe it is a great place to work. One reason is because they feel HomeBanc is a family, and they truly enjoy the company of their fellow associates. HomeBanc makes special efforts to incorporate opportunities for fun into the working environment.

Every department schedules outings for its associates. The entire department goes to an amusement park, ball game, restaurant, movie, or out to lunch. Birthdays are celebrated with cakes and celebratory cards. Weddings and baby showers are frequently held in the office. HomeBanc picks up the tab for these celebrations.

The managers often host parties, such as during the holidays, at their homes, when associates are encouraged to bring along their families. The HomeBanc Executive Team also personally serves a holiday lunch to every associate in the company. These luncheons are scheduled in each store location during December. The Executive Team travels throughout the Southeast in order to ensure everyone gets to participate in these celebrations.

I came to work at HomeBanc as an experienced Loan Officer in November of 2002. I started in a new HomeBanc office, having worked for seven other mortgage companies in Charlotte in the last 32 years. I came here expecting that the "sales pitch" that I was given by the manager to hire me would be about 50% truth, as it has always been in the past. HomeBanc was professing to be a "faith-based company" and many other proclamations [were made] about performance in the Charlotte market and how HomeBanc was a unique and different sort of Mortgage Company.

Little did I dream that everything that the HomeBanc Regional Manager told me about our wonderful company would all come true and more. I wake up smiling to come to work each day. I love the people in my office and the people I converse with in other markets. Each and every "promise" has been fulfilled 15 months later. We are indeed, different. We do put customers first and employees first. We do deliver what we promise and we do it with each and every person's best interest in mind. We do deliver better than "world-class service" and we offer our marketplace programs they cannot get elsewhere. I am proud to be a part of the HomeBanc legacy and family. I am so proud to tell people where I work and why they [should] want to come to work at HomeBanc. (Susan Webber, HomeBanc Associate)

All Hands Call

HomeBanc's values and culture are taught through constant repetition and emphasis by senior management. HomeBanc structures several communication activities with associates into its management responsibilities. For examples, once a month, all associates gather in designated meeting areas for a one-hour televised broadcast from the CEO covering all aspects of the company. The broadcast starts with national and industry-specific economic updates, followed by a discussion of strategic corporate initiatives and goals. Next, company items such as new benefits, new hiring programs, and new educational opportunities are discussed. Recognition is given to the associates who are celebrating service anniversaries. The last portion of each broadcast focuses on recognizing the nominees, runners-up and winner of the Ron Hicks World Class Service Award, noted above.

CEO hotline and open-door policy

The CEO also has a telephone "hotline" and a "hotmail" e-mail address where associates can send in questions prior to the All Hands Call or where they can express their views afterwards regarding any issue raised during the broadcast. Associates are also encouraged to use the hotline or send e-mails to the CEO to address anything that is concerning them at any time. Another avenue of communication is the managerial open-door policy, whereby associates can talk in person with any manager – all the way up to the CEO – concerning any company issue or personal concern.

CEO roundtable

Annually, the entire executive team visits each region. The CEO begins the roundtable meeting by reviewing the state of the business. Then he opens the discussion, during which associates are encouraged to bring up challenges they are facing or express their ideas regarding ways the work environment and company productivity might be improved. The appropriate executive responds immediately to each question or suggestion. If an issue is complicated or requires research, an answer is provided as quickly as possible after the meeting. Regardless, all issues are addressed. All associates located in the region are invited to the meeting and to share a meal, served by the executives.

CEO forum

CEO forums are two-day events conducted for lower-level associates in leadership and supervisory positions. The entire Executive Team attends and shares the company's vision, key initiatives, goals, and tactical plans in detail with the leadership. Each presentation is open for questions and answers. This provides for consistency of information throughout the company as leaders return to their locations and share the messages from the Forum. Approximately 150–175 HomeBanc leaders attend each forum, conducted semi-annually. They spend two entire days off-site with lodging and all meals provided.

TeamWorks

TeamWorks is HomeBanc's name for its practice of encouraging regular discussions between associates and their managers. One significant communication benefit is the practice of twice-a-year performance appraisals. These are a necessary tool to help both the associate and HomeBanc achieve desired results.

In this process, the associate initiates a two-way discussion providing input regarding his/her performance while the manager provides input to help the associate meet his/her objectives. The purpose of Team-Works discussions is to achieve results through shared goals and to improve individual skills, maximizing potential and enhancing contributions to the business.

Appraisals include objectives set for the associate and a review of performance in regard to those objectives. A review of competencies and behaviors is also included. Areas for associate development are cited and the associate is encouraged to comment on the review and to give his/her feedback regarding the information outlined and the suggested actions to be taken. Annually, the associate completes a self-assessment document, used by the manager in preparing the year-end review that results in compensation action. Associates are provided feedback to help them reach Most Valuable Performer (MVP) status. A MVP action plan is developed by the associate and leader, which is incorporated into the next review process. HomeBanc believes that each associate has the potential to achieve MVP status.

Annual meeting

At the beginning of each year, HomeBanc hosts an annual meeting – the ultimate information-sharing experience for all team members. As the HomeBanc family is not just its associates but includes their family members, HomeBanc urges its associates to bring their family members to the event. HomeBanc provides free transportation and lodging for all non-Georgia-based associates and a guest. Over a five-hour period, attendees hear the CEO present his state-of-the-company address, they watch live video presentations celebrating associate activities throughout the previous year, and they enjoy live entertainment. The day culminates with the largest awards ceremony of the year. Following the meeting, the company hosts a cocktail reception for all attendees, so they can spend some social time with each other and the executive team. In 2005 the meeting included more than 1,700 associates, their family and friends at the Atlanta Civic Center in downtown Atlanta, Georgia.

Office of People and Culture

HomeBanc's commitment to its people is evidenced by the fact that its head HR person (1) reports directly to the CEO, (2) is an Executive Vice President and equal member of senior management, and (3) heads the Office of People and Culture. HomeBanc's emphasis on people differs from that of many companies but it is illustrated by whom Pat Flood hired to head the OPC.

Pat retained a nationally recognized executive search firm, Hendrick and Struggles, to find his HR head. To assist him, he formed an advisory committee of close and valued confidants from inside and outside the company. HomeBanc took out full-page ads in newspapers like such as *USA Today*, advertising the search. Pat knew down deep he was looking for someone who cared about people as people, not just as assets or resources or as a means to an end. He sought someone who would help guard the values and protect the company from veering from its calling as it grew.

The person selected after a thorough search process was a non-corporate candidate – a minister who had built two churches in Atlanta. When you meet Dr. Ike Reighard, you are struck by a couple of things. First, he is not very corporate, and second, he has the aura, looks, and speech of a TV evangelist.

Dr. Ike is a smart, sophisticated, and deeply committed person who has put in place sophisticated hiring, training, and measurement processes, which implement and support HomeBanc's culture. Dr. Ike has an insatiable appetite for learning, a passionate commitment to making

HomeBanc "America's Most Admired Company," and a humility that describes his main job as "just to love and care for our people" as he did for the members of his church.

Dr. Ike realizes that within HomeBanc there are people from a wide spectrum of theological beliefs as well as those who hold none. He cares less about the specific religious beliefs of his associates, but more about their values and how they treat people – their actions.

Upon joining HomeBanc as a new employee, Dr. Ike said, "I was scared about moving to the corporate world. I never had worked for business, and I was over 50 years old. But I saw this as an opportunity to help Pat do something special and different in the business world to treat people (employees) as important in and of themselves, not as a fungible commodity to be used and discarded."

Dr. Ike brought a desire to make the HomeBanc not only a caring place but also a corporate leader in the areas of hiring, measuring, and training employees. He would like to make it possible for associates to take college courses at HomeBanc offices and to be able to prove to Wall Street that the cost of all of HomeBanc people programs are a good investment.

Summary

HomeBanc is different. It is unusual. Many companies espouse values and have people-first policies. Many companies do some of the people-centered activities that HomeBanc pursues. But what differentiates HomeBanc is the drive of its CEO to make HomeBanc "America's Most Admired Company," and its focus, discipline, and determination to put into practice values-centered leadership. HomeBanc's senior leadership acts on a daily basis in a manner that operationalizes its mission and core values.

Pat Flood stated to me, "My people learn about our values by watching what I do. Yes, I make mistakes. When I do, I acknowledge them openly, apologize and fix them."

HomeBanc is a corporation with over 1,300 associates and it is an example of how work can be meaningful for employees. Pat Flood is an example of a grounded successful CEO who has chosen servant leadership as his leadership model and as his reason to stay engaged in the business world.

6 Leadership lessons from Sarah: values-based leadership as everyday practice

MONICA WORLINE AND
SARAH BOIK

I arrive at a high-rise office building, one of only a few in this medium size city's downtown, at a few minutes past 8:00 in the morning. As an organizational psychologist who is studying compassion in the workplace, I have been granted permission to study a group of people who perform billing and account receivable services for the health system that owns the building; a group that I have been told displays extraordinary values and also gets results.[1] Armed with a notebook and a tape recorder, I take the elevator to the 9th floor and knock on the door marked Physician Billing. Looking through the glass door that is accessible only to those with a magnetic cardkey, I see a woman look around a cubicle wall and get up to let me in. I ask for Sarah, and she looks at me a bit quizzically as she leads me down an aisle between sets of cubicles toward the only office that has a door in this large open room full of cubicles. Sarah isn't in her office, so I am kindly deposited in the kitchen for a cup of coffee.

My first impression of the space is that I've walked into a garden rather than a billing unit. Almost every cubicle wall is decorated with silk or dried flowers of some kind, and summer is in full bloom in the paper decorations, silk flowers, and other items that spruce up the office. In the tidy kitchen, each drawer has a printed label describing its contents: "creamer, stirrers, tea" are above "coffee filters," and "hot spiced cider and hot cocoa." I think to myself that the small, clean space seems to be ready to host a party; it is fully stocked with knives, forks, drinks, cleaning supplies, and almost anything you'd expect to find in

[1] We wish to thank Foote Hospital for their support of this chapter. Extra special thanks also go to the members of the Physician Billing Unit at Foote Hospital for their participation in this research and their ongoing support. And finally, this work would not have begun nor been possible without the support and participation of the CompassionLab – Jane Dutton, Jacoba Lilius, Jason Kanov, Peter Frost, and Sally Maitlis – Monica's co-authors and collaborators in the full-scale study of the billing department.

a kitchen that serves a big group, including a refrigerator packed full of food. I meet Sarah as I'm stirring my coffee, and she greets me with a friendly conversation. She is one of the only managers I know who seems truly comfortable having a research team barge into her world. Explaining how the day will work, she leads me to a large meeting room on one end of the office. This meeting room is the site of the unit's "morning meeting," which happens sometime around 8:30 each morning.

Walking into the meeting room, I notice several tables and chairs spread about, and I'm greeted with a muffled "hello" from a slight woman who is sitting behind the largest pile of envelopes I've ever seen. I can't see her face behind the pile, but I see her hand reach up to grab an envelope and then I hear her neatly slice it open with a letter opener. She sets it aside in one of several stacks, and then reaches for another. I set up camp in a chair off to the side of the room in my role as observer. Sitting there, I am reminded of the scene in the movie *A Miracle on 34th Street* in which the post office delivers sacks and sacks of mail to the courtroom where Santa Claus is on trial, swamping the judge's podium with envelopes. I watch in wonder as Darlene, the woman behind the pile of envelopes, keeps at her work. A few people begin to trickle into the room, notice the huge pile of envelopes, and turn around to go back to their desks. After a few seconds they are back, letter openers in hand. In minutes, the room has begun to fill with people and someone shouts toward Darlene, "Do you have any more letter openers?" Darlene is new to the group, and therefore shy about the offers of help, demurring at first. But after some ribbing about the size of the pile of mail, she is encouraged to walk over to a supply cabinet at the side of the room and take out a whole box of letter openers. She passes them around, along with handfuls of envelopes, and in a few seconds the air is full of the sound of razor blades on paper. Someone calls out, "I didn't get one!" and another person walks to the supply cabinet, getting out all the letter openers she can find.

As Sarah calls the meeting to order, the whiz of razor blades is going strong. Sarah asks the group, "Who's not here today?" and people start to shout out names. They go through the list one by one, naming each person and why she is out of the office. There are a few plans for compensating for the missing hands, and then other topics of business arise. The meeting lasts about 20 minutes, features a lot of laughter, some good-natured teasing, and several questions about invoices dated after a certain point in time. At the end of the meeting, not only are the questions answered and everyone's whereabouts accounted for, but all of the envelopes from the mountain of mail have been opened and stacked in neat piles around the room. Darlene, who is a member of the "support" team in the unit, is responsible for opening the mail each day and sorting it into different processing categories. She collects the extra letter openers as people go back to their desks, her weighty task made suddenly lighter by the spontaneous coordination of so many hands.

In the mid-1990s, the physician billing unit at Foote Health System was almost non-existent, with a manager and one or two people doing billing for physicians who worked in different kinds of contractual relationships at satellite clinics. At its lowest point, it took the billing unit over 180 days to collect a dollar of accounts receivable ("Days in AR"), the chief performance measure for the unit. That was a number way too high to satisfy the growing demand for stricter financial operations in a tightening healthcare marketplace. Sarah was brought on board in part to help bring that number down, and has managed the unit since 1998. Initially her staff consisted of five billers, and she faced many daunting tasks. How to reduce the number of days in AR when Medicaid forms had to be hand-typed (due to state regulations), and any error in the duplicate copy forms required starting the entire form over again? How to reduce days in AR when the health system had decided to add more physicians to the unit's client list, and the group needed to grow fast to keep up with rising demand for billing services from new clinics? How to reduce days in AR when the turnover in employment across the health system was approaching 25% and she was likely to lose one or two of her five employees each year? How to reduce days in AR when errors in the charge entry system were increasing dramatically, at the same time that insurers were becoming more and more strict and specific about documentation for reimbursement? How to reduce days in AR when many in the industry were increasing rather than decreasing the time it took to collect money from a plethora of new insurance providers in a turbulent industry? It looked, at least to an outsider, like an almost impossible task.

When she arrived on the scene, the first thing Sarah did was to ask the billers what they needed to do their jobs better. "Post-it Notes," they answered. Expecting a much more difficult answer, a puzzled Sarah ordered a big batch of Post-it Notes from the local office supply store. "You would have thought it was Christmas when that office supply shipment arrived," she says of the billers' reactions. "They were running around whooping and hollering that they could use all the Post-it Notes they needed!" It turns out, the previous managers would not allow billers to order office supplies, and Post-it Notes were a rationed luxury. Hence Sarah tells new managers that the most important task of a leader is to attain the training and the tools that people need to do the work. Who would have imagined Post-it Notes would be such a dramatic change? "What a motivational boost, simply from providing a tool that was readily available and relatively low-cost!" Sarah comments. She would not have known about the Post-it Notes without asking – a metaphor for her overall leadership style. She assumes that the people who do the jobs are the best ones to tell her what they need in order to do their jobs better, from the tools and training that they need to the people they want and need to work with.

Today, the Physician Billing Unit averages just less than 60 days to collect a dollar of accounts receivable, beating the industry standard. They have moved from hand-typed and paper-based forms to almost entirely electronic claim processing. They have grown almost 10 times their initial size, with 41 members in the unit today. They have greatly expanded their client list, providing billing services for more clinics than ever, while they have reduced their turnover to be the lowest in the entire health system. Adequate office supplies are still celebrated in the billing department, though without quite so much fanfare – a symbol of the changes that have been wrought by a leader who listens.

How leadership based in the values of humanity, identity, engagement, participation, life, meaning, and play contributed to change in the billing department is the subject of this chapter. Sarah's role in the accomplishment of such massive growth, fundamental change, and dramatic increases in productivity, efficiency, employee satisfaction, and performance is the story we want to tell here. It's a story of leadership of a different kind, and it has everything to do with the everyday things of work, like Post-it Notes or that mountain of envelopes.

Introducing Sarah: leadership and practices of identity

Our collaboration in this chapter about Sarah's leadership lessons builds on the research that we started that day when Monica arrived in her unit. This chapter involves collaboration between Monica and Sarah that looks at that research in a new way, focused explicitly on

Sarah's role in creating daily practices that carry her leadership. Similar to what Bartunek and Louis (1996) entitle "insider-outsider" research, this chapter is based on collaborative conversations between Sarah and Monica in order to craft an articulation of Sarah's key leadership practices. By practices, we mean everyday ways of doing or accomplishing things in the unit (Orlikowski, 2002).

Sarah's practices are distilled into the quotes that begin each section of the chapter, quotes that come directly from Sarah. Following each quote, Monica articulates how the quote represents work practices in the billing unit and how those practices might look to the eyes of a scholar. Working together through multiple conversations and interviews, Sarah and Monica have created this representation of Sarah's practices in the billing department and have related the practices to the overall performance of the unit. Hence what began as a short-term collaboration has lasted over time and grown into a two-way conversation that helps us learn from each other (Bartunek and Louis, 1996). This partnership is somewhat unusual for academic writing, but we find that it is extremely helpful in our aim to bring what we have learned from one another to light.

You cannot teach common sense or values and ethics. They are instilled in a person from birth. Recognize those in a person and realize that is who they are.

Sarah says, "I always wanted to be a nurse when I was growing up. I thought it would be a noble occupation." Unlike her dreams of nursing, however, the reality of nursing school was disappointing. Just months away from finishing her degree, Sarah was involved in the care of a terminally ill cancer patient who was experiencing excruciating pain. The nursing staff had tried for days to make the patient comfortable, and Sarah's shift was the first time the patient had been able to rest. "At that point," Sarah describes, "I had a negative interaction with a 3rd year resident regarding this special patient's care and the decisions he was making. I did not follow his orders, as they would have awakened the patient who had just achieved some much-needed rest. He berated me as a lowly nurse and reported me to nursing administration. At that time it was suggested to me that perhaps I really did not want to be a nurse."

"I decided to leave nursing school that day. As a career move, I am not sorry. I vowed from that day forward that I would always try to remember that there are two sides to every situation; to look at them open mindedly, and work together for solutions. I also vowed never to treat a fellow employee as that resident treated me. He embarrassed me in front of my peers, and looked as though he was actually enjoying doing it."

Sarah received a call the next day from a doctor who was opening a private practice, and she accepted his offer to set up and run his office. Says Sarah, "That is where my fun began! I have been to many practices and hospitals since that time, and have learned many things from my superiors and my teams. One especially wise manager told me that if there was ever a time, as a manager or supervisor, that someone was not upset at me, I was not doing a good job. In her view, and now in mine, someone should always be upset about a decision or a change that has been made. If they are not, then I am not managing the team. I am not trying to be popular. She always emphasized that managing is not a popularity contest."

Sarah's experience in nursing school and her subsequent successes have shown her that a leader's work is to recognize values, ethics, and common sense in herself and in others. Sarah uses her own values and sense of the world to relate to her employees and make the decisions a leader must make. Despite her knowledge that many managerial decisions will not be popular, Sarah doesn't lose sight of empathy for her employees and their experiences. She says, "I have been where many of these billers are. I have struggled, cried, and felt that no one cared how hard it is to do it all. In remembering all of this, I feel I am able to better understand why they do what they do, why they feel what they feel, and why they need what they need on a daily basis." Sarah's practices of identity recognize that while skills can be developed or billing techniques learned, it is the deep sense of whom someone is at their essence that a leader must come to understand if she wants to engage an employee in fully supporting the organization's goals.

Conquering the envelope mountain: leadership and practices of engagement

> Don't let the slackers slack. Work with them from the second you notice them slacking. Motivate them to improve or encourage them to move on.

Within the story about the envelopes that opens this chapter, one striking detail is that no one, including the leader, asked anyone else to help open that mountain of mail. In fact, the first volunteers simply noticed the extent of Darlene's work and went wordlessly back to their desks to get their letter openers. Despite the fact that it wasn't technically their job, and that opening this much mail wasn't a daily event or a routine happening – the amount of mail was vastly larger than usual – people knew exactly how to help. While the envelope mountain isn't routine, what is routine practice is the expectation of engagement in the work of the unit, whatever that work may be.

One of Sarah's rules, in keeping with her quote above, is that no one in her unit may use the phrase, "that's not my job." For a leader who wants to create practices of engagement, everything is everyone's job when it comes to getting the critical work done. As the leader, Sarah isn't exempt from this practice; rather, she embodies and models it for others. For example, during the daily morning meeting when someone else has the floor, Sarah answers the phones. If someone doesn't understand a task, she will come and sit at the employee's desk to help her learn. Sarah's language of engagement and her model of engaged work is an important source of others' learning about the high performance norms in the unit.

The daily meeting, with its emphasis on accounting for where help might be needed because of absences or particularly heavy workloads, is another practice that builds engagement. In many manufacturing industries, a daily meeting is used to keep the plant running smoothly, but this level of daily communication is seldom employed in knowledge work or administration. Sitting together in the morning and building positive emotion, energy, and shared tasks for the day helps build employees' focus on the work of the whole unit. Shared knowledge helps limit mistakes and keep people engaged in learning. And knowing who may need help distributes the work of the unit across the formal team structures. The practice of daily meeting and discussion of tasks is another crucial way in which Sarah builds engagement.

Sarah's transparency in terms of performance requirements is another leadership practice that reinforces engagement. Once a month, Sarah shares information with the group that shows the unit's overall productivity numbers and their clinic-by-clinic performance. This monthly meeting to discuss the unit's performance and the breakdown of each team's performance creates performance pressure for all members. In addition, though, it empowers the billers to monitor their own work efficiency, and it shows them which groups are falling behind.

When a group's days in AR are rising, the other groups ask how they can help and Sarah supports their collaboration. Sarah's straightforward and transparent approach to performance data is a leadership practice that helps reinforce her expectations of high performance and high engagement in the unit's work.

Perhaps most important, however, is a deeply developed practice of stepping in when someone is *not* participating in the norms of engagement. Sarah's advice to other leaders about this leadership practice is straightforward: "Don't let the slackers slack. Work with them from the second you notice them slacking. Motivate them to improve or encourage them to move on." Sarah's leadership practices may look "nice" on the surface, but in her unit there is an unmistakable insistence on engagement. Sarah is clear that there is no shame in leaving her unit; the only shame comes when someone isn't engaged and refuses to face it. "If the work isn't for you," Sarah emphasizes, "go find work that fits your passion or interests." Sarah's first-hand knowledge of the importance of deep engagement comes from her experience of nursing school, and reinforces her practice of engaging people in the unit's performance, rewarding that engagement, and challenging those who aren't engaged.

Conquering the envelope mountain is not attributable to the heroic deeds of a leader. In this view of leadership, daily practices of engagement, supported and encouraged by the leader, set the scene for hard work and high performance. Conquering the envelope mountain is a result of daily practices of engagement that put truly put to work values such as equality, responsibility, diligence, and helping to make another person's burden lighter.

Facing the hiring squad: leadership and practices of participation

> Hiring the right person is so very important. Hire the person and the potential you recognize in that interview. If your track record of hiring the best is not stellar, then get people who are good at that to team interview with you.

"The thing that strikes me the most," remarks Kathy, a member of the billing department, "is that *we* decide who we want to hire. There aren't so many bosses out there who would let us do that. I think that is a big part of why we function so well as a group." If you ask members of Sarah's unit about selecting people who fit in the department, you will hear Kathy's comment repeated again and again. Participation in the selection of potential members, socializing new members, and creating a work environment where people want to stay are viewed within this unit as collective responsibilities. Sarah established a group interview procedure from the beginning of her tenure as the manager of the unit, convinced that her staff knows best who will fit within their work environment.

Several committees are involved in interviewing applicants for new positions after they are initially screened and interviewed by Sarah. The members of the unit take their responsibility very seriously, and have designed a set of questions that range from inquiries about qualifications and training to behavioral questions about how someone might handle a difficult issue, to questions designed to assess fit with the rest of the group. After the group interviews, the entire unit has an extensive discussion about the candidates, their qualifications, and their fit within the work environment. Once the group decides upon a preference about who to hire, the final decision to offer the job rests with Sarah. Of the more than 50 hiring decisions made in the unit since this hiring system was put into practice, Sarah has never overridden the decision of the group. "They are the ones who have to work together and take care of this person," Sarah says. "What right do I have to decide for them who they want as part of their team?" Consensus isn't always easy to reach, and not everyone is happy with every decision, but the unit has confidence in their opportunity to participate in such an enormous decision. Of course, not every decision works for the best. When that is the case, the practices of participation are such that the entire group knows that it bears some responsibility, and thus there is little opportunity for complaining or blaming.

In addition to participating in hiring decisions, the entire group participates in socialization, training, and retention activities as well. When a new member is hired, he or she is usually hired into what the billing department refers to as the "support" pod (teams are called "pods" in the billing department). The support pod is a group that is responsible for the administrative activities that all the billing pods need, such as copying, filing, mailing, and storage. New members join the support pod so that they are exposed to the basic operations of the entire unit; a practice that builds the ability to participate in the work of the entire unit. Starting off in the support pod also ensures that a level of equality remains in the group, as members all come to understand the importance of the work that happens in support.

When a job opening comes about in a billing pod, it is the unit's tradition that someone from the support pod "moves up" to a billing position. This practice of participation builds a sense of equality and mobility in the unit, creating the possibility for participation to yield a sense of accomplishment. The actual job classifications within the organizational system for those in support and those in billing positions are no different from one another, so it is solely the practices that have been built around participation in the unit that foster this sense of accomplishment. Support team and billing team members receive the same wages and benefits. The impression of mobility arises from the practice of hiring people into a pod that supports all the other teams and then allowing a newcomer to grow into a different position within the unit.

Each pod has a designated leader. The actual job of "pod leader" has been recognized by the overall health system as a position that comes with a promotion, a pay raise, and a change in job classification. The position of pod leader was invented by the billing unit, whose members had to lobby HR and convince the organization to institutionalize the new job. Sarah led her members' participation in this organizational change. In essence, Sarah's leadership practices that foster participation in running the unit have created changes that affect the entire organization. In this case, in a type of work where there is typically thought to be little room for advancement, Sarah and her employees have created a system of hiring, training, and retention that allows for three levels of growth and development. Promotion to each of these levels comes with new challenges, responsibilities, and purposes, creating an atmosphere of active participation for those who work in the unit. While sociologists have often written of workplaces such as this as "pink-collar ghettos" (Howe, 1977), leadership practices of fostering participation in the billing department have changed the character of the workplace. Today's billing department is an incubator for people's potential and self-development, capitalizing on the sense of accomplishment that comes with active participation in order to build a thriving workplace community.

Hoarding freesia body lotion: leadership and practices of humanity

> Every employee who works with you is the
> same as you...human. There may be different levels
> of hierarchy within your corporation, but when all
> the layers are peeled back, we are all the same. So treat
> every one of the employees you work with as you expect
> to be treated. This is vital to gain respect and loyalty.

An important set of practices in the billing department involves celebrating. For instance, each month the billing department celebrates
the birthdays of members who were born that month. Birthday parties
are planned, coordinated, and run by different pods within the unit. It
just so happened that Monica was there for an August birthday party.
On the day of the party, the morning meeting started off with a gift
to Marge, the only member of the unit at that time with an August
birthday. Sarah has a practice of presenting each member of the group
with a small gift, separately from the departmental gifts that others
coordinate. As it happens, Marge loved a particular brand of freesia-
scented body lotion, which had been discontinued. When she opened
the gift bag from Sarah, she found a whole complement of the discontinued freesia products. The room erupted in laughter and shouts of
surprise. "How did you get this?" Marge demanded of Sarah, who just
looked back at her with a twinkle in her eye. "You're welcome," she
replied.

How did Sarah know that Marge loved freesia body lotion, and why
does it matter? Hoarding the freesia lotion is a light-hearted example of a deeply thoughtful practice in which Sarah works to build
an authentic and caring individual relationship with each member of
her group. She interacts with each person in ways that help them feel
known, and in so doing, she helps others to build work relationships
with the same authenticity and care. Her practice of knowing everyone is a central part of Sarah's ability to build practices in the unit
that emphasize humanity. She says, "Every employee who works with
you is the same as you...human." She gets to know her employees
as people, and in so doing she encourages others to get to know their
co-workers as human beings as well. "There may be different levels
of hierarchy in a corporation," she says, "but when all the layers are

peeled back, we are all the same. So treat everyone as you expect to be treated."

Later that day, an air of secrecy surrounds the meeting room, where the door is closed and no one but the pod in charge of the party is allowed to enter. Sarah isn't in the office for the afternoon, but the birthday party goes on. At just a few minutes after 2:00, Marge's pod lines up outside the closed meeting room door, ready for the party to start. Others begin to join the line, and the intensity grows to find out what is happening behind the closed door. When it is thrown open a few minutes later, we walk in to the strains of "Happy Birthday," and discover tables covered with white tablecloths and cutout ice cream cones in a variety of bright colors. The ice cream cone theme is also reflected in decorations on the walls and hanging from the ceiling. "Oh, yeah," someone comments within earshot of me, "Marge loves ice cream. She has such a sweet tooth!" A blender fires up, and someone makes milkshakes, while others grab cake and ice cream. For about 20 minutes, people chat animatedly and enjoy their ice cream. After that, a pressure to return to work and finish the day's business creeps into the conversations, and soon people are picking up their places and wishing Marge happy birthday so that they can return to their desks.

Watching as an outsider, it seems that the celebration is an integrated part of how the members of the unit see their work. Celebrating is just as important as working; and likewise finishing the day's work isn't lost in celebrating. By 3:00 p.m., the only way you'd know there had been a party here are the ice cream cones that remain on the walls of the meeting room and the ribbons that Marge still wears in her hair. Sarah fosters relationships that recognize the fallibility and humanity of people, as well as their potential for greatness and success. As a consequence, the values of empathy, authenticity, respect, and loyalty are regularly practiced among members of the billing department, without any one person who must enforce them. That the birthday party continues without Sarah is an important tribute to the power of her leadership practices. When Sarah is away, the work of the unit doesn't suffer, nor does the quality of attention to the humanity of others. It is this regular leadership practice of attention to others' likes and dislikes, needs and dreams, desires and pitfalls that becomes the leading force in the unit for respectful interaction, humanity, and loyalty to one another and to the work that must be done.

Finding twenty dollars in your desk: leadership and practices of life

> Understand that there are a lot of influences on your
> employees' lives outside of work that impact their
> ability to perform each and every day. Then be
> understanding. They will have off days. It's OK once in
> a while.

In an interview with a long-time member of the billing department,
I hear a phrase that I've heard several times already in my few days
of research here: "This is work; that is life. Work shouldn't get in
the way of life." Unstated in that phrase, but just as present in the
members' minds, is the idea that neither should life get too much in
the way of work. There is an active agreement in place within the
billing department about the semi-permeable boundary between life
and work, due primarily to Sarah's leadership practices. Sarah is active
in promoting the boundary between life and work, as she emphasizes
regularly, "Work is like a lab coat. You should be able to take it off
and hang it up at the end of the day, then you can put it back on when
you get here tomorrow."

But Sarah's leadership practices also recognize the permeable quality
of the boundary between life and work. Over half of Sarah's employees
are single mothers who are struggling to make ends meet. All of her
employees are engaged in relatively low wage work. Many of them have
family members who are ill or elderly relatives who require their care.
Some of them experience domestic violence. Some of them have sick
or disabled children, who demand even more attention and resources.
Life, for all the talk of boundaries, is very present in this workplace.

Sarah makes sure to discuss things happening outside the department
if they are events that will affect the group. In addition, the unit raises
money to donate to disaster relief and to local charity organizations,
keeping in touch with life outside of their immediate workplace. Sarah
leads the way in coordinating care packages for members of the unit
who are ill or who are taking care of ill family members, and she
encourages others to do this as well. They understand, though, largely
through Sarah's insistence on work engagement and high performance,
that all of this life comes into the unit only as long as their work is done
as well.

Some of the women in the billing department go through divorces or other life episodes that rob them of almost everything, and they rebuild their lives with the help and support of those at work. Sarah recognizes that there is almost no way that life circumstances such as these can fail to impact members' work habits or work quality. When she knows someone is struggling, she will often bring to work what she calls "extras" to give away; she will make two potato salads instead of one, or buy two flats of soda instead of one, and bring the extra to work. Her practice of giving to those who are having trouble managing the work-life interface is done in such a way that it singles no one out. And yet, members notice Sarah's way of embodying generosity, and they adopt it and enact it as a practice as well.

One member of the unit, Terri, told the story of a painful and contentious divorce, in which her ex-husband cut her off from everything in her home, including even clothing and food. Terri had to move into a co-worker's house temporarily, having little cash on hand and no way to go home. Terri rarely talked about all of this with her co-workers, but she became increasingly tense. She described one particular day, when she was distracted from her work because she knew that she had enough gasoline in her car to take her home from work at the end of the day, but not enough to get back to work the next day. She didn't know what to do; she didn't even have enough cash to eat, much less fill the tank. Others in her work team noticed her strain on that day and, having a general sense of what was happening in her life, Terri's co-workers guessed that she needed help. When Terri went outside for her 15-minute afternoon break almost in tears, her team rallied. One teammate, Juanita, used her 15-minute break to walk to a grocery store and bring back a sack with milk and bread and a few other things in it. Juanita set the bag full of groceries in the kitchen and put Terri's name on it. Another team member left Terri a note to check the kitchen before she went home. When she came back from break and opened her desk drawer, a twenty-dollar bill caught her eye. She doesn't know, to this day, who put the twenty dollars in her desk. What she does know, though, is that her co-workers were attuned to her as a person, outside work as well as inside, and that when she was at her breaking point, her co-workers' generosity saved her.

Terri is back on her feet now, and she's continually on the lookout for others who are having a hard time. Small gifts are common in the billing department, as are practices such as bringing in extra food or vegetables from a garden or other things that might be useful. Building from the example of Sarah's leadership practices that accommodate the interface between life and work, members of the billing department are eager to repay others at work for their generosity. Work is work, and life is life in the billing department, and work isn't supposed to impinge on life. But life can't always stay outside of the workplace. "Be understanding," Sarah reminds us. "It's okay once in a while." The kind of leadership that involves being attuned to others and recognizing the forces on employee's lives outside of work is a type of leadership that might well be invisible to outsiders, but is highly visible to the unit's members. Practices of attunement to others' life circumstances and responding to another's pain have become an important way in which Sarah and the members of her staff are able to maintain their unit's high performance amid turbulent life events.

Two computer systems to one and back again: leadership and practices of meaning

> Teach, teach and then teach some more.

"We were working very hard to move from two different billing systems to one integrated electronic system," Sarah explains to me on a visit back to the billing department after my initial observation period. "And we finally did it!" Members of the unit were very happy to have an integrated system that cut down on duplication, alternate coding, and errors. In the same week that the billing department was celebrating their move to one system, however, Sarah learned from her manager that a pressing need was going to make it necessary to introduce another system of electronic billing into the unit. After all the work to integrate their electronic systems, the group would be going from two computer systems to one and then back again, with all of the attendant headaches of two different systems. "I went into our morning meeting that week," Sarah explains, "and I told the group about all the ways that this new system would make life easier and better for our patients." Someone asked if it meant that they would be returning to two different systems, and someone else asked a few questions about how it would work, but no complaints came from the group. "Don't get me wrong," Sarah says of the change, "they weren't overjoyed about it by any means, but they understood that it was necessary to take better care of our patients." Some of Sarah's most important leadership practices involve teaching her employees about how their work connects to the quality of patient care. When the billers learned that the new system, though it would make their lives worse, would make patients' lives better, they accepted the change.

As a leader, Sarah is constantly teaching. She not only teaches billing skills, but she also teaches billers about interacting with one another, building better communication, and how their work affects patients. This leadership practice has created meaning in the work for the members of the billing department. The fact that the billers think of themselves as connected to the quality of a patient's experience makes all the difference when they need to implement change. "Change is sometimes difficult for people, especially if it is a change that they don't like," Sarah says, but as a leader she repeatedly emphasizes the value of a change and the meaning of that change as she introduces it. By emphasizing the benefits of change to patient care, Sarah embodies a practice of making meaning of work that is in service of a larger goal. And in linking changes to the overall purpose of the organization, Sarah taps into one of the most powerful motivations possible – a sense of purpose. One of Sarah's employees, Angie, sums up the way she has learned to think about her job in the billing department: "I love this job. I get to fight for patients. The more their insurance will cover, they less they have to pay." Sarah's leadership practices of making meaning of the work have made billers cognizant that a patient's financial experience of the health system is just as much a part of people's health care experience as their interaction with doctors and nurses and labs and clinics.

As Sarah and her employees were thinking about ways to reduce errors that caused rejections of insurance claims, someone suggested that they visit the clinics where the charges were entered into the computer and see why staff in the clinics were making mistakes. Sarah supported the idea, and began the introduction of quarterly "clinic visits," in which the billers who provide services for a particular clinic within the health system get together baskets of goodies and go meet the staff of the clinics for which they provide services. This practice is an extension of Sarah's leadership practice of teaching and creating meaning, as it involves billers in learning about their role in the larger organizational network. The practice importantly involves bringing gifts and coming to seek information, which is crucial in making it a non-threatening and friendly "visit" rather than a tense interaction. One physician, who has now taken an avid interest in his reimbursement rate as a consequence of these clinic visits, commented to the billers who visit his clinic that he'd never met a hospital biller before. By extending Sarah's leadership practice of creating meaning, the billing department has created an innovation that exists nowhere else in the organization.

Clinic visits have become an important part of the unit's success. Because they show up with smiles and baskets of seasonal gifts or candy or homemade goodies, the billers aren't an imposition on the clinic staff, but rather a help to them. Many of the clinic staff actually look forward to the visits now and the billers and clinic staff have become acquainted, making it easier for the billers to call and get their questions answered. Further, staff in clinics understand more clearly the need for various charge entry requirements, and they can see that their errors have meaning and impact on the work of other people like themselves. These visits have changed over time, as billers have become aware of changes in the staffing of clinics that might affect the level of errors or the timeliness of charge entry. For instance, if an administrative staff member is going out on maternity leave or is absent for an extended period, the billers now make arrangements to meet with the temporary replacement workers and do some training, helping to reduce the errors and delay caused by absences and turnover. Thus, the leadership practice of teaching and creating meaning that is anchored by Sarah has spread to not only her employees, but the employees of other clinics as well.

This novel arrangement is part of what accounts for the extraordinary performance of the unit. Of her adoption of this idea, Sarah says, "Employees who are constantly learning are invaluable assets. Tap into their creativity and ideas. They have many." In this view, the work of a leader isn't to sweep an error under the rug, but rather to establish a practice of teaching and learning that creates meaning in people's work. Errors become opportunities to learn. Creative ideas become opportunities to connect to the work of the organization. Leadership practices that create meaning are vibrant; they shine through into the practices of the group as they teach one another, learn, and interact with patients and clinic staff. As a result of this practice of meaning making in the wake of opportunities and mistakes, the group becomes better at solving problems, capitalizing on opportunities, and putting valuable ideas to use in service of the organization's goals.

Dressing up Lucy: leadership and practices of play

> Levity and laughter are important pieces of a great workday! Make sure to include them so that all can enjoy. Fun does equal productivity.

I'm standing outside of Jan's cubicle, talking with her about her duties as a pod leader, when I notice a small ceramic goose sitting on the filing cabinet just outside her door. The goose is wearing a mini T-shirt that is embroidered with the hospital logo and a mini headset like those the billers wear when they are covering the phone lines. I ask Jan about the goose, and she says in surprise, "Oh, you haven't met Lucy?" I reply that I haven't, and Jan stands up from her chair to introduce me to Lucy the goose, mascot of Physician Billing. It turns out that Lucy is technically Jan's goose but she has been adopted by the rest of the unit. Everybody has contributed to Lucy's setup. As Jan explained to me, one of the billers' pet peeves is that no one's cardkey picture identification actually looks like the person; as a result, Lucy has a true identification badge around her tiny neck, complete with a picture of a dog. Lucy wears a headset and a company T-shirt, and she has a tiny in-box with actual claims resting in it. She has a set of billing manuals on her small bookshelf, a tiny trashcan, and a bulletin board with a picture of the billing unit on it. She has a mini computer, a lottery ticket, and a picture of her goose family on her wall – everything a biller goose would need. She even has a plaque for donating to the United Way fundraising campaign. As Jan was introducing me to Lucy, Marge stopped by and said, "Oh, she gave to United Way? Good going, Lucy! I'm proud of you!" Then, with a twinkle in her eye aimed at Jan, Marge added, "Oh, God, she's really gained weight. Again." We start to laugh, which urges Marge on: "Her in-box is looking a little full. Isn't she working her rejections lately?" And with that, she saunters off, leaving us howling with laughter in the middle of the office.

It would be easy to see Lucy as a diversion or a joke. But it is also possible to see in Lucy a microcosm of the world of Physician Billing. Lucy struggles to get by, buys lottery tickets in hopes of striking it rich, values her family, and keeps pictures of her work colleagues on her walls. She works, gains weight, and donates money to share with others in need. Lucy dresses up for Halloween, and has a beautiful set of cubicle decorations that change with the seasons like the cubicles around her. Lucy embodies a playfulness that is characteristic of the billing department as a whole. And as is so often the case, Sarah's leadership practices are part of the genesis of this playfulness.

As a leader, Sarah encourages playfulness, humor, and fun at work. If Sarah has a sense that tension is building, she takes out a large water gun that she keeps in her cabinet and starts a water fight in the aisleways of the unit. Every member of the billing department keeps a small water gun in her desk drawer, ready if Sarah or another co-worker decides to suddenly lighten the mood. Sometimes a biller is in the middle of work that just can't be interrupted by playtime, however, so each member also keeps an umbrella in her cubicle corner. If the umbrella is up, that person is out of the game.

Sarah supports fun and play at work because they are part of what develops high productivity. "Levity and laughter are important pieces of a great work day!" Sarah admonishes. "Fun does equal productivity." Sarah swears by playfulness as her secret to success in keeping her unit's performance numbers high.

On one of my return visits to the billing department after my initial study, I arrived during the downtown Jackson Scarecrow Festival. Organizations and groups from across the city had created scarecrows that lined the downtown sidewalks, and proceeds from the scarecrow competition were donated to charity. When I arrived at the unit, several people asked me if I'd seen Joe. As the billing department, at the time of my study, employed 30 women and no men, I was intrigued. "No, no, no," they laughed, "Joe the scarecrow!" Off I went, in search of Joe, finding him just a few steps down Main Street.

The basic structure of the scarecrow was made from burlap, straw, and wood; beyond that the unit participated in creating all of Joe's accessories. Because of the strong college football rivalry in the office, Joe turned out to have one blue and gold half (University of Michigan colors) and one green and white half (Michigan State University colors). Joe wore a half blue, half green sweatshirt, made by a member of the unit who cut two sweatshirts apart and sewed the halves back together. He had one blue button eye and one green button eye; a ski cap that was half blue with a University of Michigan logo and half green with a Michigan State logo. He proudly displayed an employee badge that read "Joe Scarecrow," and identified him as a member of the billing department. What was most extraordinary to me, though, was that each person in the unit had participated in some way in creating Joe, who stood on the street as a testament to the playfulness of the group and the fruit of Sarah's leadership practices of play.

Events such as creating Joe the Scarecrow, dressing up Lucy, having water gun fights, or potlucks keep people involved in their workplace. In Sarah's world of redundant work, these practices of play are the activities that bring people back day after day, excited to be there. In a world of low wage and low status jobs, practices of play keep people entertained and invested in the success of the group. Joe and Lucy are the symbolic products of a set of practices that nurture play as a means of high performance and low turnover. Amid a system with double-digit turnover, the billing unit experiences an ongoing average turnover rate of approximately 2%. Practices of play are a means of motivation, and the practice of playing provides threads that weave the fabric of this highly successful work unit. Playing together keeps the unit working together.

Lessons from Sarah: values-based leadership in practice

Organizational researchers use the term "practices" to refer to patterned, recurrent, situated activities engaged in by members of a human community (Orlikowski, 2002). Practices involve the repeated "ways of doing" in organizations that help to accomplish work, link people in complex ways, build resources, and make a system function over time (Orlikowski, 2002). By conceptualizing leadership as located in the practices of a community or work unit, we see a leader's job somewhat differently than we might from a command and control or even a situational leadership perspective (e.g. O'Toole, 1996; Gardner, 1999). In this view, a leader is someone who embodies, creates, and supports repeated ways of doing that put organizational values into action in everyday work (Spillane, Halverson, and Diamond, 2004).

Sarah's leadership lessons encompass seven broad practices. The first of these we call identity practices, showing ways that Sarah uses her own identity, her background knowledge and experience, and her reading of others' core identities in order to accomplish the everyday work of the unit. Sarah's early experience in nursing school provided a powerful lesson about the importance of respectful interaction and seeing situations from multiple points of view. Sarah uses this identity in her daily work as a leader.

The second set of leadership practices we call practices of engagement, because they are ways of doing that reinforce involvement with the goals, successes, or failures of the group. Sarah works daily to reinforce people's engagement in helping one another get the critical work of the unit done. She models engagement, talks engagement, and shares performance information related to her expectations for the unit. Further, she doesn't tolerate employees who will not become engaged. As she says in her second leadership lesson: "Don't let the slackers slack. Motivate them to improve or encourage them to move on."

The third set of leadership practices we call practices of participation, because they are ways of doing leadership and doing work that get everyone involved in making important decisions and thinking about possible changes. One visible and innovative aspect of Sarah's leadership is her hiring practice, which involves everyone in the unit in selecting their co-workers. Leadership that builds practices of participation is built upon the prior practices of identity and engagement, because participation requires people who are engaged in the work of the group and who are drawing from their authentic identity in order to participate fully. Leaders who foster practices of participation build an inclusive group of people who are inclined to contribute.

The fourth set of leadership practices we call practices of humanity, because they are ways of providing leadership that acknowledges the unique needs, wants, dreams, and foibles of each human being in the organization. Sarah creates leadership practices that acknowledge the uniqueness of each person, expressed in small ways, such as birthday gifts, and in large ways, such as treating each person on her team the way she would expect to be treated. Sarah's leadership practices help people recognize that when the levels of hierarchy are removed, each person is a human being with both aspirations and failings. Treating each person with human dignity is a leadership practice that builds an organization rich in respect and loyalty along with material success.

The fifth set of leadership practices we call practices of life, because they are ways of leading that emphasize the permeable boundary between life and work. Sarah leads her organization in such a way that her employees recognize that life and work are separate domains and that each is important. Sarah emphasizes that work should not overtake her employees' lives, especially as she is cognizant of the difficult and often turbulent lives of many of her employees. Sarah also leads in such a way that people understand that their lives outside of work should not overtake their ability to engage and participate in their work. The performance demands in her unit are unequivocally high. And yet, Sarah's fifth leadership lesson emphasizes that there are influences in employees' lives that impact their ability to perform their work. The only way to build an organization in which people can identify with the group, engage with its goals, and participate in a high quality manner is to recognize that compassion for employees' life situations is an integral part of a leader's work.

The sixth set of leadership practices we call practices of meaning, because they are ways in which a leader establishes links between employees' everyday activity and the overall mission of the organization. Sarah is masterful in her ability to show her employees that their mistakes matter for the experiences of real patients. Sarah emphasizes to her employees that their ability to learn can improve the experiences of patients who deal with the health system. While the billers know that they are not providing direct patient care, they also know that they are advocating for patients. Sarah emphasizes the practice of creating meaning by admonishing leaders to "teach, teach, and then teach some more." Employees who are continually learning and seeing ways in which their work has meaning are likely to reinforce other valued-based leadership practices such as being more strongly identified with their organizations, engaged in the group's work, fully able to participate in making decisions, and respectful of others in the workplace who are treated with human dignity and compassion.

The final set of leadership practices we call practices of play, because they emphasize the role of fun in high performance work. While easy to overlook as trivial or irrelevant, practices of play are the secrets to Sarah's success in managing her unit to perform to such a high level. Sarah constantly reinforces the idea that "laughter and levity are important pieces of a great work day." She starts water gun fights. She suggests people take breaks when they need them. She organizes potlucks. She is a proponent of cubicle decorating contests. Especially in work units like Sarah's, where little promotional pay or additional benefits are available as rewards, fun is a key piece of maintaining work motivation and keeping people fresh. Sarah insists that "fun does equal productivity," and her results bear her out.

Conclusion

Benjamin Zander, conductor of the Boston Philharmonic Orchestra, tells a story about a revelation that came to him late in his career: "After 20 years of conducting," he says, "I discovered that I am the only member of the orchestra who doesn't make a sound" (Zander and Zander, 2000). In that statement, Zander captures the essence of our key assertion in this chapter – that leadership, and perhaps values-based leadership in particular (O'Toole, 1996) – is located in the practices of a workplace, not simply in a person. Values-based leadership depends on creating practices – repeated ways of doing everyday work – that are in line with the values the organization strives to maintain. Sarah's leadership practices have helped her unit to achieve remarkable results, and have also built a community where people grow and thrive. Without formal leadership training, and without the benefits of a high-status, high-paid workforce, Sarah has accomplished remarkable things. Her style of leadership is to be differentiated from much writing on the subject to date, because it is a style of leadership that is embodied in daily actions and interactions. It is a leadership style built on a foundation of authentic identity – both her own and those of her employees. And it is a notion of leadership that draws on people's capacity for engagement in their work, for participation in their work environment, for making meaning of their work purpose, for human dignity and compassion, and for playful motivation. Sarah's leadership lessons help scholars and practitioners alike to see how the daily, repeated ways of doing that take place in a human community truly put values to work.

References

Bartunek, J. M. and Louis, M. R. (1996). *Insider-outsider Team Research: Qualitative Research Methods*, 40. Thousand Oaks, CA: Sage Publications.

Gardner, H. (1999). The vehicle and the vehicles of leadership. *American Behavioral Scientist*, 42: 1009–1023.

Howe, L. K. (1977). *Pink Collar Workers: Inside the World of Women's Work*. New York, NY: Avon Books.

Orlikowski, W. J. (2002). Knowing in practice: Enacting a collective capability in distributed organizing. *Organization Science*, 13: 249–273.

O'Toole, J. (1996). *Leading Change: The Argument of Values Based Leadership*. New York, NY: Jossey-Bass.

Spillane, J. P., Halverson, R., and Diamond, J. B. (2004). Towards a theory of leadership practice: A distributed perspective. *Journal of Curriculum Studies*, 36:1, 3–34.

Zander R. S. and Zander, B. (2000). *The Art of Possibility: Transforming Professional and Personal Life*. Boston, MA: Harvard Business School Press.

7 | *Leadership values that enable extraordinary success*

KIM S. CAMERON

This chapter highlights leadership lessons from positively deviant organizational performance – that is, the achievement of extraordinary success well beyond the expectations of almost any outside observer. It recounts the story of an organization that reached a level of performance that was considered impossible, so that adjectives such as spectacular, extraordinary, remarkable, and astonishing are apt descriptors. This account, based on Cameron and Lavine (2006), describes how a single organization experienced a devastating loss – the loss of mission and subsequent languishing performance – and then, despite its problematic circumstances, achieved astounding success. The chapter highlights the key role leadership values played in this extraordinary level of performance, and it explains the values that leaders in other organizations can apply in enabling their own spectacular success.

Rocky Flats

On March 23, 1951, the Atomic Energy Commission publicly announced that the nation would build a top-secret nuclear weapons plant in a rocky but flat ranching area 16 miles northwest of downtown Denver, located at the base of the beautiful Flatirons on the eastern slope of the Rocky Mountains. The site began operation in 1953 and functioned until 1989 when it was abruptly closed after a raid by the FBI. Rocky Flats was owned by the US Department of Energy (DOE) and managed by a series of weapons contractors during its years of active operation: Dow Chemical (1952 to 1975), Rockwell International (1975 to 1990), EG&G (1990 to 1995). Since 1995, the site has been operated by Kaiser-Hill, a joint venture between ICF Kaiser Engineers and an environmental engineering firm, CH2M-HILL.

Challenges

Kaiser Hill was awarded a contract to clean up and decommission the Rocky Flats nuclear production facility, but the task was ominous. First, this project represented the first clean up and closure of a nuclear weapons production facility in the world. No one in the industry knew how to accomplish this task. No one had ever taken down a plutonium production facility before.

Second, the majority of the workforce on site was represented by three unions – steelworkers, building trades, and security guards – which had a history of antagonistic relationships with the management of the previous contracting firms. Grievances were common, expectations of life-long employment were the norm, and a high degree of pride existed among the workforce regarding the skilled work they performed. Changing procedures was likely to foster serious resistance among a proud, closely knit workforce, not to mention strong resistance likely to be encountered by altering the entire organization's mission.

Third, the site included a 385-acre production area surrounded by more than 6,000 acres of open space called the "buffer zone." During its history of operation, the production areas were surrounded by three razor wire fences, prison like watch towers, and armed security guards to prevent suicide mission entrants or other subversives. Several buildings had installed inhibitors to helicopter-landing to prevent air attack. Visitors entering the facility passed through four security stations and received a "Q" clearance (requiring a full investigation of at least the past 10 years of their personal lives). A culture of secrecy, protectionism, and concealment was dominant at the facility.

Fourth, the site was one of the most polluted nuclear facilities in America. More than 21 tons of weapons-grade nuclear material was present. At least 100 tons of high content plutonium residues existed on the site with no treatment or disposal path. There were 30,000 liters of plutonium and enriched uranium solutions stored in tanks and pipes, some of them leaking, with some being buried in unmarked locations. More than 500,000 cubic meters of low-level radioactive waste and nearly 15,000 cubic meters of transuranic waste were stored in 39,500 containers. A special *Nightline* television program rated two Rocky Flats buildings as "the most dangerous buildings in America" due to their levels of radioactive pollution. Three others were ranked in the top ten. More than a dozen rooms were labeled "infinity rooms" because the levels of radioactivity registered beyond infinity on the metering devices. Contamination existed in walls, floors, ceilings, ductwork, surrounding soil, and, potentially, ground water. The prospect of cleaning up this site in any reasonable amount of time was highly improbable.

Fifth, long running battles had been fought historically between Rocky Flats contractors and government regulatory agencies, environmental groups, community representatives, and concerned citizens. Broad public sentiment existed that the facility was a danger to surrounding communities, and countless demonstrations by numerous groups had been staged from the 1960s through the 1980s in protest of nuclear proliferation, pollution, secrecy, and environmental endangerment. A demonstration involving more than 10,000 people occurred in 1969, for example, after a fire exposed the possibility of plutonium residues escaping into a wide area of surrounding terrain. The facility was almost in a state of siege by outside agencies and a concerned citizenry.

Sixth, the facility was raided by the FBI in 1989 and shut down on the spot. For years, Rocky Flats had argued that it was regulated by the Atomic Energy Commission, and therefore, the project was not subject to the inspection and oversight of the Environmental Protection Agency (EPA). However, litigation and Congressional pressure led to the EPA obtaining partial jurisdiction over Rocky Flats, and a surprise raid by the FBI in 1989 led to an immediate shutdown. In the public's eye, employees were transformed overnight from patriotic heroes engaged in winning the Cold War to polluting criminals, and they were completely barred from accomplishing the organization's production mission. For six years – 1989 to 1995 – essentially no work was accomplished at the facility as employees were waiting for production to resume but with no authorization to do so. In 1992 President George H.W. Bush announced the permanent closure of the facility as a result of the abandonment of the W-88 nuclear warhead program, but no action was taken to change the work scope from what had been outlined since 1989. Hence, the workforce was without a mission, thwarted in their desires to restart the production facility, and closely scrutinized by regulatory agencies that required large numbers of environmental reports and safety studies. Employees produced documents but were absent any meaningful work objectives.

The contract

The Department of Energy (DOE) awarded a contract to clean up the site to Kaiser-Hill in 1995 after a competitive bidding process. This was the first performance-based contract issued by the Department of Energy to encourage work toward closure rather than to manage on-going operations. That is, for the first time the contract specified that payment would be made only if work was accomplished, a dramatic change in government procedures. This first contract ran for five years, allowing DOE an opportunity to evaluate Kaiser-Hill's performance. In 2000, Kaiser-Hill was re-awarded a closure contract – in which the goal of closing the facility was added to the goal of cleaning it up – on a "no-bid" basis as a result of its performance in the previous five years. That contract was to extend through the end of 2006.

In 1995, the US Department of Energy Office of Environmental Management issued a Baseline Environmental Management Report, entitled *Estimating the Cold War Mortgage*, which provided a detailed estimate for the cost of closing facilities involved in Cold War weapons research, production, and storage. This analysis produced an estimate of a minimum of 70 years and a cost of more than $36 billion to close and clean up the Rocky Flats facility. Completion was estimated, optimistically, to occur in the year 2065. One high-ranking DOE official commented that the 70-year estimate was a gross underestimate and predicted that the more realistic number was 200 years to completion.

Extraordinary results

In light of these ominous challenges, the prospects of a successful closure and clean-up of Rocky Flats in the 70-year time frame were actually quite optimistic. Yet, what makes this story worth telling is that the entire project was completed 60 years early and at almost $30 billion savings in taxpayer funds. This chapter highlights the key leadership values that explain how this remarkable achievement was accomplished.

As the world's first nuclear production facility to be cleaned up, Rocky Flats represents a one-of-a-kind example of extraordinary success. The facility was closed, cleaned up, and will be developed as a wildlife refuge in a fraction of the estimated time. All 800 buildings were demolished, all surface level waste removed, and soil and water remediated to better than initial federally mandated standards by the end of October 2005. The estimated cost for the project is $3.9 billion (approximately $7 billion in total, including the years before Kaiser-Hill took over the project), a small fraction of the federally budgeted amount. The entire site will be able to be transformed into a Front Range wildlife refuge in October 2005, a year sooner than even the most optimistic estimates being touted as recently as 2003.

Many critics from citizen action groups, the environmental community, local and state governments, city mayors, and regulating agencies transitioned from protestors and adversaries to being advocates, lobbyists, and partners. Labor relations among the three unions (i.e., steelworkers, security guards, building trades) improved from 900 grievances to a mere handful per year, and a culture of life-long employment and employee entitlement was replaced by a workforce that enthusiastically worked itself out of a job as quickly as possible. Remediated pollution levels surpassed initial federal standards by a multiple of 13, and safety performance exceeded federal standards by two-fold and the construction industry average by four-fold. More than 200 technological innovations were produced in the service of faster and safer performance. The theme of the facility, "making the impossible possible," represents performance that exceeded by a wide margin even the most optimistic estimates.

Table 7.1 summarizes key performance changes that occurred from the time Kaiser-Hill initiated the project in 1995 until the year 2005. It highlights the dramatic success achieved on a variety of criteria – timeliness, budget, productivity, labor relations, safety and outcomes – that occurred over the 10-year period after Kaiser Hill began managing the facility.

Summary of outcomes

Despite the unusually difficult environment that characterized Rocky Flats at the outset of 1995, extraordinary results were achieved by a remarkable organization (summarized in Table 7.1). The project was completed in one-sixth the time and at less than one-sixth the cost of the original estimate. Pollution was mitigated from the most dangerous levels in America to a condition safe enough for a wildlife refuge and nature center. Despite facing a work scope in which the slightest error

Table 7.1 *Rocky Flats before and after the CH2M-HILL contract*

Performance Criteria	Beginning (Pre 1995)	Conclusion (2005)
Estimated time for completion of closure	70 Years	10 Years
Estimated closure budget	$36 Billion	Just over $6 Billion
Pollution levels	"Most dangerous rooms in America." DOE standard = 651 pCi/gm	Safe enough for a wildlife refuge. Residual soil action levels of 50 pCi/gr
Safety		
TRC = Total Recordable Case rate (# of occupationally related incidents requiring more than basic first aid)	TRC Jan 1996 = 5.0 (construction industry Avg. 4.5)	TRC July 2004 = 1.0 (construction industry Avg. 4, DOE Avg. 2)
LWC = Lost Workday Case rate (restricted days away from work); statistic is calculated by rate for 100 FTE or (# injuries/illnesses x 200,000/manhours)	LWC July 1996 = 3.2 (construction industry Avg. 4.5)	LWC July 2004 = 0.2 (construction industry Avg. 4, DOE Avg. 0.8)
Number of employees	3,500 during production. 8,000 after shutdown and before cleanup.	Steadily declining with consistent layoffs through completion in 2005.
Labor relations: employee grievances	900 in 1998.	"A handful a year." A union steward reported: "The best labor/management relations I've seen."
Relations with communities	10,000 protests; mistrust and little information flow to communities.	Model stakeholder dialogue structure. Frequent collaboration
Relations with the State of Colorado	Adversarial. Asserted that the Atomic Energy Act shielded them from state oversight	Significant and positive. State government officials were instrumental in securing federal support and helping regulators and contractor work collaboratively

(cont.)

Table 7.1 *(cont.)*

Relations with regulators: DOE *and* EPA	EPA requested FBI raids that shut down the facility in 1989	Site is a pioneer and a benchmark within DOE and EPA for clean-up and closure
Productivity	Between shutdown and closure announcement, almost no work was carried out	Ahead of accelerated closure schedule in terms of both time and cost
Organizational Culture	Secrecy, highly compartmentalized, assumptions of lifelong employment, low morale after shutdown	Collaborative, pride in closure, increased transparency, optimistic vision with a meaningful purpose

could have been disastrous, along with a set of tasks that had never been completed before, safety performance improved from levels worse than industry and federal averages to more than twice as good as these benchmarks. Safety improved five-fold, in fact, compared to the safety records being achieved previous to 1995 when absolutely no clean-up or closure work was being accomplished at all.

It is now well known that employee layoffs and downsizing are likely to create bitterness, resistance, and deteriorating performance in organizations (see Cameron, 1994, 1998). Yet, at Rocky Flats the workforce was incrementally reduced over the 10-year period from over 7,000 employees to zero with no strikes, a dramatic reduction in grievances, and labor relations rated by both union and management employees as "the best they had ever experienced." External constituencies – including various citizen groups in the surrounding communities, Colorado state officials, regulators such as the Environmental Protection Agency (EPA), and the supervisory Department of Energy (DOE) – became partners, collaborators, and contributors to the success of the project. This situation represents a dramatic shift from 10,000-person protests, lawsuits, an FBI raid, court battles, and the legislative pressures that characterized these relationships in 1995.

Exceeding almost every expected level of performance makes Rocky Flats an "extreme case" – an example so different from the norm that examining its features brings into stark relief particular features that may be hidden in normal organizations and under usual circumstances. This analysis, albeit significantly abbreviated in this chapter, is intended to highlight the values held by leaders in Kaiser-Hill, which led to this positively deviant performance. Such values may become obvious only in extraordinary circumstances.

Data sources

Information on how spectacular performance was achieved at Rocky Flats came from interviews with the actual individuals involved. Adopting this approach provided a glimpse of how these leaders experienced the dramatic change, what strategies were being contemplated, and what factors the participants themselves believed were the keys to success. It also highlighted the fact that no successful change in organizations – at least no significant transformational change – is due to a lone heroic leader or to a single vision developed by an individual at the top. It is commonplace to identify single leaders as the chief architects of spectacular successes, and people often attribute remarkable organizational achievements to a sole person's talents or genius. Icons such as Jack Welch at General Electric, Steven Jobs at Apple, Bill Gates at Microsoft, Fred Smith at Federal Express, Sam Walton at Wal-Mart, Warren Buffet at Berkshire Hathaway, and a host of others are credited with being the chief explanations for the remarkable achievements of their respective companies.

On the other hand, the story of Rocky Flats is a story of many leaders, many interwoven activities, many constituencies, and many heroic endeavors that all combined to produce a remarkable story of success. This is a key insight emerging from the analysis of this transformation – leadership comes from multiple sources at multiple times, and it must be coordinated and aligned in order for spectacular success to occur.

These individuals from whom information was gathered represent a broad spectrum of participants in the Rocky Flats project, including federal government oversight personnel from the DOE and the EPA, local elected officials, Colorado state office holders, members of the US Congress and their staff members, representatives of local and state environmental and citizen watchdog groups, managers and supervisors working in the Rocky Flats facilities, union leaders, and union members doing the daily work of clean up and closure. Each of these

groups provided unique perspectives, insightful descriptions, and helpful explanations for the success of this remarkable endeavor.

In addition to the face-to-face interviews, we also analyzed approximately 24 hours of videotaped interviews transcribed by DOE and
Kaiser-Hill as part of their efforts to understand and learn from the
legacy of Rocky Flats. Interview subjects in those tapes included
a broad cross-section of stakeholders including elected officials in
Colorado, other representatives from the State of Colorado, members
of the EPA, local community groups surrounding the Rocky Flats site,
US Congressmen who were involved in the project, and Rocky Flats
site managers from both the DOE and Kaiser-Hill.

Data were gathered primarily during the process of closure and
clean-up, rather than at the end of the project. In other words, respondents were describing processes as they were unfolding, not retrospectively after the project had been completed. It must be pointed out,
however, that our interviews and those on the videotapes were conducted after the site had enjoyed several years of success, and contributors did reflect back on and describe events regarding the history of
the site.

One caveat is in order. Despite this being a remarkable story of success, we promised to maintain confidentiality and anonymity for the
individuals who provided us with insights and quotations. Therefore,
we have not identified any individuals in the chapter – even though the
chapter focuses only on the positive leadership values displayed. Not
all data collected were glowingly positive, of course, and candid information was obtained by ensuring that names would not be associated
with individual comments or actions.

Abundance values and key enablers

The overarching leadership lesson learned from Rocky Flats can be
summarized in a single statement, although it belies the complexity
that undergirds this straightforward observation: *The impossible was
made possible by adopting an abundance value system rather than a
deficit value system.* An abundance value system is deceptively simple.

Consider the continuum in table 7.2 that is anchored on the left side
by negatively deviant performance and on the right side by positively
deviant performance (see Cameron, 2003). In the middle is normal or
expected performance.

Table 7.2 *A deviance continuum, illustrating abundance values*

	Negative Deviance	Normal	Positive Deviance
Individual:			
Physiological	Illness	Health	Olympic fitness
Psychological	Illness	Health	Flow
Organizational:			
Revenues	Losses	Profits	Generous
Effectiveness	Ineffective	Effective	Excellent
Quality	Error-prone	Reliable	Flawless
Ethics	Unethical	Ethical	Benevolent
Relationships	Harmful	Helpful	Honoring
Approach:		Deficit gaps	Abundance gaps

Most leaders pay almost exclusive attention to the gap between what is going wrong, mistakes, poor performance, or illness and the middle point on the continuum, represented by an absence of illness, effective performance, or problem resolution. This gap might be labeled a "deficit gap" or a "problem solving gap." A large majority of scientific research in fields such as medicine, psychology, and organizational studies focus on deficit gaps – i.e., addressing and overcoming problems. On the other hand, the gap between the middle and the right side represents an "abundance gap" – the gap between successful performance and spectacular or extraordinarily positive performance. This gap receives far less attention in scientific research and in the attention of managers and leaders (Cameron, Bright, and Caza, 2004). The right side of the continuum implies that leaders in organizations not only focus on being profitable, effective, efficient, or reliable in performance (represented by the middle point in the continuum), but they also focus on being extraordinary, flawless, or benevolent. Their outcomes produce benefit for more than the organization itself, since a condition of abundance makes possible the success of others outside the organization as well. The abundance approach motivates change in organizations based on the pursuit of a greater good and an opportunity to achieve positively deviant results. The right side of the continuum represents a condition of *virtuousness* – that is, the highest human condition, or the best that human beings aspire to be. The pursuit of virtuousness supplements the pursuit of personal reward and problem solving. Previous research has confirmed that abundance fosters virtuousness (Cameron, 2003).

At the heart of the Rocky Flats success story lies an approach to change represented by an abundance perspective in contrast to a deficit perspective. Rocky Flats succeeded because it was, fundamentally, a project in pursuit of abundance gap reduction rather than deficit gap reduction. Working toward the achievement of a greater good, beyond personal or even organizational success, was key to explaining the spectacular outcomes.

In this chapter, not enough space exists to explain the multiple *enablers* that made this unbelievably successful change possible – i.e., the processes, techniques, strategies, and relationships that were developed and that helped produce these outcomes (see Cameron and Lavine, 2006, for a more thorough description). A variety of enablers were important in explaining how the status quo was transformed into a new way of thinking, a new way of doing work, a new way of interpreting success, and a new set of values for those involved in the project. The most important factors in accounting for success, however, were the values held by the leaders involved in the project, which gave rise to the other enablers of success. These leaders included not only the CEO or the top management team at Kaiser Hill, but also individuals in DOE, EPA, the State of Colorado, and local citizen action groups. The leadership values that came to permeate these various groups of leaders, as they worked in collaboration with one another, help explain how and why the other enablers of success were able to occur. This chapter highlights the ten most central leadership values, therefore, because they lie at the foundation of the spectacular success that was achieved.

Leadership values

Articulating the values of Rocky Flats leaders is especially important because these values can be applicable to other organizations and other circumstances. The inherent interest in the Rocky Flats story resides, in other words, in the extent to which its leadership lessons also produce success for leaders in other organizations. It is clear that some of these leadership values are not consistent with the popular leadership literature or with much commonly prescribed consultant advice.

Nevertheless, they are crucial in accounting for the achievement of extraordinary success, dramatic change, and spectacular performance in this case. The 10 key leadership values are:

1. *The lone heroic leader is largely fictional. Effective leadership is always plural.* Single leaders with positive energy, vision, and know-how are indisputably important, of course, in producing positively deviant performance in organizations. Yet, despite the fact that these individual leaders frequently receive the lion's share of the credit for success, multiple sources of leadership are always required. At Rocky Flats, multiple leaders in multiple roles were critical to success. It was clear that no leader could have succeeded alone – multiple leaders acting in collaboration and sharing a common set of values was crucial. Spectacular organizational success simply could not have been achieved by a single leader. Supportive and aligned leaders in Kaiser-Hill and within DOE, EPA, the State of Colorado, local citizen action groups, and Kaiser-Hill's parent company, CH2M-HILL, all were essential for spectacular success. In Rocky Flats, without effective leaders in many locations, aligned in a common vision, and pursuing a clear purpose, great performance would not have occurred. *Leadership value: It is important to foster, enable, and encourage leaders throughout the organization and in other stakeholder relationships to behave like leaders. Do not rely on a single leader.*

2. *Financial incentives must create lifestyle change in order to create change in thinking.* The possibility of Rocky Flats employees receiving financial benefits that exceeded any previous remuneration package was key to the achievement of success. What was unique about this incentive system, however, was that the incentives were provided with the assumption that the workers *had already* succeeded in reaching spectacular performance. A large percentage of remuneration in the early years was paid in "script" that had little value unless spectacular levels of achievement were reached. Employees received the remuneration in advance, but it paid off only if they reached the objectives. It became possible, however, to earn much more than the normal amount of pay – in fact, lifestyle-altering levels of pay. There is much research suggesting that paying people more money does not create higher levels of satisfaction or performance. Yet, a reliance on financial incentives is the single most frequent strategy used by organizations to obtain these desired outcomes (Lawler, 2000). Pay is, by and large, not a motivator. However, when promised benefits reach a level where they could

change lifestyle – that is, when individuals can earn enough to obtain opportunities never before afforded them – pay has a chance to alter employee perspectives and organizational culture. At Rocky Flats, the incentive system was structured so that employees could earn lifestyle-changing levels of compensation, and as a result, it change the nature of their thinking. *Leadership value: Use incentives to create fundamental transformational change only if it can change lifestyles.*

3. *The profound purpose for which the organization strives must extend beyond self-interest and beyond individual lifetimes.* Every organization has a vision statement, a set of core values, and a primary mission. Most believe that they are in business to fulfill an important objective – usually to provide value in the form of financial benefits to shareholders, investors, or customers. Hardly any leader, on the other hand, wishes his or her tombstone to read that under his or her direction shareholder value increased, sales improved, market share was captured, or 99% customer satisfaction was obtained. These are important outcomes, of course, but something more fundamental, more long lasting, and more humane must be pursued if the organization is to strive for extraordinary performance. Most often profound purpose highlights a human benefit that may extend beyond a single person's life or sphere on influence. At Rocky Flats, the opportunity to create a wildlife refuge that would benefit generations yet unborn, as well as to clean up and make safe the most dangerous location in America, was a motivating vision and virtuous objective that extended beyond personal benefits. People were willing to go the extra mile, to learn new skills, to invest more creative energy, and to alter their work skills in pursuit of such an objective. *Leadership value: A profound purpose for the organization's activities must be identified which affects human beings for the better over the long term.*

4. *Symbolism must focus on what the organization aspires to become.* Most organizations have symbols that represent their identity or image – flags, logos, captions, insignias, signs, or lettering. Most images have been designed by graphic artists to portray some kind of message about the firm – what it stands for, what business it is in, or what its core attributes are. Such symbols have more meaning to employees than to the external public, of course, so the symbolism representing the organization must communicate first and foremost to employees. The symbolic message should focus on what the organization aspires to become. At Rocky Flats, relying on

stories – regarding the importance of peace gardens, the destruction of guard towers, the blowing-up of the headquarters building to get managers on-site with the workers, and creating a multigenerational legacy of replenishing nature – substituted for logos and letterheads. These stories became the symbols by which internal and external constituencies defined the organization. External symbols were replaced by internal symbols. These internal symbols focused almost exclusively on abundance values and achieving spectacular success. The values reflected in these stories, which were adopted by the organization's members, were the most powerful symbols of what the organization represented. *Leadership value: Symbols should be chosen that represent abundance aspirations for the organization and its members.*

5. *Intense bureaucracy is necessary for success – i.e., careful planning, tight controls, precise measurement, rigid accountability, and even micromanagement of crucial activities.* Bureaucracy is a dirty word in most leadership and organization literature. It is much more common to read about the need to destroy bureaucracy, break the rules, obliterate red tape, and extinguish formalization in the popular literature than to hear prescriptions to do the reverse. On the other hand, Rocky Flats was successful because of proficient execution, defect free performance, and accountability. These activities are all dependent on what is frequently eschewed as destructive to excellent performance. Without careful assessment, metrics, milestones, and standardization, this organization would never have achieved its dramatic success. Weick (ch. 3, this volume) argued that all organizations are hubris-inducing places – that is, they foster excess self-confidence and arrogance. They often reinforce successes and minimize weaknesses to the extent that potential problems are ignored and self-congratulation becomes common. Intense bureaucracy helps to moderate overconfidence by holding people accountable and ensuring accurate assessment. At Rocky Flats, a very specific and rigidly adhered to set of processes and routines were a prerequisite to accomplishing the tasks in such a rapid time frame. Projectizing the work – in which multiple standardized procedures and measures were implemented exactly – was key to Rocky Flats success. Rather than getting in the way of speed and achievement, however, these routines were followed in order to enhance them. *Leadership value: The control system must be well developed, and it must reinforce the achievement of extraordinary performance.*

6. *Trustworthiness implies perfection, but it depends on collaboration and mutual support.* The popular literature on trust suggests that consistency, equity, honesty, and discretion are key prerequisites for its presence in organizations. If individuals are treated fairly, feel that they are not being deceived, have freedom to act, and observe consistent behavior, trust is likely to be high. In addition to these attributes, however, organizations aspiring to achieve positively deviant behavior must also leave no room for aberrations from promises. In the case of Rocky Flats, a single instance of infidelity would have severely damaged trust with external constituencies. Commitments had to be strictly observed consistently. Thus, complete trustworthiness was associated with perfect follow-through on all commitments at Rocky Flats. Because of human fallibility, however, social support is required where colleagues must provide assistance, cover, advice, and even forgiveness when unwitting flub-ups occur. No individual can avoid making mistakes at some point. Hence, collaborative relationships inside the work setting make it possible to produce high reliability outcomes before outsiders first encounter the results. At Rocky Flats, such a culture enhanced the possibility of maintaining the highest levels of trust. Supportive relationships inside help foster trustworthiness on the outside. *Leadership value: High quality relationships must be built that permit perfect execution on commitments to external stakeholders.*

7. *Culture change requires a change in individuals.* Achieving extraordinary performance will not occur by reinforcing the same organizational culture. Behaving in the same ways and believing the same things will produce normal, expected, predictable outcomes. At Rocky Flats spectacular results required a fundamental change in culture. Organizational culture includes the values, assumptions, ways of thinking, norms, styles, actions, and artifacts that characterize the organization. It represents "the way things are around here." Cameron and Quinn (2006) outlined a culture change process that involves culture diagnosis, clarifying meaning, establishing strategies and tactics, identifying metrics, measures, and milestones, and developing the leadership to manage the change. A fundamental change in an organization's culture, however, also requires a fundamental change in its members as individuals. The people themselves must be different, sometimes through replacement – as occurred with some supervisors at Rocky Flats – or through a fundamental change in their orientation and values. At Rocky Flats, individuals abandoned life-long employment objectives

in favor of working themselves out of a job as fast as possible. They abandoned a secrecy culture in favor of an openness culture. They abandoned an adversarial orientation toward state and federal regulators and adopted a proactive, sharing orientation. They abandoned an antagonistic attitude toward protesters and regulators and adopted a collaborative, empathetic attitude. Leaders shifted from a profit-first stance to a generous, share-the-benefits stance. Leaders placed more emphasis on abundance-enhancement goals than on deficit-reduction goals. In other words, individuals themselves were required to undergo a fundamental internal change in order for the organization to experience the collective change required for spectacular performance. *Leadership value: In changing organizational culture, it must be ensured that individuals (especially leaders and influencers) believe differently, behave differently, and pursue abundance-based purposes and visions.*

8. *Learning from mistakes should get less priority than learning from successes.* It is common for people to advocate that wisdom and experience come from making mistakes. Thomas Watson (2005), the Nobel laureate, stated: "Would you like me to give you the formula for success? It's quite simple, really. Double your rate of failure." Oscar Wilde (1892) is reported to have said: "Experience is the name everyone gives to their mistakes." On the other hand, in circumstances in which mistakes can be very costly, destructive, or even deadly – as was true at Rocky Flats – identifying what works, which principles produce success, and how spectacular achievement can be reached should receive at least as much attention as analyzing and deconstructing errors. Rather than following the normal problem-solving model, which involves asking what the problem is, what the possible alternatives are, and then identifying which alternative is the optimal one for resolving the problem, another possibility should be considered. This approach was pursued at Rocky Flats, and it involves asking what has been a spectacular success or a peak performance, what the enablers of this success were, and which of those enablers can be carried forward to design a strategy for extraordinary success going forward. Learning from mistakes is important – and often critical – but it is often pursued at the expense of learning from successes. At Rocky Flats, more than 200 innovations were produced as a result of analyzing what was working and trying to improve on it. Building on success produced faster progress than analyzing mistakes. Of course, errors, problems, and mistakes cannot be ignored, but they often consume all of the time and attention of an

organization, and learning from success is minimized because of the threats presented by the problems. At Rocky Flats, achieving abundance objectives received at least as much attention as avoiding failures. *Leadership value: Outstanding success should be deconstructed and the key enablers and explanatory factors should be identified, then a future strategy based on these factors should be built.*

9. *Strategy should be established on the basis of what the organization can be rather than what it has been or what it is now.* Most models of corporate strategy are based on the core competencies of the organization, its strategic intent, the dynamics of the competitive marketplace, and key differentiators that can produce a sustainable advantage (Barney, 2001; Hamel and Prahalad, 1996). Such strategies will likely lead to competitive performance and reasonable levels of success. For spectacular performance to be achieved, however, strategy must be built on what is possible, on a scenario that has never been accomplished before, and on a theory of abundance. Rocky Flats could not have achieved "impossible" performance merely by trying to outperform the industry average or to achieve a sustainable competitive advantage. Great performance requires the courage to build a foundation on possibilities rather than probabilities. The vision at Rocky Flats was aimed at levels of performance never before achieved and never thought possible. The organization's strategies were then aligned with those objectives so that extraordinary success became a natural outcome. *Leadership value: Aspirations for what the organization could be must be articulated; then a strategy to achieve it can be constructed.*

10. *Virtuousness pays.* Adopting an abundance approach – that is, enabling the best of the human condition, exhibiting virtuous behaviors, fostering human thriving, being generous with resources, displaying unfailing integrity, demonstrating humility, exercising faith – has inherent value. On the one hand, demonstrating virtuousness is considered by almost everyone as admirable and fundamentally the right thing to do. It is what we aspire to do and to be as human beings. Virtually all of the world's cultures value the same inherent goodness. On the other hand, if an observable, bottom-line impact is not connected to an abundance approach, it becomes subservient to the very real pressures for improving organizational performance – usually defined as higher return to shareholders, profitability, productivity, customer satisfaction, and the like. Virtuousness must pay for it to be taken seriously in organizations, otherwise it is defined as irrelevant

at best and syrupy or saccharine at worst. The irony is that to behave virtuously in order to obtain a reward or a personal benefit ceases, by definition, to be virtuous and becomes manipulation. Fortunately, evidence exists in the Rocky Flats story, and elsewhere in scholarly literature (see Cameron, 2003), that virtuousness pays dividends. Higher organizational performance results from virtuousness than from its absence. At Rocky Flats, pursuing the best that could be imagined, reaching for the highest aspirations that could be dreamed, had a powerful affect on actually being able to achieve it 60 years early and $30 billion under budget. *Leadership value: Virtuous behaviors and values should be enabled and reinforced throughout the organization.*

Summary

Although the evidence for these ten key leadership values are not discussed in detail in this chapter – but are available elsewhere (Cameron and Lavine, 2006) – it is clear that positively deviant performance is dependent on them. Extraordinary success at Rocky Flats – which began in a deficit condition and exceeded even the most optimistic estimates of success – was dependent on these ten leadership values being demonstrated in the organization. This leadership came from multiple sources, not just from the CEO, and it was based on an abundance approach as opposed to a deficit or problem solving approach to success. In the end, focusing on closing the gaps between current performance and extraordinary levels of performance was an underlying explanation for how the impossible was made possible. Other values relating to incentives, profound purpose, symbols, control systems, commitments, culture change, learning from successes, aspirations, and virtuousness were also key drivers of spectacular success.

References

Barney, J. 2001. *Gaining Sustainable Competitive Advantage.* Upper Saddle River, NJ: Prentice-Hall.

Cameron, K. S. 1994. Strategies for successful organizational downsizing. *Human Resource Management Journal,* 33: 89–112.

1998. Strategic organizational downsizing: An extreme case. *Research in Organizational Behavior,* 20: 185–229.

2003. Organizational virtuousness and performance. In Cameron, K. S., Dutton, J. E., and Quinn, R. E. (eds.) *Positive Organizational*

Scholarship: Foundations of a New Discipline. (48–65). San Francisco: Berrett Koehler.

Cameron, K. S., Bright, D. and Caza, A. 2004. Exploring the relationships between organizational virtuousness and performance. *American Behavioral Scientist*, 47: 766–790.

Cameron, K. S. and Lavine, M. 2006. *Making the Impossible Possible: Leadership Lessons on Creating Positive Deviance.* San Francisco: Berrett Koehler.

Cameron, K. S. and Quinn, R. E. 2006. *Diagnosing and Changing Organizational Culture.* San Francisco: Jossey Bass.

Hamel, G. and Prahalad, C. K. 1996. *Competing for the Future.* Cambridge, MA: Harvard Business School Press.

Lawler, E. E. 2000. *Pay Strategies for the New Economy.* San Francisco: Jossey-Bass.

Quinn, R. E. 2004. *Building the Bridge as You Walk on It.* San Francisco: Jossey-Bass.

Watson, T. 2005. Quoted in Poor Man's College. Aapex Software, #9757.

Wilde, O. 1892. *Lady Windermere's Fan*, Act III.

8 | Principled leadership: a framework for action

MARYANN GLYNN AND
HEATHER JAMERSON

In this chapter we address a question that is fundamental to principled leadership: How can leaders lead with their principles in organizational situations that challenge their ability to act on those principles? Principled leadership is not simply about having the right values or principles, but also about being able to act on these principles when leaders find themselves in situations that may work against those principles and values.

To introduce these ideas, we offer an example that some might see as curious or even ironic: that of Kenneth Lay at Enron. Enron's recent collapse and scandalized image, along with the impending trial of its former CEO (Lay), suggest that it may not always be easy for leaders to put their principles into play. According to voluminous news reports, books, and articles about Enron, Lay's tenure with the company seemed to have been marked by his repeated attempts to communicate to both internal and external stakeholders that he was a "good" and "thoughtful" man. Likewise, he repeatedly expressed that part of his role at Enron was to guard and embody the central values of the company, namely respect, integrity, honesty, and sincerity. He claimed that, in his role of leader, he expected that Enron would reflect some of his own values and principles, particularly that of the "Golden Rule," i.e., Enron would "treat others as we want to be treated," and that the company had "absolute integrity" (as quoted in McLean and Elkind, 2004, p. 89). Prior to the allegations of Enron's impropriety, Lay stated that "ruthlessness, callousness, and arrogance don't belong here ... we work with customers and prospects, openly, honestly and sincerely" (McLean and Elkind, 2004, p. 89).

Lay's professed values of generosity and his stated desire to be a good community member seemed evidenced in his decisions to invest abundant time and resources into local area projects. Hence, Enron generously funded numerous projects ranging from hospital wings to local arts programs to the well-known baseball stadium that once bore its name, Enron Field. Indeed, during the 1990s, under the leadership of Kenneth Lay, Enron became Houston's most benevolent financial donor, and the company actively encouraged employees to embrace these professed values by involving themselves with local charities. As such, it seemed, Lay was imprinting his values on Enron, encouraging corporate social engagement as a pillar of the community in which he lived and in which the company was headquartered (Marquis, Glynn and Davis, forthcoming).

During his leadership tenure, Lay enacted these principles of community social engagement and philanthropy while Enron enjoyed unparalleled financial success. In 1999, at the peak of its stock market performance, Enron was worth an estimated $70 billion and was the seventh largest company in the United States. By all observable standards available to the public at the time, Enron's business performance and social involvement pointed to the ability of strong and effective leaders – like Kenneth Lay – to successfully blend the value of profit with the value of social responsibility (cf. Tichy, McGill and St Clair, 1997).

Yet, during this same period of time, Lay and three other top executives (Fastow, Skilling and Causey) were allegedly orchestrating one of the largest cases of corporate fraud in United States history. Lay, specifically, has been indicted on seven charges that allege that he repeatedly misled the public and investors when he knew that Enron was sinking farther and farther into debt. Additionally, he is charged with profiting from Enron's fraud by selling large amounts of overvalued stock, totaling more than $300 million in the four years that led up to the Enron crisis. Lay (and the other two defendants scheduled for trial) emphatically deny these allegations and claim that they were unaware of any fraudulent accounting practices within the company.

Whether Lay was directly involved in the fraudulent practices or not will be decided by a jury, not these authors. Yet it remains undeniable that the bankruptcy of the company has left workers without jobs and pensions, investors without returns, and California consumers temporarily without reliable energy. Recent published figures estimate that billions of dollars have been lost to each of these stakeholders, and that the fraudulent accounting practices of Enron radically and adversely impacted the lives of countless individuals and other businesses that had direct and indirect ties to Enron (cf. McLean and Elkind, 2004; Eichenwald, 2005; Independent News and Media, 2005). Also beyond question is the fact that Lay was at the helm of the Enron

Corporation during this fraudulent era and was empowered to act on his own authority. Thus, this case of leadership speaks to our primary goal in this chapter, of understanding what factors contributed to the inability of Kenneth Lay and other leaders to lead with the values that they claimed as their own.

A framework for action

The case of Enron and Kenneth Lay generates perplexing questions relevant to the enactment of "Principled Leadership." Most importantly, how do we make sense of the apparent dichotomy of values and actions demonstrated by the leader of Enron? No doubt some critics of Enron and Kenneth Lay would argue that he was a con man from the beginning, actively engaged in an elaborate plot to mislead the company, investors, and community for his own personal gain. Other commentators might suggest that Lay's values were not sufficiently internalized; thereby leaving him susceptible to the influence of impropriety that already existed within the company. However, these individual-level explanations do not seem to reconcile the humanitarian and socially engaged actions that accompanied Lay's tenure at Enron. In fact, even after the public accusation of Enron's fraudulent accounting practices, local community leaders claimed that Kenneth Lay was "one of Houston's most conscientious business leaders" (Independent News and Media 2005).

What seems more plausible to us is the argument in more recent publications on Enron that the decisions of the top executives were shaped within the larger context of societal and corporate culture during the 1990s (McLean and Elkind, 2004; Eichenwald, 2005). In these accounts, we are asked to consider explanations of leadership that include the broader environment of political, regulatory, and economic changes that gave corporations the opportunity to earn unprecedented profits in the new economy. In pursuit of these earning possibilities, proponents of this view detail the direct and indirect involvement of reputable banks (e.g., Citibank), investment firms (e.g., Merrill Lynch), and accountants (e.g., Arthur Anderson) that contributed to the massive effort to conceal Enron's growing debt, along with politicians in both the Clinton and Bush Administrations who provided the regulatory climate necessary for the scandal to occur (e.g., McLean and Elkind, 2004; Eichenwald, 2005). And, although the details of

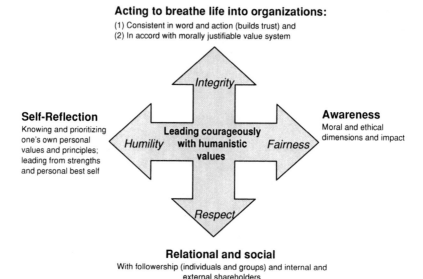

Acting to breathe life into organizations:
(1) Consistent in word and action (builds trust) and
(2) In accord with morally justifiable value system

Self-Reflection
Knowing and prioritizing
one's own personal
values and principles;
leading from strengths
and personal best self

Integrity

**Leading courageously
with humanistic
values**

Humility   *Fairness*

Respect

Awareness
Moral and ethical
dimensions and impact

Relational and social
With followership (individuals and groups) and internal and
external shareholders

Figure 8.1 Framework for principled leadership

Ken Lay's leadership at Enron may never be known, the case does raise
questions regarding the difficulty good people have in making good
decisions in bad situations. This brief illustration alerts us to the need
to understand why the good values and principles that people hold do
not always emerge as the actions of principled leadership within organizational, societal, and cultural contexts that may challenge those
values. Understanding this puzzle is the focus of our chapter.

To present our approach to principled leadership, we offer a framework for action, which is depicted in figure 8.1. This framework on
principled leadership embeds the leader contextually and relationally,
with regard to the situations that leaders face and the people with
whom leaders interact. The framework returns us to the question with
which we began the chapter: How do leaders lead with principles in
situations that challenge those principles? Our framework begins to
address this question.

Figure 8.1 shows how principled leadership occurs through a series
of steps that proceeds as follows: first, principled leadership begins
with awareness, recognizing the moral hazards and ethical decisions of
leadership actions. Next, principled leadership becomes self-reflective,
recognizing, reconciling and prioritizing one's values and then aligning

them with those of the organization. Finally, leaders courageously move to principled actions and decisions that breathe life into organizations by maintaining consistency in word and action in order to build trust with constituencies and by acting in accord with morally justifiable value systems.

Overall, we propose that principled leadership is leading courageously with humanistic values (i.e., integrity, fairness, respect, and humility) with particular sensitivity to the organizational context and social relationships, which embed leaders. The real challenge of principled leadership is not only to lead with these humanistic values but to *be* the values that are espoused – courageous, fair, humble, and honest – even in situations that challenge leaders' values and principles.

The remainder of the chapter uses this framework to explore principled leadership. Our objectives are as follows. We begin by offering a definition of "principled leadership," focusing not only leaders *doing* the right thing (leading by principles) but on leaders *being and living those principles* (leading with personal strengths and values). In doing so, we integrate leaders' ethical actions with positive organizational scholarship (Cameron, Dutton and Quinn, 2003), while considering the challenges of principled leadership in managing organizational dilemmas. Second, we outline a three-step process of principled leadership that is based on leadership awareness, self-reflection, and breathing life into organizations through action. Finally, we close the chapter by highlighting the importance of principled leadership in energizing organizations and giving meaning to organizational work.

What is principled leadership?

We begin by breaking the question of principled leadership into its constituent parts, starting with the fundamental question: What is leadership? Even with as much ink that has been spilled on the topic of leadership, it has proved to be a construct that eludes definition. In their classic tome on leadership, *Bass & Stodgill's Handbook of Leadership: Theory, Research, and Managerial Applications* (Bass and Stodgill, 1990) the authors extensively review existing definitions of leadership and conclude that definitions of leadership should be crafted to suit the purposes at hand. Echoing this pragmatism, Useem (1998, p. 4) cautions us: "A precise definition is not essential ... indeed, it may be impossible to arrive at one."

Following these leadership scholars, we take a broad perspective on leadership, conceptualizing it as "the act of making a difference," which can occur in a variety of ways, including, but not limited to:

...changing a failed strategy or revamping a languishing organization... [Leadership] requires us to make an active choice among plausible alternatives, and it depends on bringing others along, on mobilizing them to get the job done. Leadership is at its best when the vision is strategic, the voice persuasive, and the results tangible. (Useem, 1998, p. 4)

Leadership is inherently relational, linking a leader to followers, and inherently driven by some set of principles, which guide leaders as they make decisions and take actions. The relational (or social) nature of leadership is demonstrated vividly in Karl Weick's studies of Mann Gulch (1993; also see Weick's chapter in this volume). In detailing the story of wildfires on the mountain, Weick demonstrates how Wagner Dodge, in dealing with a fast-moving, unpredictable fire on steep and rocky terrain, had a life-saving solution in mind (i.e. lighting a backfire to serve as a "safety zone" for fleeing smokejumpers), but was unable to persuasively communicate this to the men he commanded, in spite of his leadership authority as crew chief; the result was the loss of 13 lives to the fire on the mountain. Incongruously, in spite of having formal authority, Dodge exerted little informal or social authority. Useem (1998, p. 54) attributes Dodge's loss – or "collapse" – of credibility as a leader to "being a person of few words... [which is] a prescription for disaster in a position of leadership."

To avoid Dodge's failure, both Weick (1993) and Useem (1998) urge leaders to recognize the need to develop social and trusting relationships with followers and to "explain yourself," through stories and narratives. As Useem (1998, p. 58) puts it, "If your leadership depends on theirs [those who work for you], developing responsibility and sharing stories is a foundation upon which it will rest." Thus, an important mandate for principled leaders is to cultivate trust in their relationships; symbols and stories can be a way of enabling others to see the leaders' trustworthiness.

The story of Mann Gulch implies that, quite literally, leadership must "breathe life" into organizations. Scott Snook delivers a similar message, in his accounting of the accidental "friendly fire" shoot down of Blackhawk helicopters in Iraq, writing that "Even the best designed organizational shells require a leader to 'breathe life' into them"

(p. 111). Making a difference, it seems, tasks leaders with two functions: first, to (literally) breathe life into organizations through social relationships and second, to do this through effective story-telling that reinforces leader-follower bonds and relationships. "All leadership takes place through the communication of ideas to the minds of others" (Charles Cooley, quoted in Gardner, 1995, p. 41).

Viewing leadership stories – as personal, relational, and visioning – stands in contrast to many popular and cultural accounts that focus on an individualized (asocial) leader making good decisions. Byron (2004), for instance, narrates "tales of CEOs gone wild" that lionize executives like Al Dunlap, Jack Welch, and Leo Kozlowski. In these stories, the leader is prominent and masterful while the social and interpersonal contexts in which leadership occurs are often invisible or an afterthought. Similarly, Khurana (2002) shows how leaders' personal charisma has become a key attribute on which organizations anchor in selecting their executives. As obvious as they may seem, these stories of leadership overlook the context in which is leadership occurs and the situational pressures that influence leadership decisions. The focus seems to be on individual traits and decision making, rather than more socially embedded, experience-based, sense-making, as Weick describes it:

When the leader says, "let's find out," what the leader really means is, let's create the story. The good story is not simply lying out there waiting to be detected. Instead, the good story comes from experience that is reworked, enacted into the world, and rediscovered as though it were something external. (Weick, 2001, p. 95)

As much as these different scholars point to the importance of thinking about the life-giving and social aspects of leadership, frameworks on leadership that incorporate these aspects are lacking. In fact, beginning with implicit assumptions of leaders as charismatic, atomistic, and infused with internalized values that lead to principled action oversimplifies the relational and social nature of leadership.

As well as being relational, leadership is also principled. All kinds of principles may motivate leadership decisions and actions. The case of Roy Vagelos at Merck is instructive on how leaders can be torn by important but competing sets of principles (Vagelos and Galambos, 2004). As the then CEO of Merck, Vagelos faced the dilemma of whether or not to invest company resources in researching and developing a drug that could potentially cure the horrific disease of river blindness, which leads to disability, early death, and decreased well-being of communities in Africa. To fund the drug would cost the company millions of dollars, as Merck had to develop, distribute, and supervise its administration in Africa. To not fund the drug, would seemingly violate not only Vagelos' personal values but also Merck's #1 stated value,

Our business is preserving and improving human life. All of our actions must be measured by our success in achieving this goal. We value, above all, our ability to serve everyone who can benefit from the appropriate use of our products and services, thereby providing lasting consumer satisfaction. (www.merck.com)

Ultimately, Vagelos decided to have his company give away and distribute the drug in perpetuity. In his decision, we can see how principled leadership must acknowledge and address sometimes-competing sets of principles. In Vagelos' case, principled leadership rested on the choice between the business principles of maximizing stakeholder value and of being a fiscally responsible company steward and the ideological principles of saving lives and delivering the stated mission of the company. How these principles shape leadership actions is the subject to which we turn next.

Understanding the structure of leadership action

As we've noted, there seems to be an overemphasis on asocial conceptions of leadership. This can be traced to the broader preoccupation in the United States with personal responsibility. Other more social values move to the margins as our culture seeks to reinforce the value of individual accountability. Whether discussing the Enron crisis, the recent prison abuse scandals of Abu Ghraib, or the timing of federal responses to Hurricane Katrina in the Gulf States, concerned citizens from around the country look to an individual or group of individuals to blame. Which leader dropped the ball, and who can we hold responsible for such horrific outcomes? In fact, our criminal justice system enforces this type of personal responsibility as individuals (and occasionally groups of individuals) are placed on trial for their actions so that society can put closure to the incident of misdeed.

Not surprisingly, this emphasis on the individual leads to an analysis of leadership that places the blame for weak leadership on individual leaders. These explanations tend to be two-fold. The first argues that the individual lacks the values necessary to make "good" leadership decisions, while the second argues that the individual does not have the skills or expertise necessary to put her/his values into action. In both cases, individuals overcome these deficits through values clarification and prioritization, and through learning the skills necessary to lead with these values. These explanations and potential solutions, however, can underestimate the social nature of leadership and the need for an analysis of principled leadership that includes a focus on the power of cultural schema and organizations in shaping leadership decisions and actions.

There is a growing body of literature within the fields of organizations (Snook, 2002), social psychology (Zimbardo, 2004, 2005), and business ethics (Gioia, 1992; Moberg, 1999; Werhane, 2002) that argues that a focus on individual action to the exclusion of attention to social contexts and cultural schema eschews the complexity of unethical (and/or unlawful) actions. These scholars point to the fact that when individuals are placed in certain types of situations, even the most ethical person can make "bad" (unlawful, unethical, or immoral) decisions. By examining how "strong" situations can elicit "weak" leadership behavior, we can see how certain structures and routines elicit certain types of thinking and behavior regardless of more individual level factors.

Briefly consider the Stanford Prison Experiment of the early 1970s as an illustration of this point. Here, Stanford students, who thought of themselves as ethical and moral people, agreed to participate in a situational psychology experiment, in which they were randomly selected to play the role of prison guards or prisoners in a life-like simulation of a prison environment. The purpose of the experiment was to try to understand what happens when good people enter into situations that challenge their personal values and ethics. As the director of the experiment, and "warden of the prison," Philip Zimbardo (2005) retrospectively describes the project as a study of the "competition between institutional power and the individual will to resist."

Zimbardo and the "guards" actively dehumanized "prisoners" through various symbolic attempts to take away their identity (e.g. giving them numbers rather than names, stripping them of their clothes and forcing them to wear uncomfortable uniforms, isolating them from family and friends), and exerting control over every aspect of their daily lives. Simultaneously, the guards became de-individuated and autonomous through their similar clothing, mirrored sunglasses, and the use of a generic title of "Mr. Corrections Officer." Within a matter of a few days, the guards resorted to immoral – indeed, inhumane – actions toward inmates in order to maintain control of the prison. Once the "prison" was dismantled, interviews with the participants revealed that neither the guards nor the prisoners could explain their actions using the values that they professed prior to the experiment. As aptly summarized by one of the guards, "I thought I was incapable of this type of behavior" (Video *Quiet Rage: The Stanford Prison Experiment*, 1971). Yet, in this case, the "strong" situation became more powerful and prescriptive than individually held values.

Perhaps even more interesting in this case were the responses of other participants in the experiment. At several points during the six-day simulation, outsiders were allowed inside the prison to provide "counsel" to the inmates. Both the legal advisor and the priest (who were legal advisor and priest to actual inmates in the California corrections system) immediately embraced their roles, giving legal advice and spiritual counsel to "inmates" rather than students who were being mistreated in an experiment that had become inhumane. Despite their professed roles as guardians of the moral and legal spheres of society, neither the priest nor the legal counsel advised Zimbardo or any other official at Stanford that the experiment had progressed into a realm of immoral, unethical or illegal actions. Even Zimbardo himself believed that the experiment was progressing successfully, until an outside observer (who did not have an assigned role within the experiment) pointed out the unethical and immoral implications of continuing the project. Only after this outside input, did Zimbardo "wake up" and immediately terminate the experiment before the scheduled date of completion. After 30 years of reflection on this experiment, and countless other projects that have tested similar hypotheses, Zimbardo concludes, "You can't be a sweet cucumber in a vinegar barrel" (2005). In other words, contextual factors and situational forces provide powerful influence on the decision-making and behavior of otherwise virtuous people.

With the help of case studies we can locate similar themes regarding the disjuncture between values and actions within corporate settings.

For instance, the case of Dennis Gioia and the Ford Pinto recall process demonstrates this type of situation (Gioia, 1992). According to Gioia, he began working at the Ford Motor Company with "a strongly held value system" that included a scathing criticism of business practices that violated ethical norms of social responsibility. However, Gioia claims that he was "quickly caught up in the game" to improve Ford's market share in the midst of strong international competition, a crippling energy crisis, and increased federal regulations in safety and emissions. As the company's Field Recall Coordinator, Gioia was in the position to make initial recommendations about future recalls and to vote in favor of or against potential recalls. Despite a stream of documentation that pointed to the likelihood of an explosion in low-speed, rear-end collisions, Gioia was slow to recommend that the Pinto be evaluated by a full departmental review board. In fact, his decision to recommend a review occurred only after he had visited the "chamber or horrors," where seeing the burnt out cars shook him out of routine ways of processing the Pinto case. Since Ford's internal standard and the laws governing recalls at the time did not provide adequate justification for the recall, the review board (and Gioia himself) voted against the Pinto recall. Only retrospectively does Gioia conclude that while his actions may have been legal and ethical, they were not moral. In other words, as Gioia was socialized within the organizational context of Ford, his actions became incongruent with his own internalized and professed values. These cases suggest that the immersion into an organizational context can become somehow ingrained in individuals over time. In these contexts, beliefs and behaviors begin to seem taken for granted, thereby replacing active decision making with routinized decision-making.

Consider how social processes condition the way in which the brain sorts information and frames potential decisions and actions. Snook (2002) and others (Weick, 1986; Gioia, 1992; Werhane, 1999) have convincingly argued that making sense of a situation occurs prior to the moment of making a decision. Snook argues that "framing the individual level puzzle as a question of meaning rather than deciding shifts the emphasis away from individual decision makers toward a point somewhere 'out there' where context and individual actions overlap" (2002: 207). This focus allows us to explore how "bad" decisions and actions can occur when good people internalize sense-making schema that exclude ethical or moral considerations.

The process of making sense begins by placing experiential stimuli into an interpretive frame or schema that organizes and filters our perception of the experience (see Senge, 1990; Starbuck and Milliken, 1988). These cognitive schemas, or mental models, impose structure upon information and organize knowledge in a way that can minimize the necessity for active cognition. Over time, mental models become reinforced through various organizational practices, routines, policies, procedures, ideas, and interactions so that our personal and collective sense making is highly structured and requires minimal (if any) effort on the part of individuals.

Significantly, this type of structured knowledge provides individuals with both an interpretation of a situation (or series of situations) and a prescriptive guide for action given this interpretation. In other words, these mental models are both descriptive and normative, as they shape our conception of what is and offer us scripts regarding the range of available responses.

Arguably these scripts operate on the basis of prototypes, which contain all the relevant information to a specific knowledge category (such as "safety problems"). All incoming data are filtered through these protoscripts, where matching information becomes organized into the existing dataset, and non-matching information gets filtered out entirely. This process of relying upon scripts thus allows sense making and decision making to occur automatically and unconsciously.

Without question, these scripts become essential to us as they facilitate efficiency and expedite decision-making processes. As certain types of situations or data become familiar, we must rely upon tried and true models of how the world works and what solutions have been successful in the past. Hence, we effortlessly believe that the schemas are accurate and that the scripts offer us viable solutions to routine problems. Gioia (1992) uses this notion of scripts to understand his own experience as Recall Coordinator. First, he argues that the scripts that he utilized regarding the Pintos were shaped by repeated input about similar vehicle accidents, thereby making this type of decision routine. Second, the job requirements themselves precluded active cognition due to the sheer volume of data that he was required to process efficiently in a workday. Third, the organizational training that Gioia received reinforced the need to remain objective and rely on formal operational procedures outlined by the company and the law, rather than training him to subjectively engage in a more reflective process of decision

making. More specifically, the context at Ford Motor Company intentionally limited the incorporation of emotions and self-reflection that
could "blur" the cost–benefit analyses he was expected to perform in
his role with the company. As seen here, over time our reliance on specific scripts becomes cognitively hard-wired, making it very difficult to
reflect upon or rethink routine decisions.

Many other cases illustrate how this type of over-reliance on scripts
can have devastating consequences. Take the case of friendly fire in
northern Iraq. Countless successful missions in Iraq gave the pilots
confidence to act on well-established and reinforced scripts that told
them to "see" enemy Hinds helicopters instead of US Black Hawk helicopters (Snook, 2002). Similarly, Wagner Dodge and his crew expected
to "see" a 10 o'clock fire at Mann Gulch, given the "tried and true"
schema that had worked in fighting other fires (Weick, 1993). The
notion of scripts helps us understand that when we expect automobile
explosions in small cars, or when we expect to see the enemy, or when
we expect to put out a fire by 10 o'clock, then this is what we see and
this is what provides motivation for our action or inaction. In essence,
we are guided in our interpretation, decision and action by socially
embedded scripts that are reinforced and maintained by the repetition
of job tasks and routine procedures that have been internalized over
time.

This analysis does not imply that the organizational scripts themselves are inherently problematic. In fact, they are generally perceived
as normatively neutral in their effort to ensure effective organizational
functioning. However, within corporate contexts, scripts can include
a limited set of objectives such as efficiency, productivity or profit, to
the exclusion or marginalization of more socially responsible goals.
When people begin to make decisions based entirely on these cognitive
scripts, they can inadvertently exclude ethical, moral or legal deliber-
ation from their framing of situations and decision-making processes.
Additionally, since schemas are both interpretive and prescriptive, the
logic of action follows these context-specific scripts in relatively predictable ways (DiMaggio, 1994). Incrementally emergent sets of procedures and routines, whether formally written or informally enacted,
combine to structure and justify actions over time. Within this context, otherwise good people can act out schema designed to achieve
a relatively narrow set of objectives that can drift away from their
internally held values or sanctioned principles.

A process for principled leadership

Organizational shells that provide layers of procedures, policies, role expectations, and institutionalized scripts may help groups of people perform relatively effectively under normal conditions; however, these shells can stifle active decision making among participants in the system. As described by Scott Snook (2002, p. 111), "to those immersed in them, such systems appear to be both omnipresent and omnipotent." As the Stanford Prison Experiment and the Pinto cases illustrate, Zimbardo and Gioia became "caught up in the game" of the dominant scripts until something "woke them up" to a broader interpretation of the situation at hand. Caught in the midst of the circumstances, these leaders began to lack a holistic interpretation of the situation and the moral implications for their decisions and actions. Here we see how schema and the organizational shells that reinforced them began to act as a substitute for strong and principled leadership. Only after disengaging from the particular context could Zimbardo and Gioia recognize the scripts in operation and reflect upon how their own values related to these dominant conceptual frames. We can speculate that one explanation for "good" and "thoughtful" Ken Lay's inability to lead with his espoused principles of respect, integrity, honesty, and sincerity at Enron may have been the normative pressures and mindless following of routinized practices that did not encourage values-based decision making.

However, principled leadership necessarily involves more than a retroactive consideration of the dominant scripts that guide decision-making and action. In other words, principled leaders must engage in an ongoing and purposeful process of rethinking the scripts that define situations and prescribe action. Werhane (1999, p. 93) refers to this as engaging the moral imagination, or "the ability in particular circumstances to discover and evaluate possibilities not merely determined by that circumstance, or limited by its operative mental models, or merely framed by a set of rule-governed concerns". Werhane argues that moral imagination begins with an individual's ability to disengage from a socially embedded script in order to consider a range of viable solutions to problems that have normative implications. In order to accomplish this, we propose a three-step process for principled leadership; the three steps are: (1) *Awareness*, making moral and ethical dimensions an explicit part of leadership decisions and action, (2) *Self-reflection* on one's personal values, the firm's values, and their alignment, and (3) *Breathing life into organizations with principled leadership*, using leadership skills of language, symbolism, and story-telling to enliven values. In all these steps, principled leadership orients itself to the social relationships in which leading is embedded; as we discussed earlier, our view of principled leadership is necessarily social and relational, both with regard to followership and to those affected by leadership actions. Next, we describe each of these three steps in the process of principled leadership.

Awareness

As an initial step, leaders must become aware of the moral and ethical dimensions of a particular situation, and evaluate the extent to which the existing conceptual models attend to these moral and ethical issues. Here, the leader must remain cognizant of the vision of the company as a whole, including both the everyday routines that insure efficiency and the overarching role of the company within the larger society. As well, leaders need to re-visit or return often to the root of their moral values. Renewing and refreshing those commitments helps keep awareness current, and returning to the root values replenishes both leaders and their values.

Questions of awareness for a principled leader to consider could be: "According to our mission and our value statement, to whom are we accountable?" And, "Do the operative schema dominating this situation take into consideration the range of stakeholders that share an interest in our operations?" One way to frame this stage of consideration includes the ability of leaders to assess the extent to which the organization aligns itself with the existing laws, the ethical norms shared by other similar organizations, and the moral obligations that it claims to hold regarding individual and community stakeholders (cf. Freeman, 2002).

Self-reflection

As the second step in this process, leaders must ensure that the values and overarching vision for the company are congruent with her/his own internalized set of values and principles. Necessarily this process begins with having a clear sense of one's personal values and being able to prioritize and articulate those values. However, this process does not end with making a list of these hierarchically ordered values. Instead, this set of values must be mapped onto the existing context and the socially embedded situation at hand to examine where they overlap and where they diverge. This process may lead the principled leader to ask questions such as: "Can I sleep with the decision that I make in leading this organization forward?" Or, "Can I be proud to tell my family members and friends what decisions I make and the actions that I take?"

Several other "tests" – or self-reflective questions – offer alternative and feasible ways for deciding if the alignment with vision and values is present; these include possibilities such as:

The Front Page Test: Would I be comfortable if this decision were on the front page?
The Golden Rule Test: Would I be willing to be treated in the same way?
The Dignity Test: Are the dignity and humanity of others preserved?
The Equal Treatment Test: Are the rights of the disadvantaged given consideration?
The Personal Gain Test: Does personal gain cloud my judgment?
The Congruence Test: Is this consistent with my own personal principles?
The Cost–Benefit Test: Does a benefit for some cause harm to others?
The Procedural Justice Test: Do the procedures stand up to scrutiny by those affected?

Questions such as these ask an honest and engaged leader to actively self-reflect on how her/his values align with both the operative mental models and the stated values of the organization. By differentiating the operative conceptual schema from the stated values in the previous stage, the leader is better able to understand the underlying tension that may exist between her/his values and the ethical and moral dimensions of a specific context. For example, if the process of self-reflection leads to a realization that the leader's values are in conflict with the overarching vision and values of the organization, principled action may involve exiting the company altogether. However, if the leader shares the overarching values and vision of the organization but diverges from the operative mental models, the principled leader may decide to take the initiative to reframe or reinterpret the situation in a way that is more congruent with the stated vision of the organization. At this point, the leader can begin to assess her/his role and potential options for principled change.

These two options for principled leadership parallel Hirschman's (1970) distinction between alternative ways of reacting to dissatisfaction with organizations: "exit," i.e., quitting or leaving the organization, or "voice," agitating in order to exert influence for change "from within." Choosing between these alternative strategies is driven by the perceived value conflict that the leader observes and by the likelihood that the leader can be an effective agent of change in the organization.

Breathing life through action

Third, leaders must begin to supplement the existing mental models that preclude active cognition with new possibilities that may appear "outside the box" to other people within the organization. At this stage, leaders begin to breathe new life into organizational shells (Dutton, 2003; Snook, 2002) by interrupting the potential progression in which minor issues lead to more complex problems, and then culminate in a disastrous crisis. Enlivening organizations with leadership principles is consistent with the "new leadership" paradigm, which sees leaders as vibrant, energetic actors in their organizations:

... effective leaders should be proactive, change-oriented, innovative, motivating and inspiring, and have a vision or mission with which they infuse the group. They should also be interested in others, and be able to create commitment to the group, and extract extra effort from and empower members of the group. (Hogg, 2005, p. 55)

Breathing life involves sense-making, updating and questioning existing mental models, rather than decision making within those models. Moreover, breathing life involves not only cognition but also collaboration; leaders don't simply provide directions, commands, or even vision, but need to develop relationships with organizational members and stakeholders. Having leaders work together with members seems a necessity; in addition, telling stories that illustrate values, inspire people and connect them to the organization gives life to leadership. Under changing mental models, leadership values and principles guide and anchor change, as well as offering points of connection between leaders and others.

Karl Weick (2001), in a chapter provocatively entitled, "Leadership as the legitimation of doubt," suggests that "... in the face of doubt, leaders are best served if they focus on animation,

improvisation, lightness, and learning" (p. 96). He explains the process by which leaders use their values to animate and breathe life into
organizations:

It is the combination of thrown-ness, unknowability, and unpredictability
that makes having some direction, any direction, the central issue for human
beings, and by implication, the central issue for leaders. Sensemaking is about
navigating by means of a compass rather than a map.... Maps may be the
mainstay of performance, but *the compass and the compass needle, which
function much like human values*, are the mainstays of learning and renewal.
If people find themselves in a world that is only partially charted, and if
leaders also admit that they too don't know, then both are more likely to
mobilize resources for direction making rather than for performance. (Weick,
2001, p. 92)

The case of Roy Vagelos at Merck again provides an insightful illustration (Vagelos and Galambos, 2004) on using his humanistic values
as a compass under uncertainty. In our opinion, his leadership decisions
and actions reveal this three-step process of breathing life into an organization by challenging the dominant mental model of economically
measured, profit driven action. Initially, we see how Vagelos engaged in
the process of "awareness," by examining the moral and ethical dimensions of the situation and the implications of his decision, considering
a wide and diverse set of stakeholders (shareholders; Merck scientists;
African communities; those afflicted with river blindness) who could
win or lose by his decision. Next, Vagelos begins to "self-reflect" on
his own values, those of his company, Merck, and their alignment. He
observed the congruence between his personal values and the two mental models, which tugged at him (i.e. corporate profitability versus saving human lives) and the overarching vision and mission of his company
(Merck's valuation of human life as a primary value) to decide to act.
And, finally, Vagelos breathes life into the organization by being willing
to see from outside the box – originally looking to other organizations
for solutions (e.g. INGOs and governments to develop and distribute
the drug) – but, with their refusal, he assumed responsibility, using his
"moral compass" to guide him through unpredictable territory.

Throughout the process, Vagelos used his skills at story-telling to
keep the founder's dream and vision alive at Merck to shareholders,
board, employees and other stakeholders. The result was a win-win
decision. In 1987, Merck & Co. announced that it had successfully

tested a drug that prevented river blindness and that *the company would make the drug available, free of charge, to anyone in the world who needed it, forever.* Vagelos' principled leadership proved to be both a lifesaver, to those suffering from the disease, and a profitable source of reputational capital for his company. As former President Jimmy Carter pointed out:

[Merck] showed that the corporate world can indeed be committed to the alleviation of suffering. Obviously, Merck doesn't get anything for these tablets – they give them away free. *What they get is the recognition by their own employees and potential customers that Merck has a heart.*

Thus, leading by principles need not be a zero-sum game.

Conclusion

Leadership, it seems, has always been storied. From ancient times to modern ones, cultures have told tales of their gods and heroes, and, more recently, iconic CEOs (e.g., Byron, 2004; Goode, 1978; Useem, 1998). Business leaders are romanticized in the press (Meindl, Ehrlich and Dukerich, 1985), often portrayed as the "corporate saviour" (Khurana, 2002) who leads by dint of their unique attributes (Weber, 1997) that imprint organizations (Biggart, 1989). And yet, as dramatic as these accounts can be, they can also be lifeless and unsatisfying. Weick (1993) alerts us to how, in the absence of trusting social relationships and a cohesive work culture, leaders can fail, in spite of their considerable expertise and drive. In this chapter, we offer an alternative to the cultural stereotype of leadership (Bligh and Meindl, 2005).

In our framework, we propose that principled leadership is social and relational, consisting of awareness, self-reflection, and actions that breathe life into organizations and overcome those situational factors that may challenge leaders' values and principles. Thus, if leaders are to succeed and "breathe life" into the organizations they lead (Snook, 2002), leading with one's principles and values must be generative and social.

References

Bass, B. and Stodgill, R. M. 1990. *Bass & Stodgill's Handbook of Leadership*, 3rd edn. New York: Free Press.

Biggart, N. 1989. *Charismatic Capitalism*. Chicago: University of Chicago Press.

Bligh, M. C. and Meindl, J. R. 2005. The cultural ecology of leadership: An analysis of popular leadership books. In Messick, D. M. and Kramer, R. M. (eds.), *The Psychology of Leadership*, 11–52. Mahwah, NJ: Lawrence Erlbaum.

Byron, C. 2004. *Testosterone Inc.* Hoboken, NJ: Wiley and Sons.

Cameron, K., Dutton, J., and Quinn, R. 2003. *Positive Organizational Scholarship*. San Francisco: Berrett-Koehler Publishers.

DiMaggio, P. 1994. Culture and economy. In N. J. Smelser and R. Swedberg (eds.), *The Handbook of Sociology*. Princeton: Princeton University Press.

Dutton, J. E. 2003. Breathing life into organizational studies. *Journal of Management Inquiry*, 12: 5–20.

Eichenwald, K. 2005. *Conspiracy of Fools: A True Story*. New York: Broadway Press.

Freeman, E. R. 2002. Stakeholder theory of the modern corporation. In T. Donaldson, P. Werhane, and M. Cording (eds.), *Ethical Issues in Business: A Philosophical Approach* (7th edn). Upper Saddle River, NJ: Prentice Hall.

Gardner, H. 1995. *Leading Minds: An Anatomy of Leadership*. New York, NY: Basic.

Gioia, D. A. 1992. Pinto fires and personal ethics: A script analysis of missed opportunities. *Journal of Business Ethics*, 11: 379–389.

Goode, W. J. 1978. *The Celebration of Heroes*. Berkeley: University of California Press.

Hirschmann, O. 1970. *Exit Voice and Loyalty: Responses to Decline in Firms, Organizations, and States*. Cambridge, MA: Harvard University Press.

Hogg, M. A. 2005. Social identity and leadership. In D. M. Messick and R. M. Kramer (eds.), *The Psychology of Leadership*, 53–80. Mahwah, NJ: Lawrence Erlbaum.

Independent News and Media. 2005. "Houston has a problem: The countdown starts at Enron," September 4.

Khurana, R. 2002. *Searching for a Corporate Savior: The Irrational Quest for Charismatic CEOs*. Princeton: Princeton University Press.

Marquis, C., Glynn, M. A., and Davis, G. F. forthcoming. Community isomorphism and corporate social action. *Academy of Management Review*.

McLean, B., and Elkind, P. 2004. *The Smartest Guys in the Room: The Amazing Rise and Scandalous Fall of Enron*. New York: Penguin Books.

Meindl, J. R., Ehrlich, S. B. and Dukerich, J. M. 1985. The romance of leadership. *Administrative Science Quarterly*, 30(1), 78–102.

Moberg, D. J. 1999. When bad people do good things at work, *Issues in Ethics*, 10 (2), Fall.

Senge, P. M. 1990. *The Fifth Dimension: The Art and Practice of the Learning Organization*. New York: Currency Doubleday.

Snook, S. 2002. *Friendly Fire: The Accidental Shootdown of US Black Hawks over Northern Iraq*. Princeton University.

Starbuck, W. H. and Milliken, F. J. 1988. Executives' perpetual filters: What they notice and how they make sense. In W. H. Starbuck and F. J. Milliken (eds.), *The Executive Effect: Concepts and Methods for Studying Top Executives*. Greenwich CT: JAL Press.

Tichy, N., McGill, A. R., and St Clair, L. 1997. *Corporate Global Citizenship: Doing Business in the Public Eye*. Lanham, MD: Lexington Books.

Useem, M. 1998. *The Leadership Moment*. New York: Three Rivers Press.

Vagelos, R. and Galambos, L. 2004. *Medicine, Science and Merck*. Cambridge: Cambridge University Press.

Weber, M. 1997. *The Theory of Social and Economic Organization*. New York: Free Press.

Weick, K. 1993. The collapse of sensemaking in organizations: The Mann Gulch disaster, *Administrative Science Quarterly*, 38: 628–652.

Sensemaking in Organizations. Thousand Oaks, CA: Sage.

Leadership as the legitimation of doubt. In W. Bennis, G. M. Spreitzer, and T. G. Cummings (eds.). *The Future of Leadership*, pp. 91–102. San Francisco: Jossey-Bass.

Werhane, P. H. 1999. *Moral Imagination and Management Decision-Making*. Oxford: Oxford University Press.

2002. Moral imagination and systems thinking, *Journal of Business Ethics*, 38: 33–42.

Zimbardo, P. 2004. A situationalist perspective on the psychology of evil: Understanding how good people are transformed into perpetrators. In A. G. Miller (ed.), *The Social Psychology of Good and Evil*. New York: Guilford Press.

Zimbardo, P. 2005. You can't be a sweet cucumber in a vinegar barrel: A talk with Philip Zimbardo. *Edge*. January 19.

9 Forgiveness as an attribute of leadership

DAVID S. BRIGHT

Forgiveness is a response to perceived negative experiences in the workplace in which the propensity toward harbored negativity is displaced or dissolved, allowing the forgiver to "refrain from causing the offender harm even though he or she believes it is morally justifiable to do so" (Aquino et al., 2003, p. 212). It is an important attribute of leaders because it buffers them against the potential harm and distraction that can result from the mistakes, misdeeds, and offenses of others (Bright, 2005). Forgiveness functions as a lubricant to the friction that occurs during the natural course of human interaction, in which the potential for inflicting or experiencing offense – via conflict, misunderstanding, hurt feelings, etc. – is an inherent possibility. Indeed, forgiveness is central to the establishment, preservation and maintenance of human relationships that make up and sustain organizations (Aquino et al., 2003).

This chapter addresses the question of why forgiveness is particularly relevant to leaders in organizations. Evidence from research on forgiveness in a unionized company, LTL Trucking, provides an illustration of (1) the three different modes of forgiveness and their effects on organizational performance, (2) differences in modes of forgiveness among different levels of employees in the organization, and (3) how greater forgiveness in the workplace has substantial organizational benefits. The chapter shows that forgiveness allows for the continuation of interpersonal connections even in the midst of conflict, turmoil, or change; in fact, it can be practiced to create lasting, transformative effects on the interpersonal relationships that make it possible for organizations to function at high levels.

The attribute of forgiveness

First, it is important to understand several basic features of forgiveness as an attribute of leadership (Cameron and Caza, 2002). Scholars

see forgiveness as a fundamental human virtue, meaning that it represents a form of moral and spiritual "goodness" in the human experience (Peterson and Seligman, 2004). Forgiveness also belongs to that
class of virtues that can be practiced only when the need for them is
invoked (Bright, Cameron, and Caza, 2005). For example, while the
virtue of integrity can be practiced continuously as a consistent demonstration of character, forgiveness is necessary only when the potential for conflict emerges. The way a person chooses to respond during
these tough moments manifest his or her propensity to forgive or to be
forgiving (Bright, 2005).

   In common usage, the word "forgiveness" invokes several very distinct connotations, making it important to be precise about its meaning
(Worthington, 2005; McCullough, Pargament, and Thoresen, 2000;
Enright and Fitzgibbons, 2000; Freedman, 1998). In this chapter I
focus specifically on forgiveness as an intrapersonal experience, where
an individual participant in an organization chooses to overcome the
potential negative emotions, thoughts, and behavioral tendencies that
occur after he or she perceives that another person or group has committed an offense against him or her. This is distinct from other usages,
such as where an organization chooses to pardon or forgo punish-
ing misbehaving members (e.g. a church forgives by refraining to expel
one its members), or where creditors forgive debtors of financial obligations (e.g. the World Bank forgives the debt of a Third-World country).
Moreover, forgiveness does not condone wrongdoing (i.e. implicitly
accept wrongful behavior), it is not reconciliation (e.g. two or more
parties may agree to work together even though they may harbor negative feelings toward one another), nor is it denial or forgetting. In lieu
of these related concepts, forgiveness has to do with the choice points
that determine how a person reacts during those moments when he or
she is naturally tempted to act on negative feelings or thoughts against
others who are seen as offensive (Yamhure Thompson and Shahen,
2002).

Case example: John and Sam

LTL Trucking is an international, unionized freight transportation
company with about 28,000 employees. Over 80% of workers are
staged in one of 29 terminals located across North America. The company is over 70 years old and has had a long history of difficult

management–union relations. The biggest labor groups are truck drivers and dockworkers. Front-line managers have a reputation for being tough-minded and hard driving.

The following simple vignette about two leaders – a manager and a union steward – illustrates the relevance of forgiveness to the practice of leadership.

John was a new terminal manager at an LTL Trucking facility. Eager to make his mark in this most recent assignment, he was on his way home from work on his first day when he saw one his terminal's trucks parked at a convenience store. Stopping to investigate, he discovered that the engine was running, the cab unsecured, and the driver unseen – all of these factors appeared to be a violation of company policy. He waited.

A few moments later the driver, Sam, exited the store with an ice cream cone in one hand and a handful of snacks in the other. John confronted Sam about the unsecured, running truck. John immediately promised a written reprimand, while Sam argued that he was just doing his job, that this was a common practice among all drivers, and that he didn't like being followed and harassed. He promised to file a grievance. This initial encounter was less than idyllic.

The next morning John returned to the terminal office, eager to establish a positive labor relationship in an early meeting with union leaders. He was shocked when he saw Sam enter the room as a union steward. Both leaders were immediately defensive, experiencing a resurgence in the negative emotions, attributions, and words that they had voiced during their previous encounter.

This experience shaped the way that these two leaders interacted with one another for about three years. Each fought hard to represent his own interests, and each continued to see the other as a rival, as a challenge to his authority or personal dignity. Still, they found ways to work through the most pressing challenges; for instance, they worked through several contract bidding cycles, finding compromises that would allow them each to save face while appearing to fight for his cause.

Then the company's senior leadership decided that a cultural transformation in the company was needed for its long-term survival. High labor costs were driving out nearly all of their unionized rivals. At the time, 50% of their competitors were much leaner non-unionized carriers. Already, the company's margin was barely 1%, and costs were rising. However, in contrast to their competitors who tried to force concessions from the union, they choose to bet on forging a new, friendlier and more collaborative relationship between union and management. The risks were huge.

As the main vehicle for igniting this shift, the company designed a series of interventions based in Appreciative Inquiry, a positive organizational development method that aims to help all employees become active, collaborative students of the organization. The intervention typically kicks off with a summit, in which several hundred employees at a given facility meet together for three days. The lead activity is usually an "appreciative interview" in which people pair up with someone they don't know – usually someone who has a very different perspective – to learn about their deepest hopes, visions, and passions for engagement in the organization. The lowest-status dockworker might interview John, terminal manager, and the CEO might interview Sam, the union steward. Usually, these conversations lead to discoveries about the humanness of every member of an organization, and this produces a new respect for the unique role that each person plays within a whole system.

Through guided discussions, employees work together to discover the best qualities that currently exist within their facility, they dream about what could be if employee–management relations were working at their best, and then they organize into action teams to work on specific initiatives that will help to put some of these ideas into practice. Management, in particular, decided to view the Union not as a begrudging rival but as a collaborative partner that brought significant value to the ability of the company to operate. For example, the CEO began touting the Union's importance in creating job stability, training highly skilled employees, and generating a strong atmosphere of safety. These meetings became widespread throughout LTL Trucking.

When the summit was introduced at John and Sam's facility, both leaders decided to take seriously the opportunity to forge a new relationship. As an example, Sam led a team of four truck-driving colleagues to develop a new marketing initiative, where truck drivers would not function merely as delivery agents but also as an active sales force. Driver Tom's assignment was to haul freight to and from a small nearby town. Tom and Sam went to John with a proposal to sponsor a breakfast for all the business owners in the town. All they needed was a small budget to buy food and reserve a banquet room.

John hesitated at first, but, based in part on his emerging esteem for Sam and Tom's leadership, he finally agreed.

True to his plan, Tom personally invited every potential and existing customer to come to a "special event." The breakfast included a program and a sales pitch, where he told the owners what he would personally do as a truck driver to ensure that their freight was handled well. He told them, "I am a truck driver for LTL Trucking, and this is what I will personally do for you to win and keep your business, because to you, I *am* LTL Trucking." He asked them what they most wanted out of a trucking service. He took their feedback back to the terminal. The result of this audacious driver's initiative was a nearly $1 million annual increase in revenue from this small town alone.

Sam's team became notorious throughout the company for similar initiatives and activities. This was an enormous change from business-as-usual where the boundaries of the truck driver function were contractually spelled out in minute detail. The results of similar activities across LTL Trucking transformed the organization. During the past four years, millions of dollars in direct cost savings have emerged. More telling is the fact that the profit margin has increased from 1% to 12%, resulting in many millions more in profitability. A cross-sectional group of employees and managers recently recommended a change in job titles for workers at all levels: dockworkers are now "freight-handling professionals," truck drivers are now "driver account representatives," and terminal managers are now "regional service coordinators." The changes have shifted fundamental assumptions about the scope of an individual's responsibilities.

The willingness of Sam and John as leaders to forgive and move beyond old grudges and a paradigm of conflict between labor and management is one reason for the emergence of these beneficial outcomes.

Three modes of forgiveness

A recent research project uncovered the dimensions of forgiveness that lead to such remarkable results (Bright, Fry, and Cooperrider, 2005). Figure 9.1 below outlines the different states of mind in individuals as they move through their reactions to offensive experiences (Bright, 2005; Yamhure Thompson and Shahen, 2002). The first box represents the ordinary, normative state of mind. All people carry with them

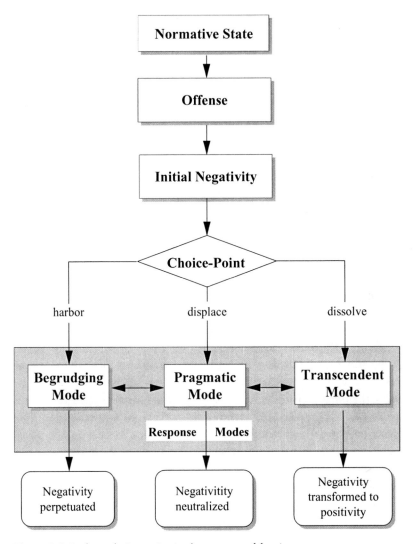

Figure 9.1 Path to choice-point in the process of forgiveness

certain expectations about how the relational world should work: how people should treat one another, how organizational policies should function, what constitutes appropriate language, what moral or ethical codes should be practiced, and so on. The operative word here is "should," that is, every person has expectations about what is right and wrong, and so long as experiences conform with these expectations, he or she feels comfortable. For instance, John's normative expectations when he first joined LTL Trucking were that company policies and the union contract were to be followed exactly. Sam's expectations, on the other hand, were that drivers should be able to work in a comfortable environment, that they should be trusted to carry out their work, and that it was unsafe and inefficient to turn off a large diesel engine just for a few minutes. It was a common practice for drivers to keep truck engines idling during very short stops.

Step two represents the catalytic moment, the point in time when a person confronts an experience in which it appears that there is a violation in normative expectations: an employee fails to perform appropriately, a manager inappropriately uses abusive or vulgar language, or in the worse cases, blatant crimes are committed. John experienced this violation of his expectations when he found the unsecured truck parked at the convenience store. In his mind it was a clear violation of the company norms he was obliged to enforce. This feeling intensified when Sam's reaction was defensive rather than conciliatory. "Why can't he just admit that he is wrong?" was a predictable reaction for John.

For his part, Sam's sense of violation occurred when he found John waiting at the truck. It was common for truck drivers to talk about being followed or stalked by company officials, an oft-cited point of resentment. He and other drivers might have felt that it was safer to leave the big diesel engine running rather than turn it off for just a few moments. His predictable reaction was, "You're harassing me. You don't trust me. I can be counted on by my job. I have a proven track record, and the fact that I'm respected by my peers is proof!"

Figure 9.1 shows that the immediate reaction in these moments is initial negativity, where the offended person feels anger, defensiveness, retaliation, or frustration. This "dissonance and distress" (Yamhure Thompson and Shahen, 2002, p. 407; Janoff-Bulman, 1992) is a normal outgrowth of a mismatch between one's expectations and experiences, and it represents a choice-point (Glidewell, 1970). It is at this moment that forgiveness may or may not emerge.

The final box in Figure 9.1 illustrates that people tend to draw on one of three modes when responding to offensive experiences. The begrudging mode perpetuates negativity; the pragmatic neutralizes negativity, and the transcendent mode transforms negativity into positive ends (Bright, 2005; Bright, Fry, and Cooperrider, 2005). The remainder of the chapter discusses these three reactions to violated expectations, and it illustrates the consequences of each one of the three responses.

Table 9.1 *Embedded assumptions in modes of response to offense*

Begrudging	Pragmatic	Transcendent
Self-protection	Self-interest	Self + Other
Survival-fight	Suvival-engage	Learn
Compete	Compromise	Transcend
Negativity	Neutrality	Positivity
Forgiveness is an illusion	Forgiveness is a necessity	Forgiveness as life choice

The begrudging mode

At one extreme is begrudgement, which fosters the choice NOT to forgive but, rather, to hold on to the negativity. This mode is invoked when people feel threatened or disabled in their relations with offenders, making the need for self-protection a paramount concern. They may look for ways to justify the harboring of deep negativity, for example by creating stories that they have to fight back to survive in a highly competitive world where there are only winners and losers. People who choose this response mode may see forgiveness as an illusion and, at best, they use the possibility of forgiveness as a bargaining chip in the negotiations.

The initial begrudging mode selected by Sam and John led to a strained relationship that lasted for nearly three years. The assumptions that shaped this conflict were deeply rooted in over 70 years of animosity between union and management. Emotions, particularly negative ones, are contagious in organizations (Barsade, 2002). It is common for stories of egregious activities to be told and retold for many years. With each retelling of an offensive story, the anger, frustration, and animosity is reinforced and perpetuated. In LTL Trucking, there were tales of workers in this organization who kept mental score of the perceived offenses that others had committed against them, drawing on these slights as justification for acting out in retaliation. This included about 25% of the workers in Sam and John's company (Bright, 2005; Bright, Fry, and Cooperrider, 2005).

The outcome of this conflict, as reflected in table 9.1, was the perpetuation of deep-seated negativity. The deleterious impacts of such deep-seated negativity on both people and the organization leads to revenge, incivility, and conflict (Bies and Tripp, 1997; Andersson, 1999; Mikkelsen and Einarsen, 2002). Needless to say, dysfunctional workplace relationships have a negative impact on the performance of organizations (Dutton et al., 1997).

The pragmatic mode

In contrast, a pragmatic response to offense fosters a minimal form of forgiveness in which people actively work to neutralize the intrapersonal negativity associated with the violation of expectation. The basis for doing so, however, is highly utilitarian. People might talk about the necessity of working together to achieve common aims, but they are focused on their own self-interests even when it is in their best self-interest to find a workable relationship with those who have offended them. "It's not worth it to hold on to these [negative] feelings," was a common statement heard in interviews at LTL Trucking. This statement indicates an awareness of the personal costs of deep-seated negativity, leading many to find ways to overcome it. Thus, compromise is common, and forgiveness – at least to the point of displacing the negativity – is seen as necessary for sustained interpersonal interaction.

In LTL Trucking, the pragmatic mode was by far the most frequent. Through Sam and John's negotiations as leaders on both sides of the management–labor divide, they had to find a way to put aside the negative feelings that came from their initial encounter. By their own account, this was not an easy process. They described several encounters where they "put aside" (i.e. displaced or neutralized) their negative feelings toward each other in order to push for a common agenda that would allow both of them to successfully accomplish the aims of their respective constituents. This willingness to find ways to come together was a predominant theme among most workers' responses to offense, with over 90% invoking this mode in their general approach to the daily work interactions (Bright, 2005; Bright, Fry, and Cooperrider, 2005).

The transcendent mode

The third response identified in figure 9.1 is the transcendent mode, which describes a deeper form of forgiveness. Adopting this response enables the offended person to transcend negative emotions, to think broadly about the negative experience, and to consider how it might lead to positive outcomes. For instance, when people select this response mode they are concerned not only with themselves but also with others. Negative experiences present an opportunity for learning. People try to identify what good can come from the offense. From this perspective, forgiveness becomes a life-choice and an opportunity for achieving one's highest potential as a person or leader.

In Sam and John's case, they now talk about what they have learned from each other during the years since they forged a new relationship. Sam is learning from John about the fundamentals of the business, including the challenging tradeoffs that must be considered in making decisions. He also describes how he helps John engage a style of management that is supportive of workers. For his part, John has discovered how to recognize and draw on the best qualities of his workforce. Whereas they were once confrontational and antagonistic, they are now collaborative and supportive in their work relationship. LTL Trucking's dramatic improvement in performance can be ascribed, in part, to the fact that at least 40% of its workers were choosing the transcendent mode in their responses to common workplace offenses (Bright, 2005; Bright, Fry, and Cooperrider, 2005).

Benefits of transcendent forgiveness

To understand *why* a transcendent mode of forgiveness has positive effects on organizational performance whereas a begrudging mode has negative effects, consider John's insistence on reprimanding Sam, while Sam promised a grievance in retaliation. Each action was seen as offensive to the other, each had strong feelings about the encounter, and each had choice-points about how to respond to the negativity that he felt toward the other. It is hard to imagine that improved organizational performance in LTL Trucking would have been possible if labor employees had not overcome their animosity toward managers and vice versa.

Fredrickson (1998) demonstrated that negative and positive feelings operate in very distinct ways on how people think. When people's experiences are dominated by negative emotions, they instinctively invoke a survival mode, a natural fight-or-flight impulse (Bion, 1959). This means that they are mostly concerned with how to protect themselves and others whom they see as members of their social group. This protection or fight mode is consistent with the assumptions of begrudgement. The range of action possibilities is very predictable and narrow:

seek revenge on those who have hurt you, destroy them or their success if possible, make them suffer as much as you have suffered. In other words, negative feelings are associated with a *narrowing* effect on the alternatives people can consider in the ways they relate to one another (Fredrickson et al., 2000, 2003).

In contrast, positive emotions are associated with an *expansion* of thought-action possibilities. When people experience sensations such as happiness, contentment, or wonderment, they are primed to think creatively, playfully, and innovatively. Moreover, the range of issues to which they can pay attention increases dramatically. Positive emotions also create an "undoing" effect, meaning that they literally heal the mental and emotional ruptures that are associated with acute experiences with negativity (Fredrickson et al., 2000).

Fredrickson's work suggests that adopting a transcendent mode of forgiveness, in contrast to a begrudging mode, fosters positive emotionality and creates opportunities for others to experience positivity as well. People tend to feel positive emotions when they experience psychological safety, a sense of trust in their relationships with others, and being forgiven for offenses. When people are offended, the sense of trust is broken, or there is a lack of forgiveness, the narrowing effect of negativity will spiral. One of the ways transcendent forgiveness leads to enhanced organizational performance, in other words, is that it creates a positive mental and emotional mindset in which people can draw on the healing, restorative power of positive emotions.

Modes of forgiveness among different employee groups

The study of LTL Trucking also explored potential differences in the propensity of different categories of employees to be forgiving (Bright, 2005). First, a survey was created and distributed to a cross-section of employees at two LTL facilities, and 125 questionnaires were returned. Employees read three potentially offensive scenarios. For example, a peer scenario depicted a co-worker having a "bad day" who intentionally performed work incorrectly, then refused to correct it when requested to do so. As a result, the respondent was forced to make up for the co-worker's lack of performance. Respondents read this story then responded to questions about how forgiving they would be if they were affected by the offense. A score assessing the propensity to be forgiving in each scenario was created, and differences between managers,

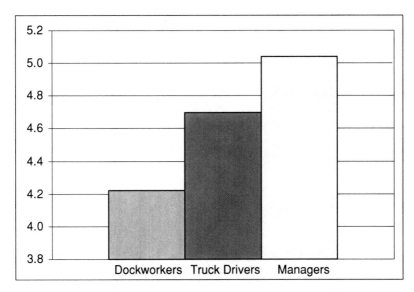

Figure 9.2 Comparison between work groups in mean scores of forgiveness

truck drivers, and dockworkers were statistically explored. The mean scores are summarized in figure 9.2, showing that dockworkers were the least likely to be forgiving, managers were the most likely to be forgiving, and truck drivers were in between. The differences were statistically significant. Forgiveness appears to be strongly associated with job position (e.g. a person's relative level in organizational hierarchy).

Additional evidence for the relationship between forgiveness and employees' job position was found by examining the responses of 45 interviewed workers who talked about their reactions to offenses in the workplace. These results are summarized in table 9.2 (Bright, 2005). More dockworkers and truck drivers than managers were likely to choose the begrudging response mode. Almost equal proportions of dockworkers, truck drivers, and managers selected the transcendent forgiveness mode, as indicated by the shaded area, although that response mode was rare. Most employees most of the time selected a pragmatic mode of forgiveness – "I will forgive if it benefits me" – although the transcendent and pragmatic modes combined were the most frequently selected category. The key summary finding in these analyses is that LTL Trucking's front-line managers tended to be more forgiving than other employees.

Table 9.2 *Frequency of response mode by employee group*

Mode of Forgiveness	Dockwrkrs	Drivers	Mgrs
Begrudgement only	1		
Begrudgement & pragmatic	5	4	
Pragmatic only	5	4	6
Pragmatic & transcendent	5	6	5
Transcendent only		1	1
Begrudgement & transcendent			1
All modes		1	
Total	16	16	13

Why are managers more forgiving?

Whereas it is impossible to say for sure, the nature of managerial work may help foster more pragmatic and transcendent modes of forgiveness and fewer begrudging responses. That is, the role of managers seems to require an advanced ability to cope with offense.

First, it is possible that people who have a more forgiving propensity are attracted to managerial roles in which interpersonal interactions are more frequent. The role of a front-line manager in LTL Trucking, as in other organizations, is highly demanding. He or she coordinates the work of up to dozens of workers, competes with other managers for resources, and tries to foster good communication with leaders and customers. In this role, maintaining good relations is imperative for success, and the consequence of holding grudges could be damaging both for relationships and for the company. Several managers talked of a certain persona as the ideal manager: tough-minded, but able to "let things slide off his back." It might be that those who are not able to address their own negativity would not be selected for these positions, or if they are, might not last.

Conversely, this demanding environment may influence people in management positions to become more forgiving if they do not already possess the capacity for it. The more the job requires high quality relationships, the more likely that forgiveness is required to be success-ful. It is possible that any manager who does not learn to be forgiving, or to manage his or her own negativity, does not survive long in the role. If managers were to predominantly draw on the begrudging response mode, they could perpetuate retaliation from workers, a distraction in terms of time and efficiency. As one manager noted, "Your main focus is how the union feels that day. If your guys are already pissed off because of something from last week, it just falls apart from there."

In contrast, the potential significance of forgiveness to leaders is substantial. Forgiveness can be employed by leaders to resolve conflict (Butler and Mullis, 2001), to increase the value of human resources (Kurzynski, 1998), as a means to rebuild cooperation (Bottom et al., 2002), and to promote an atmosphere of restorative justice (Bradfield and Aquino, 1999). For forgiving leaders themselves, the biological effects of forgiveness include physiological and psychosocial healing, and reduced illness and stress (Thoresen, Harris, and Luskin, 2000). It is related to greater creativity and learning, mental stability, enhanced cardiovascular fitness (McCullough et al., 2000), and emotional stability (Exline and Baumeister, 2000; Enright and Fitzgibbons, 2000). Leaders who have experienced forgiveness tend to be happier and more tolerant (Enright and Fitzgibbons, 2000), and those who have a forgiving disposition (Cameron and Caza, 2002) may have better social relationships, and greater life satisfaction and self-esteem (Ashton et al., 1998). These benefits of forgiveness for leaders are not trivial, and thus it should not be surprising to see a tendency toward forgiveness among managers who are placed in leadership positions.

Benefits of forgiveness to organizations

Forgiveness may also have a positive impact on organizational performance when it is practiced widely. In particular, forgiveness creates both buffering and amplifying effects in organizations. It buffers the organization from harm, and it amplifies positive effects.

Buffering effects

A buffering effect is evident when organizations are more resilient to challenging circumstances, when they able to withstand stressful, difficult circumstances. For instance, researchers have found that forgiveness was a significant factor in the ability of organizations to recover from downsizing (Bright, Cameron, and Caza, 2005; Cameron, Bright, and Caza, 2004). Downsizing is usually associated with highly negative outcomes among surviving employees: perceptions of injustice, life disruption, and personal harm (Cameron, Kim, and Whetten, 1987; McKinley, Sanchez, and Schick, 1995). Begrudgement is common, as evidenced by blaming, holding animosities, seeking vengeance, and displaying self-interest (Staw, Sandelands, and Dutton, 1981). Exceptions to these negative patterns emerge when employees forgive leaders for taking the decision to downsize, buffering the organization by enhancing resiliency, commitment, and a sense of efficacy (Masten and Reed, 2002; Dutton et al., 2002). Forgiveness deepens and enhances the ability to absorb the threat and trauma of downsizing and to bounce back from adversity (Dienstbier and Zillig, 2002; Fredrickson et al., 2000), and by enhancing the preservation of social capital and collective efficacy (Sutcliffe and Vogus, 2003). These findings imply that organizations benefit from forgiveness when they experience difficult circumstances mainly by relying on forgiveness to buffer the trauma. Resilience, healing, and restoration are more likely.

Amplifying effects

Forgiveness also creates an amplifying effect within organizations. Because forgiveness has the potential to transform negative to positive emotions, it can lead to a contagion effect in organizations (Barsade, 2002). Where one person expresses forgiveness, others are also more likely to forgive, leading to a replication of virtuousness and an elevation in positive well being (Fredrickson, 2003). In turn, positive emotions build high-quality relationships among organization members (Dutton and Heaphy, 2003; Bolino Turnley, and Bloodgood, 2002). Observing and experiencing forgiveness unlocks an upward spiral, and increasing social connections in an organization (Feldman and Khademian, 2003). In essence, virtuous actions such as forgiveness lead to and inspire more virtuous actions.

The LTL Trucking case provides some evidence that the buffering and amplifying benefits of forgiveness were in play. One benefit of a transcendent mindset among employees is that they come to see each other as "more human," more like oneself, and therefore, more forgivable. At one facility, the number of employees who expressed a willingness to draw on a transcendent mode of forgiveness increased substantially in the months after their participation in the organizational intervention based in appreciative inquiry. That is, focusing on a positive future helped employees become more inclined toward choosing transcendent forgiveness. Considering that LTL Trucking had a long history of labor–management conflict, fostering a more positive approach to employees' willingness to select transcendent forgiveness was a necessary condition for forging a new culture of collaboration. The indirect results, in terms of profitability and employee innovations, were impressive – note again the improved margin of profitability (an increase from 1% to 12%), a transformation in employee culture leading to a flattened leadership hierarchy, and numerous employee contributions of ideas that improved the bottom line.

How might leaders exercise transcendent forgiveness?

An adequate treatment of suggestions for practicing forgiveness is beyond the scope of this chapter, though many authors have written extensively on the topic (see especially Gustafson Affinito, 1999; also Enright and Fitzgibbons, 2000; Rye et al., 2000; Worthington, 2005). However, the results of this case analysis suggest not only many benefits of transcendent forgiveness, but also means to practice it.

One key idea in transcendent forgiveness is the ability to learn from negativity in one's experiences. The way that leaders shape their own normative expectations about appropriate and inappropriate activity within an organization sets the stage for both offense and forgiveness. How does a leader choose to interpret the mistakes and missteps that potentially lead to the experience of feeling offended? On one hand, leaders can choose to see any perceived slight, in either human or performance issues, as an opportunity for learning rather than keeping score, discovery rather than retaliation, and as a moment for personal and organizational development. Fostering this transcendent perspective reduces the likelihood that a person will be offended in the first place.

When a leader does feel offended, the degree of forgiveness is determined by how actively he or she chooses to use the experience as an opportunity for development, growth, and learning on the one hand, or as a moment to simply "get over" or "get through" on the other hand. The literature suggests several ideas for how to forgive, including the following:

- *Acknowledge the wound.* A first step to forgiveness is to recognize that one is suffering the effects of an offense. Acknowledging one's own feelings of hurt, anger, or disappointment is a first step toward choosing how to deal with the experience, even if others are unaware that a person feels offended. Writing one's feelings in a journal can help this process. Write down a description of the offending event, outline the implicit assumptions that made the moment feel particularly egregious, and capture emotions and thoughts. It may also be helpful to talk with a very close confidant, especially someone who is far removed from the situation. It may not be helpful to bring out one's feelings and thoughts in the immediate environment of the offense, though this depends on the strength of existing relationships.

- *Reframe perceptions of the offense and the offender.* Reframing encourages the offended leader to find out more about the offender and the circumstances that led to the offense. When a leader invokes his or her curiosity, he or she is now cognitively positioned to become other-focused and willing to learn, rather than self-focused and more inclined to accuse. Questions to ask might include any of the following:
  - What experiences in the offending party's background may cause the offending activity, for example, in one's upbringing or current home life?
  - What are the basic assumptions about work or life that shape the offending person's perspectives and conclusions?
  - How might I act if I were in this person's shoes?

  The discovery of answers to these questions can guide the leader to greater understanding, and often help him or her to feel greater empathy with the offending party's life experiences. Research shows that when people have empathy for others, it is easier to forgive them because we tend to see them as a reflection of ourselves.

- *Separate the question of justice or other issues from the question of forgiveness.* Justice deals with the social consequences of action, which should be debated and decided through the legal structure of organizations. Forgiveness focuses on how one deals with the intrapersonal emotions and thoughts that are induced by offense. A person can forgive without forgoing the right to justice. Similarly, a person can forgive without reconciling, condoning, or sending the wrong message. The greatest beneficiary of forgiveness is the forgiver.

- *Choose to forgive.* Forgiveness is active, not reactive. Indeed, the basic tenet of forgiveness is that it is a choice to exercise control over and to transform one's own reactions to potentially negative interpersonal experiences.

- *Find strength in one's belief structure.* Though forgiveness has strong secular impact (Arendt, 1958), it is discussed and encouraged in most spiritual traditions. For this reason, most people find that the capacity for forgiveness is often directly linked to a community of spiritual practice or tradition. When leaders link to their most deeply held belief structures, they often find a reserve of strength that encourages transcendent forgiveness.

At the level of organizations, forgiveness can have an influence on the way that a company learns from its past. Research on high performing organizations suggests that they learn from mistakes, and may even try to recreate them (Weick, Sutcliffe, and Obsfeld, 1999; Weick, 2003). When forgiveness is a prevalent practice within organizations, it allows people to focus on opportunities, rather than on vengeance. Leaders will foster organizational benefit when they encourage organization members to forgive one another of mistakes and misdeeds, while simultaneously addressing the systemic causes of human error. In this sense, organizations may be more effective to the extent that they forgive, yet don't forget.

Summary

The ability to exercise forgiveness is an important attribute of those who aspire to exercise strong leadership. Leaders in key positions have more influence on the culture and atmosphere of an organization than do other employees. They set an example that is contagious and that others draw on as a model for responding to challenging circumstances within an organization. Forgiveness is an important factor that helps create an atmosphere where relationships can develop in a more collaborative direction. Forgiveness is a means to repair workplace relationships (Aquino et al., 2003), and when organizations require that people work interdependently, it can mitigate the occurrence of damaged connections.

An understanding of forgiveness in the workplace serves to enhance such benefits for employees and foster greater organizational performance (Cameron, Bright, and Caza, 2004). That is, a better understanding of forgiveness helps enhance the propensity to forgive, which, in turn, is central to the establishment, preservation and maintenance of interpersonal connections in organizations. Successful managers and leaders practice forgiveness as a strategy for maintaining the benefits of positivity in their own experiences, and as a way to help encourage healthy, effective relationships among others. Forgiveness can be fostered as a common practice within an organization, and the results of this study of LTL Trucking highlight the fact that forgiveness is a key attribute of effective leadership and improved organizational performance.

References

Andersson, L. M. 1999. Tit for tat? The spiraling effect of incivility in the workplace. *Academy of Management Review*, 3: 452.

Aquino, K., Grover, S. L., Goldman, B., and Folger, R. 2003. When push doesn't come to shove: Interpersonal forgiveness in workplace relationships. *Journal of Management Inquiry*, 12 (3): 209–216.

Ashton, M. C., Paunone, S. V., Helmes, E., and Jackson, D. N. 1998. Kin altruism, reciprocal altruism, and the Big Five personality factors. *Evolution and Human Behavior*, 19: 243–255.

Arendt, H. 1958. Irreversibility and the power to forgive. In H. Arendt (ed.), *The Human Condition*. 233–247. Chicago, IL: University of Chicago Press.

Barsade, S. G. 2002. The ripple effect: Emotional contagion and its influence on group behavior. *Administrative Science Quarterly*, 47 (4): 644.

Bies, R. J., and Tripp, T. M. 1997. Revenge in organizations: The good, the bad, and the ugly. In R. W. Griffin, A. O'Leary-Kelly, and J. Collins (eds.), *Dysfunctional Behavior in Organizations*. Thousand Oaks, CA: Sage.

Bion, W. R. 1959. *Experiences in Groups*. New York, NY: Basic Books.

Bolino, M. C., Turnley, W. H., and Bloodgood, J. M. 2002. Citizenship behavior and the creation of social capital in organizations. *Academy of Management Review*, 27 (4): 505–522.

Bottom, W. P., Gibson, K., Daniels, S. E., and Murnighan, J. K. 2002. When talk is not cheap: Substantive penance and expressions of intent in rebuilding cooperation. *Organization Science*, 13 (5): 497.

Bradfield, M., and Aquino, K. 1999. The effects of blame attributions and offender likableness on forgiveness and revenge in the workplace. *Journal of Management*, 25 (5): 607–631.

Bright, D. S. 2005. Forgiveness and change: begrudging, pragmatic, and transcendent responses to discomfiture in a unionized trucking company. Unpublished dissertation, Case Western Reserve University, Cleveland, OH.

Bright, D. S., Cameron, K., and Caza, A. 2005. The ethos of virtuousness in downsized organizations. Working Paper: Department of Organizational Behavior, Case Western Reserve University.

Bright, D. S., Fry, R. E., and Cooperrider, D. L. 2005. Forgiveness from the perspectives of three response modes: Begrudgement, pragmatism, and transcendence. *Journal of Management Spirituality and Religion.*

Butler, D. S., and Mullis, F. 2001. Forgiveness: A conflict resolution strategy in the workplace. *Journal of Individual Psychology,* 57 (3): 259.

Cameron, K. S., Bright, D. S., and Caza, A. 2004. Exploring the relationships between organizational virtuousness and performance. *American Behavioral Scientist,* 47 (6): 766–790.

Cameron, K., and Caza, A. 2002. Organizational and leadership virtues and the role of forgiveness. *Journal of Leadership and Organizational Studies,* 9 (1): 33–48.

Cameron, K. S., Kim, M. U., and Whetten, D. A. 1987. Organizational effects of decline and turbulence. *Administrative Science Quarterly,* 32: 222–240.

Dienstbier, R. A., and Zillig, L. M. 2002. Toughness. In C. R. Snyder and S. J. Lopez (eds.). *Handbook of Positive Psychology:* 515–527. New York: Oxford University Press.

Dutton, J. E., Ashford, S. J., Wlerba, E. E., O'Neil, R., and Hayes, E. 1997. Reading the wind: How middle managers assess the context for issue selling to top managers. *Strategic Management Journal,* 15 (5): 407–425.

Dutton, J. E., Frost, P. J., Worline, M. C., Lilius, J. M., and Kanov, J. M. 2002. Leading in times of trauma. *Harvard Business Review,* 54–61.

Dutton, J. E., and Heaphy, E. D. 2003. The power of high-quality connections. In K. S. Cameron, J. E. Dutton, and R. E. Quinn (eds.). *Positive Organizational Scholarship: Foundations of a new discipline:* 263–278. San Francisco: Berrett Koehler.

Enright, R. D., and Fitzgibbons, R. P. 2000. In R. D. Enright and R. P. Fitzgibbons (eds.), *Helping Clients Forgive: An Empirical Guide for Resolving Anger and Restoring Hope.* Washington DC: American Psychological Association.

Exline, J. J., and Baumeister, R. F. 2000. Expressing forgiveness and repentance: Benefits and barriers. In M. E. McCullough, K. I. Pargament, and C. E. Thoresen, *Forgiveness: Theory, Research, and Practice:* 133–155. New York: Guilford Press.

Feldman, M. S., and Khademian, A. M. 2003. Empowerment and cascading vitality. In K. S. Cameron, J. E. Dutton, and R. E. Quinn (eds.). *Positive Organizational Scholarship: Foundations of A New Discipline:* 343–358. San Francisco: Berrett Koehler.

Fredrickson, B. L. 1998. What good are positive emotions? *Review of General Psychology*, 2: 300–319.

2003. Progress on the Broaden-and-Build Theory of Positive Emotions. Paper presented at the Positive Links Presentation, University of Michigan, September 8. Access at www.bus.umich.edu/Positive/Learning/pastpositivesessions.htm.

Fredrickson, B. L., Mancuso, R. A., Branigan, C., and Tugade, M. M. 2000. The undoing effect of positive emotions. *Motivation & Emotion*, 24 (4): 237–258.

Fredrickson, B. L., Tugade, M. M., Waugh, C. E., and Larkin, G. R. 2003. What good are positive emotions in crises? A prospective study of resilience and emotions following the terrorist attacks on the United States on September 11th, 2001. *Journal of Personality & Social Psychology*, 84 (2): 365.

Freedman, S. 1998. Forgiveness and reconciliation: The importance of understanding how they differ. *Counseling & Values*, 42 (3): 200–216.

Glidewell, J. C. 1970. *Choice Points*. Boston, MA: Colonial Press.

Gustafson Affinito, M. 1999. *When to forgive: A Healing Guide*. Oakland, CA: New Harbinger Publications.

Janoff-Bulman, R. 1992. *Shattered Assumptions: Towards a New Psychology of Trauma*. New York: The Free Press.

Kurzynski, M. J. 1998. The virtue of forgiveness as a human resource management strategy. *Journal of Business Ethics*, 17 (1): 77–85.

Masten, A. S., and Reed, G. J. 2002. Resilience in development. In C. R. Snyder and S. J. Lopez (eds.). *Handbook of Positive Psychology*: 74–88. New York: Oxford University Press.

McCullough, M. E., Pargament, K. I., and Thoresen, C. E. (eds.) 2000. *Forgiveness: Theory, Research, and Practice*. New York: The Guilford Press.

McKinley, W., Sanchez, C. M., and Schick, A. G. 1995. Organizational downsizing: Constraining, cloning, and learning. *Academy of Management Executive*, 9: 32–44.

Mikkelsen, E. G., and Einarsen, S. 2002. Basic assumptions and symptoms of post-traumatic stress among victims of bullying at work. *European Journal of Work & Organizational Psychology*, 11 (1): 87–111.

Peterson, C., and Seligman, M. E. P. (Eds.) 2004. *Character Strengths and Virtues: A Handbook and Classification*. New York: Oxford University Press.

Rye, M. S., Pargament, K. I., Ali, M. A., Beck, G. L., Dorff, E. N., Hallisey, C., Narayanan, V., and Williams, J. G. 2000. Religious perspectives on forgiveness. In McCullough, M. E., Pargament K. I., and Thoresen, C. E.

(eds.), *Forgiveness: Theory, Research, and Practice*: 17–40. New York: The Guilford Press.

Staw, B. M., Sandelands, L. E., and Dutton, J. E. 1981. Threat-rigidity effects in organizational behavior: A multilevel analysis. *Administrative Science Quarterly*, 26: 501–524.

Sutcliffe, K. M., and Vogus, T. J. 2003. Organizing for resilience. In K. S. Cameron, J. E. Dutton, and R. E. Quinn (eds.). *Positive Organizational Scholarship: Foundations of a New Discipline*: 94–110. San Francisco: Berrett Koehler.

Thoresen, C. E., Harris, A. H. S., and Luskin, F. 2000. Forgiveness and health: An unanswered question. In M. E. McCullough, K. I. Pargament, and C. E. Thoresen (eds.), *Forgiveness: Theory, Research, and Practice*: 163–190. New York, NY: Guilford.

Weick, K. E. 2003. Positive organizing and organizational tragedy. In K. S. Cameron, J. E. Dutton and R. E. Quinn (eds.), *Positive Organizational Scholarship: Foundations of a New Discipline*, 66–80. San Francisco: Berrett Koehler.

Weick, K., Sutcliffe, K. M., & Obsfeld, D. 1999. Organizing for high reliability: Processes of collective mindfulness. *Research in Organizational Behavior*, 21: 81–123.

Worthington, Everett L. 2005. *Handbook of Forgiveness*. New York: Routledge.

Yamhure Thompson, L., and Shahen, P. E. 2003. Forgiveness in the workplace. In R. C. Giacalone and C. L. Jurkiewicz (eds.). *Handbook of Spirituality and Organizational Performance*: 405–420. New York: M. E. Sharpe.

10 Values and leadership in organizational crisis

EDWARD H. POWLEY AND
SCOTT N. TAYLOR

Shattering glass and gunfire are not typical sounds in work organizations. But in one school organization, that taken-for-granted assumption shifted when an army fatigue-clad gunman broke into a five-story university building and began shooting at students and staff on a late Friday afternoon in May. Approaching the gunman, a student known for his gregarious personality and leadership qualities was shot and killed instantly while his friends ran from the building. Ninety others hid in offices, closets, and classrooms as the lone gunman roamed the building for seven hours, evading police and holding building occupants under siege.

This chapter presents how leaders in one organization dealt with a major traumatic event in which the core values and social fabric of the organization were threatened. We address three specific themes. First, we briefly mention the increasing importance of paying attention to such crisis events, both because they are increasing in number and frequency, and because there is still much to learn about their complexity. Next, we look at the nature of organizational healing inasmuch as it is also an area in need of greater attention from organizational scholars and practitioners. Third, we explore values-based leadership and its role in coping with crisis and healing through a presentation of narrative accounts of the school shooting incident. We conclude with some general thoughts about values-based leadership in organizations.

Tragedy on the rise

Events such as the one described in this chapter seem to be on the rise. A series of *New York Times* studies demonstrated the pervasiveness of mass violence. Of 100 rampage killings examined, all spanning 50 years, 32 shootings occurred in the workplace, 20 were in schools, and 11 were at restaurants (Butterfield et al., 2000; Fessenden, 2000; Goodstein and Glaberson, 2000). Moreover, multiple shootings and mass violence have grown significantly. In the 18 years between 1966 and 1983, the annual average for rampage killings was 0.66; by contrast, from 1984 to 1999, the average jumped to 5.4 incidents per year (Fessenden, 2000). Other kinds of crises such as natural disasters around the world demonstrate the wide-reaching effect these events can have on individual lives as well as organizations, local and national governments, and even the international economy. While this chapter emphasizes leaders' impact in a single organization, we believe the concepts are generalizable to other organizations touched by crisis, such as natural, technological, or human-induced disasters.

According to Gordon and Wraith (1993), the main feature of trauma is "rupture," in which continuity of time, relationships and attachments, the perceptions of self and others, and expectations about the future all are torn apart. The tragedy in New Orleans, Louisiana resulting from Hurricane Katrina in August 2005 is an apt example in which many government institutions and corporations experienced ruptures. Ruptures in the timing of assistance became a critical issue; relationships and attachments among victims as well as government leaders were disrupted or destroyed; the changes in perceptions of self and others were highlighted daily on the national news as victims, police, and local officials were interviewed; and expectations about the future of the region were changed completely.

Similarly, the shooting incident analyzed in this chapter not only damaged organization members' psychological safety but also affected the organization's core culture and identity. Organization members had only recently moved into a multi-million dollar university building, designed by a world-renowned architect as a symbol of the institution's core values of innovation, entrepreneurial spirit, and forward-thinking management training. The shooting and subsequent standoff with police had the potential to harm the core identity and brand quality of the organization by associating its new building with violence and death.

Healing the social fabric

In our view, leadership is not a position but rather a relationship (Quinn, 2004). Thus, anyone can possess leadership characteristics and play a leadership role. Moreover, the way values-based leaders respond to others has a transformative impact. For example, leaders supporting the healing process consciously care about making connections with, between, and among organization members. Through their actions during or after crisis, they mindfully reach out to other organization members beyond the boundary of their department or organizational unit. Their primary intent is to engage with employees, encourage, offer support, and build up those affected by the events. They build strength by gathering organization members to share emotions and stories, and by drawing on their own character and strength. As a result, the organization's social fabric, bound together by the social relationships inherent in organizations and beyond, is thereby nurtured through support networks and opportunities to gather (Powley & Cameron, 2006).

Healing refers to the reparation and mending of the social fabric, continuity, expectations, and shattered self-concepts, all of which are necessary if an organization is to return to a healthy state of functioning. Healing has been addressed somewhat by organizational scholars when talking about the emotional work of managers (Frost, 2003), but it remains an under-explored concept in organizations. Healing is different from resilience (bouncing back from trauma) (Sutcliffe & Vogus, 2003), adaptation (adjusting to changes or coping with aberrations: Cyert and March, 1963; Levinthal, 1991), and hardiness (being durable or tough: Maddi and Khoshaba, 2005). These concepts refer to organizational attributes enabling organizations to withstand major trauma or damage resulting from external or uncontrollable events (as opposed to making mistakes and human error). Healing refers to the ways an organization may use those attributes to regain health.

More specifically, healing refers to the process of becoming sound, healthy, and whole after suffering illness or harm. Physiological healing is the result of successful medical or pharmaceutical treatments aimed to alleviate pain and suffering. The nature of the healing process – the process of restoring one to health – is a useful analog to healing at a collective or organizational level. While healing has not been addressed widely in organizational research, one examination of healing looks at the responses of children exposed to traumatic experiences such as war, violence, death, and victimization. A key finding from this work is that "the healing of trauma cannot be accomplished by an individual alone." It always requires social intervention and collective support (see Ayalon, 1998; Jareg, 1995; Lumsden, 1997; Terr, 1991).

Building on these findings, we propose that at the collective level, healing refers to coordinated activity by several individuals who aim to restore harmony, security, and integrity to individuals in their care. The role of leaders, then, is to help organizational units return to health by being attuned to and concerned for the social relationships of their organizations. The degree to which organizational leaders accomplish this is based upon their level of concern and care for organization members and, by virtue of their positions, their ability to reach out towards others. This requires specific actions and interactions among organization members and organization leaders. We note again that effective organizational leaders in crises are not necessarily those who hold a managerial position; rather effective leaders are those individuals who act in extraordinary ways with the intent to help heal the organization as a whole as well as its members.

Values-based leadership behavior

A key theme in leadership research is concerned with understanding *who* a leader is and is seeking to become, and *how* he or she responds to others, as opposed to just what a leader does (e.g. Boyatzis and McKee, 2005; Quinn, 2004). This aspect of values-based leadership is not new in the leadership literature, but arguably has never been emphasized to the extent seen today. It manifests itself under the names of servant leadership (Spears and Lawrence, 2004), spiritual leadership (Fry, 2003), authentic leadership (Gardner et al., 2005), resonant leadership (Boyatzis and McKee, 2005; Goleman, Boyatzis and McKee, 2002), the fundamental state of leadership (Quinn, 2004), and the eighth habit (Covey, 2004), to name a few. In each case, the attributes are markedly similar. Leaders (more than ever) must be in touch with their personal identities, their values, and their ideal aspirations *and* these internal resources should be guides dictating how leaders seek to lead others. Covey (2004) refers to the phenomenon in terms of voice: "Find your voice and inspire others to find theirs." Quinn (2004) describes leading with values as being internally directed, other-focused, externally open, and purpose-centered; that is, one begins to transcend self-serving needs in favor of others:

In the fundamental state of leadership, we ... become less externally directed and more internally directed .... We begin to transcend our own hypocrisy, closing the gap between who we think we are and who we think we should be. In this process of victory over self, we feel more integrity and we feel more whole. Our values and behavior are becoming more congruent. Our internal and external realities are becoming more aligned . . . We also become less self-focused and more other-focused. (p. 22)

Boyatzis and McKee (2005) describe this internally directed and other-focused quality as *resonant leadership*: leaders who are "awake, aware, and attuned to themselves, to others, and to the world around them" (p. 3). In fact, research has shown that empathy is positively related to perceived leadership. In other words, leaders are thought to be more empathetic (Kellett, Humphrey, and Sleeth, 2002). Resonant leaders are also mindful, seeking to "live in full consciousness of self, others, nature, and society"; face challenges with hope, inspiring "clarity of vision, optimism"; and "face sacrifice, difficulties, and challenges, as well as opportunities, with empathy and compassion for the people they lead and those they serve" (Boyatzis and McKee, 2005, p. 3).

These characteristics describe what we mean by values-based leadership. That is, anyone, regardless of managerial position can display values-based leadership. Moreover, it manifests itself primarily in relationships and interactions among organization members. In particular, values-based leadership in crises is focused on helping the organization and its members experience healing. The psychological literature refers to these attributes as the "character" of the leader (Peterson and Seligman, 2004), character defined as "the sum of the moral and mental qualities which distinguish an individual or a race; mental or moral constitution; moral qualities strongly developed or strikingly displayed" (*Oxford English Dictionary*, 2005).

Here we focus on a specific type of character strikingly and consistently displayed by values-based leaders in moments of crisis. Bednar (2003) effectively describes leader behavior as:

[The] capacity to recognize, and appropriately respond to other people who are experiencing the very challenge or adversity that is most immediately and forcefully pressing upon [the leader]. Character is revealed, for example, in the power to discern the suffering of other people when we ourselves are suffering . . . [and] is demonstrated by looking and reaching outward when the natural and instinctive response is to be self-absorbed and turn inward. (p. 2)

We believe the behavior Bednar describes is consistently found in moments of organizational crisis where values-based leadership is present; it is the essence of what a values-based leader does in crisis because of *who* he or she is. Their behavior is a manifestation of their unique character. We present several examples to illustrate how leaders responded to the school shooting and helped restore the organization to health. These responses illustrate the importance of leadership character in demonstrating a unique form of values-based behavior.

A tragic shooting

The break-in and subsequent shooting spree created tremendous damage to the school's physical space and the social architecture. Repairing the physical damage alone cost the school approximately a quarter million dollars, but the cost to the social infrastructure was inestimable. Observing the actions and interactions of those involved and affected by this event highlighted the extent to which leaders in the organization demonstrated value-based leadership. Hidden behind reports about the expected actions of official leaders are stories of organization members demonstrating values-based principles. Their actions in assisting and supporting others reflect deeply held organizational values and beliefs, which are indicators of the kinds of virtuous actions required for an organization to heal after crisis.

The business school of a mid-western private university in the United States was the site of the shooting in 2003. After one victim was fatally shot and two victims were wounded, the school became the scene of a hostage taking with approximately 90 building occupants. The gunman exchanged gunfire with and evaded police officers, sharp shooters, and SWAT throughout the seven-hour siege. Outside, police officers secured the area surrounding the building, evacuated and closed surrounding buildings, and redirected traffic – all while family members waited outside and the local media descended upon the campus. Amidst echoing gunshots from inside the building, a small number of students and staff members escaped. Helicopters circled overhead. Faculty, staff, and students inside and outside watched and waited. It was close to 11.00 p.m. before those in the building reunited with family and friends, SWAT officers cornered the gunman in an upstairs classroom, and took him into custody.

Over the next week, while the school building remained closed as a crime scene and construction workers repaired damage from the gunfire, the school and university offered times for faculty, staff, and students to reunite and share personal experiences of the incident. Acting quickly, school administrators and staff outlined a course of action and began the healing process. They developed strategies regarding upcoming graduation events; when and how to retrieve personal effects from the building; and a process for communicating with staff, faculty, students, and alumni. One week later, the school held a memorial service, and faculty, staff, and students symbolically and ceremoniously re-entered the business school building.

Method

To identify examples of individuals leading with values, we examined narrative accounts based on many individuals who were present or involved in some way during the crisis incident. The narrative accounts represent composites of stories and experiences from multiple interview participants (described in detail below). The approach to data gathering in this investigation consisted of open-ended, semi-structured interviews that allowed participants to share their thoughts, feelings, and experiences related to the incident. The first author conducted interviews over several months after the incident with approximately 60 individuals who were members of the school and university community. This approach enabled us to discover organization members' motivations and perceptions as well as their actions and interactions – and whether the actions individuals took – represent the idea of leading with values.

We felt that the procedure for conducting a narrative description of the aftermath of the shooting required *inviting* volunteer participants to share their experiences and reactions to the trauma. That is, in order to acknowledge that the incident produced deep psychological and emotional wounds in some individuals, and therefore some people may not wish to re-live the events associated with the break-in and its aftermath, the first author sent e-mail invitations to approximately 800 faculty, staff, and students providing them with a chance to be interviewed. Within two weeks, at least 60 members of the organization voluntarily responded to the e-mail and asked for an interview. We made great efforts not to pressure any individual to participate, and in very few cases was any individual contacted directly. The respondent sample, therefore, is biased in favor of those willing to discuss the incident within a few weeks after it occurred.

In the interviews, participants were invited to first share their personal stories of the event in narrative form. They were then asked to describe events that stood out regarding the organizational responses to the incident. They also discussed other stories that were particularly remarkable and memorable. Finally, they provided information about how their background might have affected the way they experienced the incident. These in-depth interviews represented one attempt to capture the full range of emotions, motivations, and experiences as recounted by the participants. Thus, they were the means by which we could determine whether behaviors represented leading with values, as opposed to merely fearful or self-protective responses.

Having participants describe the events in this way served several purposes. First, the open-ended questions "allow[ed] respondents to construct answers, in collaboration with listeners, in ways they find meaningful" (Riessman, 1993, p. 54). That is, the interview process gave participants the opportunity to respond in ways they felt most comfortable. Having individuals share their stories aloud was also an act that had a healing effect itself, inasmuch as storytelling has the capacity to heal organization members (Fredriksson and Eriksson, 2001; Swatton and O'Callaghan, 1999). Whereas retelling traumatic events can stir up negative emotions, guilt, and sorrow again, the act of story-telling in the presence of an interested and empathetic listener tends to have the opposite effect, such that sharing stories of trauma and crisis usually has a restorative effect (Herman, 1997; Pennebaker and Harber, 1993). For example, Herman (1997) noted, "Sharing the traumatic experience with others is a precondition for the restitution of a sense of a meaningful world," and "the response of the community has a powerful influence on the ultimate resolution of the trauma" (p. 70). In other words, the process of publicly sharing stories and experiences prepares individuals and organizations to experience healing, although the content and motivation of those stories may or may not lead to the fulfillment of that potential.

Stories of values-driven leaders

Using a qualitative data analysis process derived from the nursing literature (Fredriksson and Eriksson, 2001), the stories and experiences were analyzed to uncover examples and themes of virtuousness and healing. To capture themes of organizational healing, we revisited narratives or "realist" tales (Van Maanen, 1988) from a number of participants in a qualitative study of the incident. These accounts represent actions of ordinary organization members acting as leaders to support and help fellow colleagues. We chose a narrative approach (Ludema, 1996; Nye, 1997; Swatton and O'Callaghan, 1999) for this qualitative study because we wanted to retain a broader perspective of the story, and it allowed us to orient the research toward organization members, their experiences, and their reactions to the events.

From our research, we learned that the narratives of individuals have several common characteristics. First, it goes without saying that people's backgrounds or contexts made a difference in how they acted, that is, their training and previous experience influenced their actions and interactions during and after the shooting. Second, organization members were positioned such that they could step forward as leaders. Third, they were mindful of others, being attuned and aware of others who might need the unique help they could provide. Individuals leading with values drew on established relational networks and cultivated important new ones. We believe these four characteristics were key factors in explaining value-based choices and leader character, which led individuals towards assisting others and helped them reach outward when the instinct was to turn inward (Bednar, 2003). We have classified leadership examples into four categories: *going beyond formal roles, building a collaborative community, leading others to safety, and the victim's leadership*. Using these categories, we retell the events of the shooting and police standoff in order to illustrate the leaders' impact on the organization's ability to come together, heal, and move forward.

Going beyond formal roles

The first responders, after the police and emergency medical personnel, were the school administrators. As the building occupants were escorted from the building six or seven hours after the break-in, they boarded a bus and were taken to a different location on campus for a police debriefing. School leaders greeted building occupants as they descended the bus. These individuals remember being pleased to see the Dean. Other people were present, but the building occupants did not recognize them and, instead, focused on the school leaders who were waiting for them. "There were other people there," a faculty member recounted. "But for the most part, I didn't recognize them. But the Dean, I wanted to shake his hand. So I shook his hand." A staff member remembered being very impressed that the Provost and the Dean were waiting at the buses. "The Dean has never hugged me in his life," she said, "and I've hugged the Dean at least five times since this." What is perhaps more remarkable is that the Dean was five hours away by car from the university when he received a phone call about the shooting. He turned around on the highway and sped all the way back to the university, arriving just as staff members and students came off the buses. Demonstrating personal compassion and caring for organization members as individuals was an important signal indicating that school leaders valued and understood the individuals for whom they had responsibility. Adopting the role of nurturer and concerned friend had high healing potential because it extended beyond the formal roles required of university administrators.

The university president attended memorial services for the victims, school employees, students, and the community, each time expressing personal grief and mourning with others. With regard to the victim's family, he was especially compassionate and understanding. He modeled for organization members what it means to be a caring human being. He not only played a critical role as the representative of the university, but, more importantly, he responded as a human being who was willing to share personal grief and empathy. A student present at the memorial service observed him choking up as he expressed his emotions over the loss. At another event, the president was described as displaying appropriate amounts of emotion, and instead of wanting to rush through the ceremonies and events, he took time to meet with people, talk to them about their experiences, and be available to listen. This allowed others to manage the logistics of the response while he spent time with the staff or students. Instead of isolating himself from others to "manage" the response, he embraced the opportunity to meet with them.

The night of the shooting the university president joined with others at the school's library to meet with family members of the building occupants who were finally released from the police. Just as the Dean greeted individuals coming off the buses, the university president greeted them as they came into the library. "There was a family collected around talking among themselves, and he walked up and introduced himself," observed one student at the library. Many felt that the university president's professional background in psychiatric medicine enabled him to respond as a caring and thoughtful individual. He showed compassion for organization members as he listened to their stories but also demonstrated great poise and complete control at the same time. He made a point to meet with individual families, expressing sympathies, and say, "I'm so grateful you're okay." These actions might have been expected, but the presence of school and community leaders at midnight demonstrated a personal level of commitment and caring to the school and its people.

Among some building occupants there was a sense that even though most of the school leadership was not in the building during the incident, they were "suffering vicariously." A staff member said, "They were going through our suffering. They were concerned with the anguish, the fear, all of that. I'm sure in their individual ways, they were right there with us. It really was a sense of 'We were all in this together.'" These moments of caring, the consoling and comforting those affected by trauma, represent the unspoken part of leadership in such circumstances – an aspect of leadership perhaps unnoticed due to its highly situational and personal impact.

Building a collaborative community

The relationship between the university and the city, already on reasonably good terms, was brought to a new level of collaboration as the university president and mayor held several meetings together. These meetings were not only of strategic importance, but they served a healing function as well, signaling that others could have confidence that the organization would make it through the crisis. "It seemed that the key people that needed to be back in charge and have the brave face were putting on the brave face at least for the more formal functions," a student remarked. The university president and mayor provided personal responses themselves as well as official press releases. One student was impressed that the president and the mayor were personally involved in the event from the very beginning. The president and the mayor sent an E-mail to the entire university community that carried the theme: "We are part of the community. The university is part of the community. We have been affected by this incident, and the community is affected by it too. It is not an isolated act." The university president and the mayor treated the event as a community issue. One university administrator who saw them work closely together through the events noted:

When it came time to do a news conference or make a statement, they did those things together. They treated this as a community issue as opposed to a university problem or city problem. You could easily imagine a scenario when it takes hours to bring something to closure, you can imagine university officials pleading to city officials and saying, and "Why didn't you bring that to closure faster?" Instead, you had plant services folks and construction administration folks giving the blueprints and plans so that they can figure things out together, and anybody who knows the building knows the challenges.

In another instance, a department chair gathered with his faculty and staff inside their office space to talk about what had happened, to share their individual stories in their workspace. He had grown up listening to stories from survivors of the holocaust, learning how to listen and ask questions of others who had experienced that trauma. His inclination in this instance was a concern for his colleagues and staff members. As the department members connected with each other, sharing their personal experiences while they walked through their office space together, they discovered new ways to support and help each other back to work. As a departmental leader, the chair felt the need to bring people together to listen together to each other's experiences. He viewed his job as asking questions and facilitating the conversation because, as he said, "I felt it was important." Building a collaborative community was an important way to assist the healing process.

The point is that several leaders with formal roles went beyond their official duties to facilitate the healing process. Whereas officials often succumb to the threat-rigidity response during crisis and revert to official responses, imposition of formal structures, and finger-pointing (Cameron, Kim, and Whetten, 1987), as in the case of the hurricane disasters in the summer months of 2005, these leaders engaged with organization members personally and empathetically. They responded collaboratively with the broader community. They demonstrated a level of virtuousness that helped organization members heal. They chose to reach outward when the instinctive response would have been to turn inward. All these efforts occurred at a time when these leaders were personally dealing with the trauma themselves and when their administrative responsibilities had increased markedly because of the crisis.

Leading others to safety

The incident created a situation where organization members not holding formal leadership positions nevertheless took on important leadership responsibilities. Several examples underscore leading in this way when people courageously sought out others and led them to safety. In one instance, a female faculty member distinctly remembered a faculty colleague, not known for being a "caretaker," calling out to others in the department to secure the administrative assistants in an office. He had just finished a telephone conversation with an MBA student about an upcoming course when he heard screaming outside his office. He politely took a message, and ran to look out an interior window into the atrium where he saw the victim lying on the floor. He returned to his office to call security who told him to take as many people as he could with him into the office and lock the door. After calling out to the staff members, he brought them into his office and rolled some metal filing cabinets in front of them to protect against stray bullets. There they stayed for six hours until SWAT officers arrived.

At about the same time, another faculty member aided a number of colleagues and students to safe areas. She had been sitting in her office on the fifth floor when she heard a loud crash, presumably the sound of shattering glass or the first gunshots. She continued to work until she heard approaching sirens. Imagining that someone was hurt, she descended to the main level and entered the atrium. By this time, the atrium had been vacated and was quiet. Then she heard more shots and recognized them immediately as gunfire. Instead of running for the nearest exit, she found her way back to the stairwell and returned to her department, warning her colleagues about the shooting and advising them to secure themselves in their offices. At first, they froze in disbelief, but then they acted quickly. She left her department office again, this time searching the exposed study carrels one and two floors below, directing graduate students to secure offices.

In still another instance, two staff members heard the gunshots and began to warn others throughout the building. They alerted one student as he was entering the elevator to the atrium where the gunman was shooting. They both ran to another part of the building, warning more people and eventually spotting the gunman before making contact with police. Once on the phone, they provided information about possible places the gunman might go and the whereabouts of others in the building.

Outside, a university counselor arrived on the scene and not only began meeting with people who had come out of the building, but began to organize support groups in various areas around the university. With his director away from the office for a family event, this counselor mobilized counselors in the resident halls, the counseling office, and in the surrounding buildings, all the while being inundated with calls and pages from his office assistant, about therapists offering to help, students seeking assistance, and police providing instructions. In each case, he contacted counseling staff in different locations and coordinated their movements across campus. Once the university's central administration organized a more formal response, he made his way to a primary meeting place for students, friends, and family at a location across campus in order to coordinate the support effort. "I recognized that I was the one to do it, but if somebody else wanted to take over, and offered to do so, that would be fine. In the meantime, I would be happy to do what I think needs to be done, and I was happy to take on as much consultation as need be." His team of counselors was readily available, due to his leadership efforts, which extended beyond his formal position.

These incidents provide examples of individuals who adopted leadership roles in the way they responded to circumstances facing them. These emergent leaders demonstrated what Boyatzis and McKee (2005) refer to as being awake, aware, and attuned to themselves and to others. Specifically, at the time that it was required, they demonstrated mindfulness of the situation, the potential dangers to others, and the opportunity they possessed to offer help.

The victim's leadership

Ironically, the victim himself – both in life and in death – displayed one of the most dramatic examples of values-driven leadership. He demonstrated what Quinn (2004) referred to as the "fundamental state of leadership": being internally directed as opposed to being externally directed. The student victim had just finished his first year in the MBA program and was the president-elect of the Black MBA Student Association. He was known as an engaging leader and one who was self-reflective and driven by his own values. Confronting conflict or discomfort was not unusual for him because of his commitment to inclusion and integration across ethnic and cultural barriers. He was a team builder and consensus creator rather than a divider. On the day of the shooting, he had come to the building briefly and was about to leave when the gunman broke through the glass doors and entered the atrium. Moments before his death while his fellow students dove for cover or ran from the building, he reportedly walked toward the gunman trying to calm him down and talk to him. He died while behaving congruently with his values.

Throughout the memorial services, vigils, and prayer gatherings given in his honor, he was described as charismatic, a genuine friend, and role model for all, and as someone who crossed racial and ethnic divides. In life, his value of inclusion and friendship transcended himself, and in death, he brought many people together from a wide range of backgrounds. The memorial service was an extraordinary experience for many. A staff member noted, "It was a beautiful collection of people who had come together to celebrate the life of the student." An administrator remarked that the service at the university was multicultural: "There were Indians, Hindus, and Sikhs, and Chinese, and all kinds of backgrounds and cultures in the chapel."

This story demonstrates that leadership is not just an activity of formally designated individuals, but it can be demonstrated by any individual behaving congruently with values. Even those who have died can exercise leadership. Values-based leaders produce impact through the exercise of values, the consistency with core principles, and the demonstration of a core purpose. Great figures of history, whose examples still serve as a form of leadership today, remain influential primarily because they enacted their values in a consistent and congruent way; that is, an individual's legacy and example are emblematic of values-based leadership. In this crisis, the display of leadership values left the most lasting impressions and affected many lives for the better.

Conclusion

We have outlined four categories of stories in which leaders or emergent leaders demonstrated themes associated with values-based leadership. The four categories included *going beyond formal roles, building a collaborative community, leading others to safety,* and *the victim's leadership.* In this description, we have illustrated that values-based leaders reach outward when the natural and instinctive response could easily have been inwardly focused. Values-driven leadership influenced how this organization managed the crisis, and, as a result, how the organization itself was able to re-establish a sense of identity, strengthen values, and restore relationships that were ruptured by the event. Organizational leaders fulfilled their formal roles as they coordinated events and administered the details of the crisis, but they went beyond formal roles and manifested their personal values by meeting with families and encouraging individual employees and students. Organization members reported that leaders went beyond their formal responsibilities by responding in compassionate and caring ways. Moreover, leaders who were aware of and attuned to organization members' needs, offering a personal touch to a colleague or staff person, significantly influenced the outcome for many. Some faculty and staff members also became emergent leaders in the face of the trauma when they responded in value-driven ways, for example by looking after others' concerns before their own. In some instances, this meant risking their lives for others.

Organizations and leaders faced with difficult events may respond with a threat-rigidity response (Staw, Sandelands, and Dutton, 1981) in which the organization or its leaders turn inward, display self-protective behaviors, blame others, become critical or cynical, and turn down opportunities to connect with others or to share information. Alternatively, they can respond virtuously (Cameron, 2003), as many did in this case, with compassion, caring, mutual support, courage, and faith. These examples of leaders acting with care, compassion, and empathy demonstrate the power of leading with values. People are affected more personally and more deeply when leaders express their core values than when the formal roles of leadership are carried out. One alternative does not exclude the other, of course, but formal leadership roles can often omit the expression of core values. Organizing, controlling, establishing vision, setting strategy, and administering rewards all are critical parts of the leader's responsibilities, but, as this crisis incident illustrates, values-driven leadership has the most impact on organizational healing, resilience, and effective functioning.

Organizations are centers of human relating. Leaders acting congruently according to a fundamental set of values – and an external focus toward organization members – represent an important element of human relating. Organizations will increasingly face natural, technological, or human-induced crisis, and therefore values-driven leaders in organizations must tend to the social relationships and connections that determine whether an organization emerges stronger from crisis.

Organizations will need leaders who have character and deeply held values, who have the capacity to recognize and appropriately respond to their organization members mindfully, and who are attuned to organization members' needs and concerns. As both organization members and managers demonstrate values-driven leadership, they represent an important source of hope and courage that enables organizational healing.

References

Ayalon, O. 1998. Community healing for children traumatized by war. *International Review of Psychiatry*, 10: 224–233.

Bednar, D. A. 2003. The character of Christ. Address given at Brigham Young University, Idaho, Religious Lecture Series (January 25).

Boyatzis, R. E., and McKee, A. 2005. *Resonant Leadership*. Boston, MA: Harvard Business School Press.

Butterfield, F., Fessenden, F., Glaberson, W., and Goodstein, L. 2000. How the study was conducted. *New York Times*, 28.

Cameron, K. S. 2003. Virtuousness and performance. In K. S. Cameron, J. E. Dutton, and R. E. Quinn (eds.) *Positive Organizational Scholarship: Foundations of a New Discipline*, 48–65. San Francisco, CA: Berrett-Koehler.

Cameron, K. S., Kim, M. U., and Whetten, D. A. 1987. Organizational effects of decline and turbulence. *Administrative Science Quarterly*, 32(2): 222–240.

Covey, S. R. 2004. *The 8th Habit: From Effectiveness to Greatness*. New York, NY: The Free Press.

Cyert, R. M, and March, J. G. 1963. *A Behavioral Theory of the Firm*. Englewood Cliffs, NJ: Prentice-Hall.

Fessenden, F. 2000. They threaten, seethe and unhinge, then kill in quantity. *New York Times* (April 9): p. 1.

Fredriksson, L. and Eriksson, K. 2001. The patient's narrative of suffering: A path to health? An interpretative research synthesis on narrative understanding. *Scandinavian Journal of Caring Sciences*, 15(1): 3–11.

Frost, P. J. 2003. *Toxic Emotions at Work: How Compassionate Managers Handle Pain and Conflict*. Boston, MA: Harvard Business School Press.

Fry, L. W. 2003. Toward a theory of spiritual leadership. *The Leadership Quarterly*, 14(6): 693–727.

Gardner, W. L., Avolio, B. J., Luthans, F., May, D. R., and Walumbwa, F. 2005. Can you see the real me? A self-based model of authentic leader and follower development. *The Leadership Quarterly*, 16(3): 343–372.

Goleman, D., Boyatzis, R., and McKee, A. 2002. *Primal Leadership: Realizing the Power of Emotional Intelligence*. Boston, MA: Harvard Business School Press.

Goodstein, L. and Glaberson, W. 2000. The well-marked roads to homicidal rage. *New York Times* (April 10), p. A1.

Gordon, R. & Wraith, R. 1993. Responses of children and adolescents to disaster. In P. Wilson and B. Raphael (eds.), *International Handbook of Traumatic Stress Syndromes*: 561–575, New York, NY: Plenum.

Herman, J. 1997. *Trauma and Recovery: The Aftermath of Violence – From Domestic Abuse to Political Terror*. New York, NY: Basic Books.

Jareg, E. 1995. Main guiding principles for the development of psychosocial interventions for children affected by War, ISCA Workshop, Stockholm, Sweden.

Kellet, J. B., Humphrey, R. H., and Sleeth, R. G., 2002. Empathy and complex task performance: Two routes to leadership. *The Leadership Quarterly*, 13(5): 532–544.

Levinthal, D. A. 1991. Organizational adaptation and environmental selection: Interrelated processes of change. *Organization Science*, 2(1): 140–145.

Ludema, J. D. 1996. Narrative inquiry: Collective storytelling as a source of hope, knowledge, and action in organizational life, Unpublished doctoral dissertation, Case Western Reserve University, Cleveland, OH.

Lumsden, M. 1997. Breaking the cycle of violence: Are "communal therapies" a means of healing shattered selves. *Journal of Peace Research*, 34 (4): 377–383.

Maddi, S. R. and Khoshaba, D. M. 2005. *Resilience at Work*. New York: American Management Association.

Nye, E. F. 1997. Writing as healing. *Qualitative Inquiry*, 3(4): 439.

Oxford English Dictionary. 2005. New York: Oxford University Press.

Peterson, C. and Seligman, M. E. 2004. *Character, Strengths, and Virtues*. Oxford: Oxford University Press.

Pennebaker, J. W. and Harber, K. D. 1993. A social stage model of collective coping: The Loma Prieta earthquake and the Persian Gulf War. *Journal of Social Issues*, 4(40): 125–145.

Powley, E. H. and Cameron, K. S. 2006. (In press). Organizational healing: Lived virtuousness amidst organizational crisis. *Journal of Management Spirituality and Religion*.

Quinn, R. 2004. *Building the Bridge as You Walk on It: A Guide for Leading Change*. San Francisco, CA: Jossey-Bass.

Riessman, C. K. 1993. *Narrative Analysis: 30*. Newbury Park, CA: Sage Publications.

Spears, L. C. and Lawrence, M. (eds.). 2004. *Practicing Servant-leadership: Succeeding Through Trust, Bravery, and Forgiveness*. San Francisco, CA: Jossey-Bass.

Staw, B. M., Sandelands, L. E., and Dutton, J. E. 1981.Threat-rigidity effects in organizational behavior: A multilevel analysis. *Administrative Science Quarterly*, 26(4): 501–524.

Sutcliffe, K. M. and Vogus, T. J. 2003. Organizing for resilience. In K. S. Cameron, J. E. Dutton and R. E. Quinn (eds.) *Positive Organizational Scholarship: Foundations of a New Discipline*: 94–110. San Francisco, CA: Berrett-Koehler.

Swatton, S. & O'Callaghan, J. 1999. The experience of "healing stories" in the life narrative: A grounded theory. *Counseling Psychology Quarterly*, 12(4): 413–429.

Terr, L. 1991. Childhood traumas. *American Journal of Psychiatry*, 148: 10–20.

Van Maanen, J. 1988. *Tales of the Field: On Writing Ethnography*. Chicago IL: University of Chicago Press.

11 | *Making more Mike Stranks – teaching values in the United States Marine Corps*

MICHAEL B. PARKYN

Why the Corps has values

Mike Strank released the American flag into the February wind that blew from behind. He steadied his five weary men as they raised a makeshift flagpole atop which the Stars and Stripes whipped straight and true. Across Iwo Jima and offshore, Americans paused briefly in recognition of the flag's message – they would prevail. In one modest act, the six Marines forged an enduring symbol of the honor, courage, and commitment upon which the Marine Corps depends upon in peace and war.

Sergeant Strank, who later died leading his men on that island, embodied the qualities found in the best of leaders. He forged the group of men who raised the flag; he steadied them morally and mentally through trial after trial just as he steadied them physically on that windy February day; and he remained committed to their success and well being until the day he died. One of his contemporaries, Joe Rodriguez, offered

Everybody idolized Mike. He was a born leader, a natural leader, and a leader by example. Harlon, Ira and Franklin all loved him. Even his lieutenant, Lieutenant Pennel, stood somewhat in awe of Mike.[1]

How did Mike Strank become such a "natural" leader? Some declare that he was made into a leader at Marine Corps boot camp; others insist that leaders like Mike are born and not made. To the US Marine Corps, the argument misses a simple point: the Corps and America will never have enough Mike Stranks – we will always need more. From this point rises one important question: *how do we make _more_ Mike Stranks?*

---

[1] James Bradley, *Flags of Our Fathers*, New York: Bantam Books, 2000, p. 105.

How Marines fight – maneuver warfare

To answer this question, we need to know how the Marines function – how Marines win battles. Answering the "how" will further illuminate the "who" – the Mike Stranks – who make the Corps successful. Only then are we prepared to discern the process employed by the Marines to produce leaders who enable the Corps to employ its core capability.

What is maneuver warfare?

Marines advocate a style of fighting known as *maneuver warfare*. While linear warfare practitioners focus on smashing the enemy in contests of force against force, maneuver warfare practitioners attempt to pit their force's strengths against enemy weakness in order to *shatter the enemy's cohesion*, rendering enemy forces incapable of fighting.

Maneuver warfare relies on speed. Physical speed allows maneuver forces to arrive where the enemy is not. Decision-making speed allows maneuver forces to perceive opportunity before the enemy perceives its own vulnerability.

Maneuver warfare also relies on surprise. Given superior speed in physical and decision-making realms, maneuver forces attempt to attack vital points in the enemy's system that are the least prepared to defend against attack.

Finally, maneuver warfare relies on focus. In the capstone doctrinal guide simply titled *Warfighting*, the Marines make clear that maneuver warfare doesn't attempt to avoid violence; rather, it depends on the ability to focus effort, including violence, at appropriate points in time and space.

Clearly, this approach to warfare was a departure from the methodology used to defend against the Soviet threat during the Cold War. The Maneuver Warrior would require much more mental agility, creativity, and the ability to think critically than was required of the Cold Warrior.

Three Block War

> You say to your soldier [in Europe] "Do this" and he doeth it; but I am obliged to say [to the Americans] "This is the reason you ought to do that" and then he does it.
>
> Friedrich von Steuben
> Revolutionary War Inspector General

At the Cold War's end, visionaries within the Corps attempted to characterize the way of future war. Recognizing that the United States faced no aggressor that would be willing to face US forces in traditional combat, these visionaries predicted that war would move with the world's population – towards littoral and urban areas. They chose the "Three-Block War" as their term for the conflict of the future. In coining this term, the Corps characterized an environment in which Marines on one block provide humanitarian relief efforts while Marines a block away battled enemy guerilla forces. At the same time, Marines on a third city block battled a well-equipped conventional foe.

This most chaotic area, where command and control reached its limit, is a most important area. It is where the enemy is paralyzed; his will is broken. It is where we protect the people who need protection, and kill those who need to be killed. When operations go as planned, it is where victory is won. When operations go awry, it is where the world's media chronicles the resulting tragedies.

The Three Block War focused on the hard reality of the modern battlefield's unpredictability, which has grown to a degree that defies the military's most capable centralized control mechanisms. The Three Block War didn't envision the possibility that friendly forces would fight beyond the bounds of their command and control structures – *it guaranteed it.* An understanding of the mission underpins success in the Three Block War. Marines cut off from timely guidance need to know the ultimate desired end state of any operation, and the larger purpose served by the end state. Armed with this knowledge, the Marines can adapt their methods as the tactical situation changes in order to achieve the results desired by their seniors. Like the teaching of core values of the Marine Corps, arming Marines with the "why" of the mission is nothing new. It is why our Soviet adversaries reputedly complained that American forces failed to adhere strictly to predictable tactics. It was also apparently essential to the first American soldiers, the Continental Army, who exasperated Baron von Steuben with their insistence on understanding the bigger picture behind their orders.

If the Corps wanted to execute maneuver warfare principles in the Three Block War, it needed more than fast-thinking headquarters and trustworthy officers. It needed to cultivate the ability to execute maneuver warfare principles among those who most routinely operated beyond the boundaries of effective command and control networks. To outsiders, this seemed a dilemma without solution – the least trained, least educated, least mature members of the force were potentially the most influential. Much of the promise and burden of maneuver warfare would be borne by young enlisted Marines.

The Strategic Corporal

The Marines solved this dilemma head-on by teaching *every* Marine how to use speed, surprise and focus to shatter an enemy's cohesion. The emblematic young Marine, employing maneuver warfare tenets in a decentralized environment with the trust of his fellow Marines, is referred to as the *Strategic Corporal*.

In arriving at the concept of the Strategic Corporal, the Marine Corps returned to an essential strength. The Corps' leadership recognized that the ability to decentralize and win in combat hinged upon a combat organization's cohesion, their ability to act in unison even when not moving shoulder-to-shoulder.

Cohesion, in turn, resulted from the shared experiences from recruit depots to officer candidate school to shared heroes. Cohesion resulted from shared priorities and ways of doing business. Cohesion resulted from shared values.

Marines who hold common values and beliefs can trust one another, communicate with one another, and harmonize with one another in the most challenging of circumstances. A service ethos – a shared set of core values – facilitates the trust, communications, and harmony – the oneness – that becomes cohesion.

Core values of the Strategic Corporal

> Honor, courage, commitment – these are our core values. They are values that ALL MARINES must inculcate and demonstrate in their every action. These values are our ethos. Weave this ethos through the very fabric of your being, and you earn the right to wear the title of United States Marine.
>
> MCRP 6-11D, *Sustaining the Transformation*

Ask any retired Marine, regardless of age, when the core values of honor, courage and commitment were introduced to the Marines. "They were always there," will be the answer, because they accurately capture the ethos – the shared values – that have enabled Marines to prevail through the worst of struggles. Previous expressions regarding service to the Corps included Shakespeare's "Band of Brothers" reference from *Henry V*, "First to Fight," "Soldiers of the Sea" and "Every Marine a Rifleman."

Association with tangible images proved effective in the Corps. In speeches to Marines, General John A. Lejeune, 13th Commandant of the Marine Corps, referred to Marine victories in World War I when characterizing the Corps. He further personalized each Marine's identification with and debt to the victors of those battles. When instituting annual celebration of the Marine Corps birthday on November 10, 1921, General Lejeune referred to an "eternal spirit" that was common to Marines:

This high name of distinction and soldierly repute we who are Marines today have received from those who preceded us in the corps. With it we have also received from them the eternal spirit which has animated our corps from generation to generation and has been the distinguishing mark of the Marines in every age. So long as that spirit continues to flourish Marines will be found equal to every emergency in the future as they have been in the past, and the men of our Nation will regard us as worthy successors to the long line of illustrious men who have served as "Soldiers of the Sea" since the founding of the Corps.

The close-knit society of the Corps celebrated the "illustrious men" of World War I, including Major Dan Daily and Captain Lloyd Williams of "Retreat, Hell! We just got here!" fame. These blue-collar heroes, models of martial virtue to thousands of Marines, were joined by machine-gunning Sergeant John Basilone of Guadalcanal and pugnacious fighter pilot Gregory "Pappy" Boyington during World War II. Later Marines guided on the exemplary stars of Korean War hero, Colonel Lewis "Chesty" Puller of the Chosin Reservoir, and Lieutenant Wesley Fox of Vietnam's "Walking Dead."

In 1992, General Carl E. Mundy, Jr., 30th Commandant of the Marine Corps, first explicitly framed the values that had been shared implicitly among Marines for so many years. In his "Commandant's Statement on Core Values of the United States Marines," General Mundy defined the three values:

HONOR: The bedrock of our character. The quality that guides Marines to exemplify the ultimate in ethical and moral behavior; never to lie, cheat, or steal; to abide by an uncompromising code of integrity; to respect human dignity; to have respect and concern for each other. The quality of maturity, dedication, trust, and dependability that commits Marines to act responsibly; to be accountable for actions; to fulfill obligations; and to hold others accountable for their actions.

COURAGE: The heart of our Core Values, courage is the mental, moral, and physical strength ingrained in Marines to carry them through the challenges of combat and the mastery of fear; to do what is right; to adhere to a higher standard of personal conduct; to lead by example, and to make tough decisions under stress and pressure. It is the inner strength that enables a Marine to take that extra step.

COMMITMENT: The spirit of determination and dedication within members of a force of arms that leads to professionalism and mastery of the art of war. It leads to the highest order of discipline for unit and self; it is the ingredient that enables 24-hour a day dedication to Corps and Country; pride; concern for others; and an unrelenting determination to achieve a standard of excellence in every endeavor. Commitment is the value that establishes the Marine as the warrior and citizen others strive to emulate.

Having explicitly defined three core values, the Corps needed to implement them. But while the Corps deliberately recruited people with the potential to live by these values, they recognized that there was a vast difference between a person with untapped potential and the Marines they needed. They required a process for changing one into the other.

Transformation

The 31st Commandant of the Marine Corps, General Charles C. Krulak, first characterized the process now known as "Transformation." Through this process, Marines embrace the core values that form our ethos; these core values coincide with our nation's highest ideals. Over time, these Marines become better at helping the Corps win our nation's battles; they reinforce the legacy of our Corps; and through their citizenship beyond the Corps, they inspire others like them to serve in the Corps. From conception, Transformation was intended to continue throughout the entirety of every Marine's service.

Transformation employs the stories of the Corps' heroes and the core values as common, consistent elements in messages that are delivered through a variety of means. The aggregate is a service-wide, career long, comprehensive education in values.

Process is articulated through T/E Continuum

Transformation is articulated through a system of learning the Corps refers to as the Training & Education Continuum. The continuum addresses all aspects of a Marine's learning; it includes the common combat skills training learned by all Marines, unit training that Marines receive in their combat organizations, skill progression training that Marines receive in order to progress within their specialty, and the professional military education and training (PME/T) that Marines receive during their service. PME/T is designed "to equip Marines with the skills, confidence, understanding, and vision to exercise sound military judgment and decision making in battle."[2] A large share of the PME/T Continuum aims at improving Marines' leadership abilities.

When?

Unlike most corporate leader development initiatives, the Corps' Transformation begins *before hiring*. By revealing outright the Corps' two functions – to make Marines and win the nation's battles[3] – recruiters dissuade those who are not likely to hold values that would allow these people to adopt our ethos as their own value. As handpicked examples of "our kind of people," recruiters attract people like them – people who have the makings of good Marines – to the Corps like raw iron filings to a magnetized, polished steel sword. Through effective recruiting, Marine recruiters perform the bulk of the screening effort, allowing recruit depots and the Officer Candidate School to concentrate on training.

Also unlike most corporate efforts, the Corps' Transformation is not conceived as a punctuated, terminal effort. The opposite is true – the architects of Transformation intended that it would continue throughout a Marine's service, until the day that a Marine returned to civilian life.

[2] MCO 1553.4A, *Professional Military Education*, Quantico, VA: Marine Corps Combat Development Command, 20 December 1999.
[3] MCRP 6-11D, *Sustaining the Transformation*, Quantico, VA: Marine Corps Combat Development Command, 28 June 1999.

How – vehicles for transformation

The Marine Corps Values Program, a center of gravity for Transformation, is implemented in three phases. The initial phase, a training-based program, takes place at recruit depots and Officer Candidate Schools. The second phase, reinforcement education, takes place at formal schools. The third phase, sustainment education, takes place at the small unit level.[4]

Three more programs provide the vehicle for transformation. The Reading Program provides for individual exploration, education and growth on a continuing basis. Mentoring adds growth-oriented guidance counseling to leadership and core values education. The Performance Evaluation System spans the length of a Marine's service, allowing the Corps to choose its best for the future.

Phase I: Values training

The first days of any Marine's life in the Corps are harried ones. Would-be officers are referred to not as Marines but as *candidates*; their enlisted peers are called *recruits*; both groups have yet to earn the title Marine.

Although officer candidates will not learn the basic infantry tactics taught at recruit depots – officers spend six subsequent months at the Basic School for that – the objectives of the recruit depots and Officer Candidate Schools are similar. Both organizations

- Screen potential Marines to ensure suitability
- Evaluate potential Marines for leadership ability
- Immerse potential Marines in the Marine culture

Putting applicants under stress allows evaluators to determine an individual's suitability for becoming a Marine, and that individual's potential to lead. By challenging would-be Marines in a stressful environment, instructors achieve some ground truths: will this candidate function well under hostile conditions? Does the candidate value the group's needs over individual needs? Is the candidate competitive? The instructors also immerse applicants in the Marine culture, which itself

[4] ALMAR 49/96, *Implementing Instruction for the Marine Corps Values Program*, Washington, DC: US Marine Corps, 1996.

Integrity

Knowledge   Justice

Courage   Enthusiasm

Decisiveness   Bearing

Dependability   Endurance

Initiative   Unselfishness

Tact   Loyalty

Judgment

Figure 11.1 The leadership traits of the US Marine Corps

induces stress. The immersion also conveys some essentials to these people: after courses of instruction in which they are taught 14 leadership traits, 11 leadership principles and the three core values, they have the continuing presence of their instructors, who act as living models of all that a Marine should be. Finally, these same noncommissioned officers – upon whom the Corps' maneuver warfare doctrine rests – make significant input in evaluating future Marines for their leadership potential.

The scene is the same, whether it takes place at one of the two recruit Depots or Officer Candidate School: a group of harried young people, hopelessly out of their element, fatigued and hungry, rush from training evolutions to classroom instruction and back again. Often thrust into situations with no clear answers, these would-be Marines find their old behaviors are woefully inadequate in the profession of arms. Whether assigned as leaders of their peer group for instructional purposes, or as team leaders in combat problem solving exercises, they encounter situation after situation in which the best solutions are achieved by employing the traits and principles. Immediate, clear feedback, usually delivered by instructors from the noncommissioned officer ranks, reinforces the necessity of employing the traits and principles. Initial training prepares Marines to lead.

- Be technically and tactically proficient

- Know yourself and seek self-improvement

- Know your Marines and look out for their welfare

- Keep your Marines informed

- Set the example

- Ensure the task is understood, supervised, and accomplished

- Train your Marines as a team

- Make sound and timely decisions

- Develop a sense of responsibility among your subordinates

- Employ your unit in accordance with its capabilities

- Seek responsibility and take responsibility for your actions

Figure 11.2 The leadership principles of the US Marine Corps

High-pressure circumstances, simple lessons, visual examples and immediate feedback form the vehicle of choice for leadership instruction of new Marines. General Charles C. Krulak, the 31st Commandant of the Marine Corps, referred to the process as "inculcation" – impressing upon the mind through frequent, repetitive instruction. The Latin root of "inculcate," *inculare*, translates loosely as "trample," a fitting characterization for the physical nature of values instruction in this early stage of a Marine's service.

Phase II: Reinforcement training

Following Officer Candidate School, commissioned officers receive formal instruction in the continuum at five venues along the path from candidate to General; enlisted Marines attend instruction at six venues following graduation from one of the recruit depots. Some are conducted exclusively at resident schools, while others appear in optional nonresident versions. For purposes of progression in service, the Marine Corps consider resident and nonresident education to be equivalent. This ensures that all Marines, regardless of assignment, will be afforded the education that is so vital to their development.

Attempting to perpetuate the Corps' famous battlefield successes in World War I, the 13th Commandant, Lieutenant General John A. Lejeune, set broad policy for the functioning of the Corps in *The Marine Corps Manual*. Commenting on the the battlefield cohesion present within the Marines in France, Lejeune noted:

A spirit of comradeship and brotherhood in arms came into being in the training camps and on the battlefields. This spirit is too fine a thing to be allowed to die. It must be fostered and kept alive and made the moving force in all Marine Corps organizations.

Recognizing that commissioned and noncommissioned officers act together to lead Marines at all echelons, the Marine Corps University characterizes points of coincidence along the educational tracks of officers and noncommissioned officers. In doing so, the University attempts to ensure commensurate education in leadership and moral development.

Each school delivers instruction that is tailored to the required growth of the Marines in attendance, and fosters long-term change. The education they receive at each school is commensurate with the leadership challenges they will face in the next several years. Where once they led through personal direction and force of personality, they now prepare to assume a sequence of leadership roles, characterized by the University as Leading Marines, Leading Leaders, Developing Subordinate Leaders, Developing Command Climate, and Leading Change. Although the themes of leadership are consistent, the roles and sophistication change.

The common foundation exists in the 14 leadership traits, 11 leadership principles, and three core values.[5] In their most basic presentation – during initial training – the traits and principles illustrate tangible, virtuous manifestations of the Corps values to Marine recruits and officer candidates. During reinforcement education, Marines confront progressively more complex issues with analysis that is based on the same traits and principles. Each stage of education targets a degree of comprehension that touches on the foundational traits and principles, yet builds sequentially upon lessons from the Marine's last formal military education.

---

[5] Alternately referred to as Corps values.

As the issues confronting Marines become more complex, Marines must better understand the drivers behind the 25 traits and principles. With continuing education, Marines strengthen their foundation in the three core values. The values are then connected to common frames of reference for Marines, allowing them to work in progressively diverse and challenging situations while maintaining cohesion with their fellow Marines and upholding the character of the Corps. The most senior of Marines have the opportunity to examine the philosophical underpinnings of the core values, and understand the effects of interacting with other military organizations and nationalities that hold different value sets.

Phase III: Sustainment education

MCRP 6-11B, *Marine Corps Values: A User's Guide for Discussion Leaders* provides a ready reference for small unit discussions on core/Corps values. Using vignettes to illustrate the application and misapplication of core values in a Marine setting, the *User's Guide* provides leaders at all levels with all of the required material and guidance for conducting effective seminar-setting discussions that help sustain the momentum of growth Marines experience in formal schools.

Unit discussions – using personal and historical example. Unit discussions offer an immediate benefit – significant expansion of the time during which Marines are educated. Because the discussions are conducted within a peer group, they cause a second-order effect that transcends the first – they allow each Marine to influence the other Marines in the group. The aggregate values of the Marines in the group – the group's *ethos* – will become the guiding force of such discussions and will, as a result, be reinforced.

Professional Reading Program

The Marine Corps Professional Reading Program was created to augment formal PME and unit discussions by allowing Marines to work through a by-grade list of selected works with warfighting themes. Originally published as a text message for dissemination to all units, the reading program has grown into a dynamic, web-based venture under the stewardship of the Marine Corps University, with the active support of the Commandant of the Marine Corps.

Of six objectives stated when General Alfred M. Gray, 29th Commandant of the Marine Corps, conceived the Professional Reading Program, the first was "To impart a sense of Marine values and traits." Commandant Michael Hagee, who recently reinvigorated the program, intends that the program should "[contribute] to the growth of aggressive and informed leaders."[6]

A quick look at the Professional Reading Program web page will confirm this objective. The works, divided into selected readings for Marines of every rank, form an eclectic mix of material ranging from current to classic, from science fiction to the reality of the US Constitution. Many of these works are employed at resident schools. Accompanying a short synopsis of each book is a discussion guide for leaders, allowing the Professional Reading Program to provide ready support to unit discussions. Table 11.1 shows the current iteration of the Marine Corps professional reading list.

The Professional Reading Program allows Marines the opportunity for self-paced and unit-guided education in leadership. As a component of leadership, values education receives a significant boost from this program.

Mentoring

If Professional Military Education acts as a series of bricks paving the path of a Marine's service to country, mentoring represents the mortar holding the bricks together. The Marine Corps Mentoring Program was conceived:

To facilitate genuine concern between leaders and their subordinates and between team members; to increase unit cohesion; to focus leaders on the development of the "whole Marine," connecting both professional and personal development to mission accomplishment; to foster and strengthen relationships of accountability and responsibility between Marines and adherence to our core values 24 hours a day, 7 days a week; and to better equip our Marines to handle the increased challenges of today's operational climate.[7]

---

[6] MARADMIN 007/05, *Marine Corps Professional Reading Program*, Washington, DC: US Marine Corps, 2005, p. 1.
[7] USMC Training and Education Command, *Mentoring*, http://www.tecom.usmc.mil/mentoring/, September 24, accessed 2005.

Table 11.1 *The Marine Corps professional reading list*

Enlisted ranks	Title
Private and Lance Corporal	*A Message to Garcia* *Rifleman Dodd* by C. S. Forster *The Killer Angels* by Michael Shaara *The Soldier's Load* by S. L. A. Marshall *The Defense of Duffer's Drift* by E. D. Swinton *Black Hawk Down* by Mark Bowden *Constitution of the United States*
Corporal and Sergeant	*The Red Badge of Courage* by Stephen Crane *Battle Leadership* by Adolph Von Schell *With the Old Breed at Peleliu and Okinawa* by E. B. Sledge *The Bridge at Dong Ha* by John Miller *Gates of Fire* by Steven Pressfield *The United States Marines: A History* by BGen. E. H. Simmons *The Last Full Measure* by Jeff Shaara *Flags of Our Fathers* by James Bradley *Fields of Fire* by James Webb *Tip of the Spear* by Sgt. G. J. Michaels
Staff Sergeant	*The Art of War* by Sun Tzu (Griffith translation is recommended) *The Forgotten Soldier* by Guy Sajer *Pegasus Bridge* by Stephen Ambrose *We Were Soldiers Once and Young* by Harold Moore and Joseph Galloway *Phase Line Green – The Battle for Hue 1968* by Nicholas Warr *The Village* by Francis West *This Kind of War* by T. R. Fehrenbach *The Arab Mind* by R. Patai *Attacks!* By Erwin Rommel
Gunnery Sergeant	*Semper Fidelis: The History of the US Marine Corps* by Allan Millet *Navajo Weapon* by Sally McClain *Citizen Soldiers* by Stephen Ambrose *Breakout* by Martin Russ *My American Journey* by Colin Powell

Table 11.1 (*cont.*)

	Unaccustomed to Fear by Roger Willcock
	The Savage Wars of Peace by Max Boot
	Command in War by Martin Van Creveld
Master Sergeant and First Sergeant	*Bayonet Forward!* By Joshua Chamberlain
	Seven Pillars of Wisdom by T. E. Lawrence
	Defeat into Victory by William Slim
	Band of Brothers by Stephen Ambrose
	Strong Men Armed by Robert Leckie
	The Mask of Command by John Keegan
	War in the Shadows by R. B. Asprey
	The Face of Battle by John Keegan
Master Gunnery Sergeant and Sergeant Major	*First to Fight* by Victor Krulak
	Fortune Favors the Brave by Bruce Myers
	Reminiscences of a Marine by John A. Lejeune
	No Bended Knee by Merill Twining

Officer ranks

Warrant Officer	*Small Wars Manual*
	MCWP 6-11, *Leading Marines*
	Victory at High Tide by Robert Haint
	The Armed Forces Officer by S. L. A. Marshall
	The Quiet American by Graham Greene
Officer Candidate, Cadet, Midshipman	*Beat to Quarters* by C. S. Forester
	A Message to Garcia by Elbert Hubbard
	The United States Marines: A History by BGen. E. H. Simmons
	MCDP-1, *Warfighting*
	Chesty by Jon Hoffman
Second Lieutenant	*Rifleman Dodd* by C. S Forester
	On Infantry by John English and Bruce Gudmundsson
	This Kind of War by T. R. Fehrenback
	Cleared Hot by Bob Stoffey
	Fields of Fire by James Webb
	Chancellorsville by Stephen W. Sears
	The Easter Offensive by G. H. Turley
	The Face of Battle by John Keegan
	The Arab Mind by R. Patai

(*cont.*)

Table 11.1 (*cont.*)

First Lieutenant and Chief Warrant Officer 2	*The Ugly American* by William Lederer and Eugene Burdick *Reminiscences of a Marine* by John A. Lejeune *A People Numerous and Armed* by John Shy *All for the Union* by Elisha Hunt Rhodes *The Storm of Steel* by Ernst Junger *Once an Eagle* by Anton Myrer *Company Commander* by Charles B. MacDonald *The Forgotten Soldier* by Guy Sajer *Utmost Savagery* by Joseph Alexander *Attacks!* By Erwin Rommel
Captain and Chief Warrant Officer 3	*The Art of War* by Sun Tzu (Griffith translation is recommended) *Fields of Battle* by John Keegan *Goodbye, Darkness* by William Manchester *From Beirut to Jerusalem* by Thomas Friedman *Unaccustomed to Fear* by Roger Willcock *Command in War* by Martin Van Creveld *Eagle Against the Sun* by Ronald Specter *Stonewall in the Valley* by Robert G. Tanner *The Savage Wars of Peace* by Max Boot *Infantry in Battle* compiled by George C. Marshall *Field Artillery and Firepower* by J. B. A Bailey *Terrorism Today* by Christopher Harmon
Major and Chief Warrant Officer 4	*Grant Takes Command* by Bruce Catton *The General* by C. S. Forester *On War* by Karl von Clausewitz (trans. Howard and Paret) *European Armies* by Hew Strachan *The Guns of August* by Barbara Tuchman *The Mask of Command* by John Keegan *A Bright Shining Lie* by Neil Sheehan *Crucible of War* by Fred Anderson *Strategy* by B. H. Liddell Hart *The Glorious Cause* by Robert Middlekauff *For the Common Defense* by Allan Millet and Peter Maslowski *Battle Cry of Freedom: The Civil War Era* by James M. McPherson

Table 11.1 (*cont.*)

	The History of the Peloponnesian War by Thucydides ("Landmark" version by Strasser recommended)
Lieutenant Colonel and Chief Warrant Officer 5	*A Revolutionary People at War* by Charles Royster *Defeat into Victory* by William Slim *Patton: A Genius for War* by Carlo D'Este *The Army and Viet Nam* by Andrew F. Krepinevich *Seven Pillars of Wisdom* by T. E. Lawrence *One Hundred Days* by ADM Sandy Woodward *The Lexus and the Olive Tree* by Thomas L. Friedman *Supplying War* by Martin Van Creveld *Masters of War* by Michael I. Handel *The Roots of Blitzkrieg* by James S. Corum *Frontiersmen in Blue* by Robert M. Utley
Colonel to General	*Abraham Lincoln and the Second American Revolution* by James McPherson *Supreme Command* by Eliot Cohen *All Quiet on the Western Front* by Erich Remarque *War and Peace* by Leo Tolstoy *Military Innovation in the Interwar Period* by Williamson Murray and Allan Millet *The Rape of Nanking* by Iris Chang *Dereliction of Duty* by H. R. McMaster *Diplomacy* by Henry Kissinger *Carnage and Culture* by Victor Davis Hanson *Crusade in Europe* by Dwight D. Eisenhower *Memoirs of General W. T. Sherman*, ed. by William S. McFeely *Feeding Mars* by John Lynn *Eisenhower's Lieutenants* by Russell S. Weigley *Fleet Tactics and Coastal Combat* by Wayne P. Hughes Jr. *Generalship: Its Diseases and Their Cure* by J. F. C. Fuller *Inventing Grand Strategy and Teaching Command* by Jon T. Sumida *The Campaigns of Napoleon* by David G. Chandler *The Conduct of War* by J. F. C. Fuller

Mentoring recognizes that the development of Marines, especially new Marines, depends on continued good influences. As the days of common squad bay living pass, young Marines spend more time in close proximity to the older Marines who teach by example. Mentoring acts as a vehicle for the maintenance of close professional relationships between Marines and their seniors in their organizations.

The Commandant of the Marine Corps charges commanders to assign a mentor to every new Marine in the unit. By teaching counseling techniques to all Marines and ingraining the value of mentoring to all Marines, the Corps also facilitates the creation of ad hoc mentoring relationships that spring up when younger Marines encounter older professionals whom they admire.

Through the promotion of mentoring, the Marine Corps sustains and brings continuity to the "bricks" that represent periodic formal education. During 20 years of service, the average Marine officer amasses only three years of formal education following graduation from the Basic School. Without mentoring, this Marine will receive only three years of sustainment education in values. However, the same Marine receives *seventeen* additional years of reinforcement in core values through mentoring. As the prime vehicle for values education during 85% of this Marine's twenty-year service, effective mentoring is essential to Transformation.

Performance evaluation

While mentoring is designed to guide future long-term performance, the performance evaluation system "supports the centralized selection, promotion, and retention of the most qualified Marines of the Active and Reserve Components."[8]

Performance evaluation's two components – Proficiency and Conduct marks for enlisted Marines through the rank of corporal, and fitness reporting for all other Marines – put teeth into the core values program. Each report covers a myriad of items that factor into the rating of a Marine's performance. Each report requires reporting seniors to base part of the Marine's evaluation on the adoption of core values in his/her daily life.

---

[8] MCO 1610.7D, *Performance Evaluation System*, Washington, DC: US Marine Corps, 2004, 1002.

Pro/Con

Entry-level enlisted Marines are evaluated with Proficiency and Conduct markings. Pro/Con markings employ simple criteria that allow seniors to characterize the young Marine's performance with a pair of numbers on a one-to-five scale. The conduct marking in particular refers to the Marine's development along the lines illustrated by the traits and principles. More than a grade on obedience to the law, conduct includes

Conformance to accepted usage and custom, and positive contributions to unit and Corps. General bearing, attitude, interest, reliability, courtesy, cooperation, obedience, adaptability, influence on others, moral fitness, physical fitness as effected by clean and temperate habits, and participation in unit activities not related directly to unit mission, are all factors of conduct and should be considered in evaluating the Marine.[9]

Fitness reporting

The fitness report (FITREP) provides the primary means for evaluating a Marine's performance. Headquarters Marine Corps (Manpower and Reserve Affairs) employs FITREPs in supporting the Commandant's efforts to select the best-qualified personnel for promotion, augmentation, resident schooling, command, and duty assignments.

The FITREP maintains solid connections to the core values through the traits and principles. Of fourteen graded areas in a FITREP, nine employ title and context from one of the traits or principles. Three more employ descriptors that refer to traits or principles. The FITREP employs all 25 traits and principles in some capacity of evaluating Marines.

Performance evaluation summary

Again and again during their service, Marines are subjected to the litmus test of performance evaluations. Proficiency and Conduct markings and fitness reporting allow the Marine Corps to characterize each Marine's internalization of the Corps values and apply that characterization in selecting, promoting and retaining Marines for future service.

[9] MCO P1070.12K, *Marine Corps Individual Records Administration Manual*, Washington, DC: US Marine Corps, 2000, 4005.6A.

Conclusion

Cohesion is achieved by fostering positive peer pressure and reinforcing our core values to the point that our Corps values become dominant over self-interest.[10]

The adoption of maneuver warfare as its doctrinal approach to war required the Marine Corps to grow critical thinkers. Acknowledgment of the Three-Block War battlefield brought the Corps to realize that maneuver warriors were needed throughout the ranks, down to the most junior Marine.

Inspired by General Lejeune, the Corps evolved a series of themes and truths into three core values, which, by virtue of universal adoption, became the Corps' ethos. We try to create cohesive organizations by fostering the development of the three core values in all of our Marines. When Marines adopt these behaviors, the Corps creates self-sustaining success.

To the three-block warrior, working alongside like-minded people is its own reward. That person whose beginning was analogous to the raw iron has now become the polished, magnetized steel, that the Marine recruiter first represented at the start of Transformation – a model for the new Marine, and a magnet for the Marines of the future. Through a broad spectrum of war games, simulations, exercises, group discussions and individual effort, the Corps implements these core values through five primary vehicles: initial values training, reinforcement education, sustainment education, mentoring, and performance evaluation.

One must observe the Marine Corps from a distance in order to fully appreciate the beauty of Transformation. Up close, where trees are individual, the observer sees a poster or a short training session or a mentor helping a new Marine or a Marine being evaluated for future potential. Once the observer retreats to a distant point of observation, the trees coalesce – the individual vehicles used to teach values combine into a single, self-sustaining process. Here is the beauty of the forest – the more effectively we achieve the Transformation in our Marines, the more the process of Transformation becomes self-sustaining. The more the process becomes self-sustaining, the more we win battles and

---

[10] MCRP 6-11D, *Sustaining the Transformation*, p. 73.

maintain the trust of the nation that tasks the Marine Corps to remain the most ready when the nation is least ready.

When Mike Strank and his brother Marines raised the flag at Iwo Jima, they created an enduring image that validated General John Lejeune's efforts to institutionalize success through the creation of Corps-wide values; Sergeant Strank's image continues to inspire our Corps and our nation today. More importantly, Mike's values, reflected in his leadership, left a lasting, positive image in the Marines under his charge. Honorable, courageous and committed fully to his Marines, he created a group whose values were encapsulated by its most silent figure, Ira Hayes, when Hayes explained his relationship with his fellow Marines and the bond between all Marines with five simple words: "They'd never let me down."

Index